Resource Conflict and Environmental Relations in Africa

Kelechi Johnmary Ani
Editor

Resource Conflict and Environmental Relations in Africa

palgrave
macmillan

Editor
Kelechi Johnmary Ani
Department of History and Strategic Studies
Alex Ekwueme Federal University Ndufu-Alike Ikwo
Abakaliki, Nigeria

Afrocentric Governance of Public Affairs
North West University
Potchefstroom, South Africa

ISBN 978-981-19-7342-0 ISBN 978-981-19-7343-7 (eBook)
https://doi.org/10.1007/978-981-19-7343-7

This Palgrave Macmillan imprint is published by the registered company Springer Nature Singapore Pte Ltd.
The registered company address is: 152 Beach Road, #21-01/04 Gateway East, Singapore 189721, Singapore

This book is dedicated to every soul that has remained passionate about transforming the African environment from a theatre of conflict and resource curse to a land of sustainable development.

Foreword

The African continent is blessed with rich human and natural resources. These resources are the central pillars of national developments within the African continent and in other parts of the globe, where many of the African descendants and her mineral resources are exploited in the quest to attain societal transformations. Ironically, the presence of these resources in many African nations is the major cause of intra-class conflict among the elites of those nations. The struggle for control, exploitation and expropriation of these resources has been the major cause of wars in Africa. One regrettable feature of natural resource exploitation in Africa is that these resources are produced for exports to Europe and North America without any addition of value through processing. Thus, African nations have remained the primary producers and exporters of natural resources. The consequence is that the bare export of natural resources has not been able to drive economic development in Africa. Another concomitant feature of natural resources exploitation in Africa is environmental degradation. The process of natural resource exploitation in Africa has often ran counter to the globally approved standard for sustainable development. Natural resource exploitation is usually carried in Africa without sufficient considerations of their impact on the environment.

This book, *Resource Conflict and Environmental Relations in Africa*, clearly captures the rich mineral resource deposits in the African continent and how these resources have become the central drivers of conflicts, violence, militia activities, agitations and other forms of insecurity that threatens the security of lives and properties. This has led many scholars to describe the natural resources endowment of Africa as a curse in disguise. The manifest impact of this resource curse and the neo-colonial wind of underdevelopment within the African continent were extensively discussed using the push and pull effects of environment endowments during Sierra Leone Civil War, Niger Delta crisis and Angola resource crisis as specific case studies. The book also captures the place of climate change, rule of law and conflict resolution processes in the changing nature of mineral resource and environmental conflicts in Democratic Republic of Congo, Nigeria, and a number of other African countries.

Finally, the book is a concise but detailed analysis of the political economy of mineral resource exploration, exportation and management by domestic and international actors in Africa. It captures the reasons how these resources, while driving a low level of economic development, engender so much violence and conflict in course of the bid for their acquisition and exploitation.

In conclusion, I strongly recommend this twelve-chapter book for global scholars, students, researchers, policymakers and analysts as well as those searching for the fountain of knowledge in Mineral Resource and Environmental Studies, African Political Economy, Environmental History and African Development Studies.

Professor Thaddeus Chukwuka Eze
Professor of Law
Vice Chancellor
Renaissance University Ugbawka
Enugu, Nigeria

Preface

Resource endowment is a fundamental determinant of environmental governance dynamics across African states and societies. The government of many African countries do not make the extra effort to turn their mineral resources into secondary products but hastily sale them abroad in order to make quick money. Unfortunately, the resource exploration process is done by multinational corporations in such a dehumanizing way that naturally undermines the natural environment thereby generating group and communal resistance.

This book presents the multiple push and pull effects of resource competition in Africa. The chapters interrogate how the competitive quest to control access to environmental resource between government and non-governmental actors have led to some positive and negative effects, while emphasizing that resource endowment has become a major driver of conflict in Niger Delta of Nigeria and Cabinda region of Angola as well as creating strong armed conflict in many parts of sovereign African states. The study reveals that the war in Sierra Leone was fundamentally sustained by diamond exploration and trade thereby accounting for the popular resource curse theory that has undermined the development of many African states. The role of climatic factors in influencing the nature of man's relations in Egypt and African international relations was also discussed.

Finally, the content of the book would help in advancing the path towards the promotion of peaceful environmental relations and politics in the African continent. I therefore strongly encourage policymakers, researchers, students and environmentalists to diligently read through the contents of this academic work and eke out new theories and ideas on the management of resource curse and climate change in Africa.

Abakaliki, Nigeria Kelechi Johnmary Ani

Acknowledgements

Special appreciation goes to all the scholars whose works have been cited in the process of the development of this book. May God bless the contributors and those who assisted in the review of all the chapters and editorial phase of the book. I wish to specially appreciate the motivation from my family, contributors and reviewers during the development of this intellectual work. Special thanks goes to all the staff of Springer staff who have shown passionate interest towards the production of this book. I really appreciate Sandeep Kaur, Aparajita Singh, Saranya Siva, Aurela Heumadar, Melvin Lourdes and others technical support staff that helped to ensure that this book became a reality.

Contents

Notes on Contributors

Abutu Freeman Gabriel Adikwuoyi Ph.D. holds a Bachelor of Arts in History, Masters of Arts History and Doctor of Philosophy from the Benue State University, Makurdi. As an upcoming scholar, he is a regular Member of the Historical Society of Nigeria and has articles published in reputable journals and books locally and internationally. Currently, he is a Lecturer in the Department of History and International Studies Admiralty University of Nigeria Ibusa Delta State.

Emmanuel Obiahu Agha Ph.D. is a Lecturer in the Department of Sociology, Alex Ekwueme Federal University, Ndufu-Alike, Ikwo, Nigeria. His research interests include industrial sociology, human resource management, security and development studies

Kelechi Johnmary Ani Ph.D. holds a Bachelor of Arts in History and International Relations from Ebonyi State University, Abakaliki (Second Class Upper). He bagged a Postgraduate Diploma in Education and a Master's Degree in International History and Diplomacy from the University of Maiduguri, all in Nigeria. He proceeded to North West University, South Africa where he graduated with a doctorate degree in Peace Studies. He has peace, conflict, terrorism, African diplomacy, politics and history as his areas of research interest.

He is an Extraordinary Professor in Afrocentric Governance of Public Affairs Research Entity, North West University South Africa and also a Lecturer in the Department of History and Strategic Studies, Alex

Ekwueme Federal University, Ndufu-Alike, Ikwo, Ebonyi State, Nigeria. He is a Visiting Scholar, Masters in International Relations, University of The Gambia and currently a Visiting Senior Lecturer in the Department of History and International Studies, Renaissance University Ugbawka, Nigeria. He was a Post-Doctoral Research Fellow in the Department of Politics and International Relations, North West University (Mafikeng Campus), and currently, a Senior Research Fellow at the University of Johannesburg, both in South Africa.

Timothy Chibuike Anyanwu is a Lecturer in the History Department of Alex Ekwueme Federal University, Ndufu-Alike, Ikwo. Currently, he has attended many conferences and has a number of publications. He is also doing his Ph.D. programme in International History at the University of Nigeria, Nsukka.

Vincent Okwudiba Anyika is an interdisciplinary scholar in the Department of History and Strategic Studies, Alex Ekwueme Federal University, Ndufu-Alike, Ebonyi State. He has worked as Travel and Tourism consultant for VIP Express Tourism Limited, Port Harcourt for five years before joining the Alex Ekwueme Federal University. He holds a B.A. in History and Diplomatic studies from the prestigious University of Port and M.A. in History and International Studies from the Ignatius Ajuru University of Education, Port Harcourt, the premier state-owned University of Education in South-South Nigeria. He is a member of the Society for Peace Studies and practice (SPSP) and the Historical Society of Nigeria.

Lawson Onyema Chukwu is a postgraduate student in the Department of History and International Studies, University of Nigeria Nsukka. His areas of research interest include peace, conflict and international relations

Anthony Dibua is a postgraduate student in International Relations at the University of Westminster, London, United Kingdom.

Chinyere Samuel Ecoma Ph.D. is a Reader (Associate Professor) of History in the Department of History and International Relations, Veritas University, Abuja. She taught previously in the Department of History and International Relations, Ebonyi State University, Abakaliki; Department of History and International Studies, Babcock University, Illishan Remo, Ogun State; Instructional Facilitator, National Open University of Nigeria (Calabar Study Centre); and Department of History and International Studies, University of Calabar, Calabar Cross River State before joining Veritas University, Abuja. She is an Honorary Member of the International Scholarly Committee of the Interdisciplinary Scholarly Book Series within the Eschaton Library, Kraków, Poland.

Emmanuel Metu Egbule Ph.D. is priest with the Anglican Diocese of Ikeduru, Imo State, Nigeria. He has a Ph.D. in Religion (Biblical Studies) from Imo State University, Owerri, Nigeria, and Postgraduate diploma in Education from the National Teacher Institute Ibadan. He is the National Assistant secretary of Nigeria Association of Biblical Scholars (NABIS) and its Coordinator in the South East Nigeria. He is Lecturer in the Department of Religious and Cultural Studies at the Alex Ekwueme Federal University, Ndufu-Alike, Ikwo Ebonyi State, Nigeria. He has special interest in Igbo cultural studies, African cultural Hermeneutics and Missions in Igbo land. He has done extensive research on Igbo communal life and currently writing a work on "Igbo communal Life a stepping Stone for Ecumenism". He believes that the principles of Igbo communal life when contextualized make for transformational possibility in contemporary Africa.

Nnenna I. Enwo-Irem Ph.D. is a Lecturer in the Department of History and Strategic Studies, Alex Ekwueme Federal University, Ndufu-Alike, Ikwo Ebonyi State, Nigeria. Her areas of research interest include gender studies and social history.

Maryam Jungudo Ph.D. is a Senior Lecturer in Department of History, Nigerian Army University Biu, Nigeria. Her areas or research interest include aqua-conflict in Africa, peace, security and gender studies.

Chukwuemeka Nwosu Ph.D. is a Professor in the Department of History and International Studies, Faculty of Humanities, Imo State University, Owerri, Nigeria. He holds B.A. and M.A degrees from the University of Calabar, Calabar Nigeria. He also holds a Ph.D. in African-American history from the Department of History and International Studies, Imo State University, Owerri, Nigeria. He holds LL.B., B.L., degrees from the University of Calabar, Calabar Nigeria, and the Nigerian Law School, Abuja, Nigeria. A Solicitor and Advocate of the Supreme Court of Nigeria. He has been teaching courses in Foundations of International Law and Diplomacy; he also teaches Foundation of Diplomacy in the Department of History and International Studies; African Diaspora History, Strategic Studies, Foreign Policy and Diplomacy, and International Relations. He has interest in contemporary security studies.

Goldpin Nelson Obah-Akpowoghaha Ph.D. is Political Theorist, Peace and Conflict Studies Expert. He obtained all his degrees in Political Science from the prestigious Obafemi Awolowo University formally called the University of Ife (i.e. B.Sc. Ed.; M.Sc.; and Ph.D. in Political Science). He was a Postdoctoral Fellow at North West University, Mafikeng, South Africa and an Associate Professor in the Department of Political Science, University of The Gambia. He is a member of Nigerian Political Science Association (NPSA); Social Studies Association of Nigeria (SOSAN); and a reviewer to British Journal of Education, Society and Behavioural Science.

Professor Victor Ojakorotu Ph.D. earned his doctorate degree in International Relations from the University of the Witwatersrand, South Africa. He earned the University of the Witwatersrand, Postgraduate Merit Award, 2002, 2003 and 2004; and Laureates, Governance Institute, CODESRIA, Dakar (2002). He is a NRF rated Professor of African Environmental Politics. He is currently the Deputy Director, School of Government Studies, North West University South Africa.

Reuben Edafenene Ojighoro Ph.D. is a Lecturer in the Department of Religious Studies, College of Education, Warri, Delta State, Nigeria.

Victoria Nnenwogo Okafor graduated from the Department of History and Strategic Studies, Alex Ekwueme Federal University, Ndufu-Alike, Ikwo, Nigeria. Her area of research interest includes environmental studies and economic history.

Ikemefuna Taire Paul Okudolo Ph.D. is presently a Postdoctoral Research Fellow in the Indigenous Language Media in Africa Entity (ILMA-Entity) at the North West University, Mafikeng, South Africa. His postdoc is focused on Africa studies. He received his Ph.D. in political science. His first two degrees are in public administration. He bagged the academic degrees at the Ambrose Alli University, Ekpoma, Edo State, and the University of Lagos, respectively. He is an editor in the News Agency of Nigeria (NAN) since 2008, where he has been involved in several beats including education, judiciary, environment and food security.

Yemisi Olawale is a postgraduate student in the Department of History and International Studies, University of Illorin, Nigeria. His research interest includes peace conflict and African international relations.

Chijioke Francis Onyebukwa Ph.D. bagged a Doctor of Philosophy in International Relations in 2017 from the Department of Politics and International Relations, Faculty of Human and Social Science, North West University Mafikeng Campus, South Africa. His areas of research interest include peace, security, conflict and conflict management, diplomacy as well as politics and electoral violence in Africa. He co-authored *The Struggle for Leadership Relevance between Nigeria and South Africa*, Berlin: Lambert Academic Publishers in 2013 with Ojakorotu Victor and Maseng Jonathan Oshupeng. He was a Senior Researcher in Governance, Politics and Conflict with African Heritage Institution Enugu State Nigeria before joining the Department of International Relations, Madonna University, Okija, Nigeria. He has also worked as an Academic Writing Consultant at the Academic Development Center, North West University Mafikeng from 2014 to 2016.

Ogunnowo Ruth Oore-Ofe Ph.D. holds a Bachelor of Arts degree in History from Obafemi Awolowo University (OAU), Ile-Ife, Nigeria. She has a Master's degree in International Affairs from the Legon Center of International Affairs and Diplomacy of the University of Ghana, Legon Ghana. Her areas of research interests include diplomacy and diplomatic communication, peace and conflict studies, and contemporary history, with special interest in African studies. For a keen interest in communicating in at least one foreign language in Africa and anticipating an edge in the career of International Relations, she enrolled in the French tutorials for foreigners at the Centre Beninois des Langues Entrangeres (CE.BE.LAE) of the University of Abomey Calavi, Cotonou Republic of Benin and Alliance Francaise, Lagos, Nigeria. She bagged a doctoral degree in International Relations from North West University, Mafikeng, South Africa.

List of Tables

CHAPTER 1

Introducing Resource Conflicts and Governance in Africa

Yemisi Olawale, Kelechi Johnmary Ani, and Goldpin Nelson Obah-Akpowoghaha

Introduction

The link between natural resources and conflict has raised numerous questions in extractive industries, especially in developing countries in the post-cold war (Ruben, 2007; Hamid et al., 2022; Hamid and Cederman, 2022; Jesse, 2020; Alexis, 2020). The discussion has even intensified

Y. Olawale (✉)
Department of History and International Studies, University of Illorin, Illorin, Nigeria
e-mail: yemisiwaleisaac@gmail.com

K. J. Ani
Department of History and Strategic Studies, Alex Ekwueme Federal University, Ndufu-Alike Ikwo, Abakaliki, Nigeria

G. N. Obah-Akpowoghaha
University of The Gambia, Kanifing, Gambia
e-mail: akpowoghaha@gmail.com

K. J. Ani (ed.), *Resource Conflict and Environmental Relations in Africa*,
https://doi.org/10.1007/978-981-19-7343-7_1

given the consistent and higher demands for natural resources globally (Joshua et al., 2017; Olanrewaju et al., 2020). Given this link, it has raised several questions. Is it a coincidence that several resource-rich countries have records of conflicts and governance challenges in their extractive sector? What is the connection between natural resources and conflict? In what ways can natural resources translate into sustainable growth and development and many more are questions academics and policymakers have over two decades continue to dissect. Put differently, the issues of natural resource governance in developing countries are widespread and perturbing. DR Congo and Sierra Leone in Africa to Peru in Latin America to Iraq and Kuwait in the Middle East have records of natural resource conflict and governance difficulties. As some of these countries continue to extract their natural resources, new challenges emerge from which have continuously sustained discussion and research about natural resources (Beevers, 2019; Hamid and Cederman, 2022; Ojakorotu, 2018).

That the African continent remains one of the resource-rich continents globally is not news. The fifty-four countries are blessed with abundant renewable and non-renewable resources. Among African renewable resources include—water, land, forest, and fish and non-renewable include minerals, metals and oil among others. Ayee (2014: 15) notes that the continent of Africa has more than global resources of vital solid minerals among which include cobalt, manganese, gold, platinum, uranium, and oil. In 2008, solid minerals and petroleum resource extraction in Africa were estimated at $1 trillion (Forstater et al., 2010). The importance of natural resources to economic growth and development cannot be underestimated. Natural resources are an important source of revenue, and employment opportunities that raises standard of living, human development index, economic growth and increase state economic status in global economic relations (Omotola, 2010; Mukoro, 2010; Clayton, 2016). However, it is important to state that the above positive features of natural resources are only achievable if the rich natural resources governance is available to manage the extraction and utilisation of revenues (Auty, 2001; Collier and Hoeffler, 2002). In this case, references can be made to Norway, Canada and Botswana.

On the other hand, the availability of natural resources and their abundance can translate into underdevelopment riddled with crises of natural resources governance, conflicts, instability and civil wars, inequality and abject poverty, and corruption among others. These negative features are the product of natural resource mismanagement and the absence of a sustainable governance mechanism. The African extractive sector has been characterised by the negative aspect of natural resources mismanagement and its outcomes. Within this premise, Kiiza et al. (2011) contend that the abundance of natural resources in the African continent can be described as a curse rather than a blessing. Put differently, the availability of abundant natural resources, years of extractions and billions of resource revenues in Africa have not translated into any sustainable development. Africa remains a poor continent that grapples with growth and development challenges.

There are records of high-intensity conflict caused and prolonged in Angola, the Republic of Congo, the Democratic Republic of the Congo, DRC, Nigeria and Sudan and low-intensity conflicts in Burundi, Chad, Djibouti, Senegal and Uganda (SIPRI, 2000). The bewildering aspect of the resource crises is that countries with little or no resources like African countries performed better on development indicators (Eyene and Reeta 2021). In a report published by the Natural Resource Governance Institute in 2017, only two African countries—Ghana (oil and gas) and Botswana (mining)—out of thirty-one African countries assessed were ranked 'good' in terms of resource governance (NRGI, 2017). The remaining twenty-nine countries' natural resources sector falls within the category of 'satisfactory', 'weak', 'poor' and 'failing' (NRGI, 2017). In most extant literature on African natural resources, the 'resource curse' dominates the perspectives of scholars, academics and policymakers (Frankel, 2010; Salah, 2020).

Against this backdrop, the chapter provides an overview of Africa's natural resources conflicts, governance and management. Apart from the introduction and conclusion of the chapter, the first section provides a conceptual overview of the interconnection between natural resources and conflict. The next section surveys various resource-based conflicts in Africa and their outcomes on Africa's economic growth and security. The last section examines natural resources governance in Africa from the perspective of accountability and transparency. The chapter relies on secondary data source drawn from books, journals and country-based reports.

Explaining Africa Resource Conflict Through Greed and Grievances Approach

Several scholars have sought to examine the causes of natural resource conflict from various theoretical standpoints. Among these theories are relative deprivation theory, theory of greed and grievances, collective action theory and frustration-aggression theory (Ojakorotu, 2018). However, the chapter's discussion is anchored on the greed and grievances theory to explain the dynamics, causes and intersections of conflicts and natural resources in Africa. The greed and grievances theory provide political, economic and social explanations for the causes of natural resources conflict in Africa. The theory is shaped by the research of Paul Collier and Hoeffler (2002). In Collier and Hoeffler's pioneering contributions (1998), abundant natural resources is considered a dominant factor causing conflict. Through Collier and Hoeffler's (1998) statistical analysis of civil war causations at the country level, these authors claim that abundant natural resources is associated with a higher risk of conflict. The theory contends that conflict over natural resources can be explained from two possible perspectives: grievances or greed (atypical opportunity) (Collier 2000).

Collier and Hoeffler (2004) argue that civil wars are caused by 'greed' rather than 'grievances'. Collier and Hoeffler (2004) contend that resource conflicts and their prolongation can be traced to the greed of combatants (actors) in such resource conflicts. According to the theoretical position, conflict over natural resources is caused by greedy behaviours of actors (combatants, militias and ethnic warlords) who start conflicts and insurgency in their state extractive sectors in them to control the extraction of resources, personal self-enrichment as well as to possess a degree of power within the state (Madubuko, 2015). Collier and Hoeffler (2004) considered combatants as war entrepreneurs and war capitalist with the sole aim of securing profits. On the aspect of grievance, Collier and Hoeffler (2004) contend that grievances cannot be considered the primary cause of civil wars, and even in the case where grievances are considered, they serve as ideological covers for rebels and combatants in natural resources conflict to further achieve their undeclared motives and interest in conflict.

However, despite the overarching contributions of Collier and Hoeffler (2004) regarding the greed and grievances position, it has come under serious criticism for its rebel-centric and pro-state biases position (Koubi et al., 2014; Ross, 2015; Olanrewaju et al., 2020). These criticisms are propelled by the need to gain a wider understanding of the causes of civil war beyond Collier and Hoeffler's submissions. Fearon and Laitin (2003) contend that conflicts in extractive actors cannot be explained only through the greediness of rebels and other combatants as advanced by collier and Hoeffler. The extractive sectors are characterised by a multiplicity of actors (the government, civil societies, local community and oil multinational cooperation) among others. Hence, Fearon and Laitin (2003) advanced the position that civil wars in extractive sectors must factor in resource curse outcomes, which points out the failure of natural resources governance and opportunistic leaders who siphon extraction sector revenues than providing public goods and good governance to their countries' entire populations.

The research of Hamid et al. (2022: 12–22) in particular made significant advances in the greed and grievance theory. Hamid et.al. (2022) contend that Collier and Hoeffler's isolation and emphasis on greed as the principal cause of conflict and the criminalisation of insurgents and rebels can lead to the prolongation of natural resources conflict. On the other hand, there is a need for more constructive arguments to understand insurgents' behaviour in the extractive sector. Drawing from Cederman et al. (2013) study of inequality, grievances and civil war as our theoretical point of departure, Hamid et al. (2022) critically examine the place of inequality and grievances in civil wars. According to Ali and Cederman, the 'link between extraction and conflict depends on how extractors that is the actors responsible for the extraction, and the affected communities interact'.

In their submission, Hamid et al. (2022)'s study shows that the extractive sector and conflict involve multiple actors and beyond rebels. In the case of grievance, Hamid et al. (2022) categorise community grievances into distributive, migration induced, political and environmental. The authors contend that beyond greed, these grievances can serve as a focal cause of rebellion and insurgency behaviour rather than greed. Hamid et al. (2022)'s contributions also stem from their discussion of extractors' reactions as a prime factor that shapes the behaviour of insurgents or rebels. Extractors can either respond through repression, accommodation or corporate social responsibility. In the case of repression, violent conflicts are bound to ensue. While this study does not intend to validate Collier and Hoeffler's priority of greed as a principal cause of the civil wars or Hamid et al. (2022)'sinequality and grievance approach, it embraces the position that resources conflicts involve multiple actors with various interests guided by greed and grievances often caused by the failure of sustainable natural resources governance in the extractive sector.

Natural Resources and Conflict in Africa: Intersections

Natural resources are not evenly distributed on the earth's surface (Odewumi and Patrick 2005: 192). Various parts of the world differ in climate, soil, topography, water bodies, natural vegetation, mineral wealth and other natural endowments (Odewumi and Patrick 2005: 192). Various scholars have defined natural resources. Okoli and Uhembe (2015: 39) define natural resources as nature-given material assets that can be harnessed by mankind to sustain life and create wealth. Abiodun (2007: 16) also conceives natural resources '¦as all non-artificial products situated on or beneath the soil, which can be extracted, harvested or used, and whose extraction, harvest or usage generates income or serves other functional purposes in benefiting mankind. Examples of such resources include solid minerals, metals, wildlife, fish, timber, wood, petroleum resources and oil, natural vegetation and water.

Various scholars have also defined natural resource conflict. According to Coser (1956), conflict implies "the struggle over values, interests, claims to status, power, and resources in which the opponents make attempts to neutralise, injure, or eliminate their rivals." Conflicts over natural resources can also be classified into two: violent and non-violent (Kyem, 2021: 24; FAO, 2000). Non-violent conflict over natural resource conflicts refers to low-level disputes and disagreements over access, ownership, allocation and use of natural resources (FAO 2000). Most of the time, violent conflicts over natural resources are the product of failures to resolve them non-violently. UNO (2012) also claims that the transformation of non-violent conflicts into violent ones are driven by factors such as ethnic division, povertyPoverty and inequalityInequality, poor governanceGovernance, economic marginalisation and failure of cooperative or peaceful strategies, assume a violent identity. In Africa, natural resource conflicts are primarily violent while the less-known are non-violent and are turning into violent cases in no time given the poor management.

Several scholars' study has expanded the scope of knowledge on the relationship between natural resources and conflict. In describing the negative outcomes between natural resources and conflict, Richard Auty conceptualised it as a 'resource curse'. The resource curse is one of the influential arguments that accounts for conflict over natural resources. The term 'resource curse' was coined by Richard Auty to describe how resource-rich countries could not use their wealth to boost their economic growth. The resource curse argument is hinged on the idea that the abundance of natural or mineral resources, particularly, oil and gas in their teemingness quantity, has not yielded any significant development rather than poor growth, conflict and instability. Put differently, rather than rapid and sustainable growth and development, and resource-rich countries are faced with sluggish growth and development (Auty and Gelb, 1986; Gelb, 1988; Auty, 2001). The similar arguments of the resource curse are mirrored in other scholars' research. Karl (1999) calls it the paradox of plenty; Akpan (2003) conceptualised it as 'tragedy at midday'; Collier and Hoeffler (1998, 2004), Elbadawi and Sambanis (2000) and Lujala et al. (2005) conceptualised it as 'spoils of nature'; and Umoh (2010) calls it the crisis of abundance. In essence, the existence of extractive commodities in most rich mineral resource states has been considered not beneficial to this state in the light of growth and development indices. Many of these states elope in internal strife due to natural resources governance between the state and sub-state actors such as militias and warlords (Collier and Hoeffler, 1998, 2002).

Scholars like Schellens and Diemer (2020) note that theories of natural resource conflict revolve around two theoretical standpoints, 'too little' or scarcity theory and 'too much' or abundance theories. The scarcity theory is a cause of conflict that stems from issues arising from environmental degradation, population rise and migration (Mildner et al., 2011). Based on Homer-Dixon (1994), scarcity of natural resources can exacerbate conflict from three standpoints, decreasing supply caused by overexploitation and pollution; economic deprivation following environmental scarcity; and environmental stress caused by migration flows. Apart from the scarcity theory, the relationship between resource and conflict can be located in the abundance thesis which is generally summarised under the resource curse (Auty 1993). From the abundance standpoint, Schellens and Diemer (2020) studies show exploitation of resources for personal enrichment, the emergence of resource-dependent and authoritarian government, the absence of strong government institutions to guide proper allocation and utilisation of resources and extractive sector dependency lead to vulnerable economy which in turn fuels conflict in areas where it is abundant.

Abiodun (2007) in his studies contends that natural resources' linkage with conflict can be categorised into three, namely 'as a source of conflict', 'as a factor in conflict prolongation' and 'as a means of resolving conflicts'. Abiodun (2007) notes that natural resources become a source of conflict when there are disputes over the quantity and quality of extracted resources between actors involved; disputes and politics over the ownership, management and control of natural resources extraction (in terms of actors involved such as oil multinational cooperation, democratic or authoritarian regimes, the role of civil societies and community stakeholders) and the process of extraction (effects on communities, dangers constituted to livelihood [Abiodun 2007]).

In terms of prolongation of conflict, Abiodun (2007) contends that natural resources played prolonged conflicts through the provision of revenue to prosecute and sustain the conflict. This is evident in the case of Angola, DR Congo, Sierra Leone and Sudan. Also, natural resources prolong conflicts in an attempt by actors involved in the conflict to control extractive sites and the peace belligerency thesis (Abiodun 2007). Natural resources conflict becomes prolonged when actors are involved in preventing peace missions because their control of extractive industries can become endangered (Abiodun 2007). Natural resources also prolong conflicts given that the multiplicity of stakeholders involves in the conflicts such as national government, local militia, warlords, civil and ethnic societies, and external actors. Lastly, natural resources have also promoted the need to resolve conflicts (Abiodun, 2007). In this case, neighbouring states or international organisations benefitting directly or indirectly from the extractive sector often show concern for the need to resolve conflict to curtail the spillover effect and ensure that the extraction of a particular natural resource is not compromised. In this case, the granting of presidential amnesty to ethnic militia and warlords in the Niger Delta region of Nigeria and the establishment of the ECOWAS Monitoring Group into resolving the Liberia and Sierra Leone crises are excellent case studies.

Hamid et al. (2022)'s study additionally provides a critical perspective on the interconnection between natural resources and conflict. In Hamid et al. (2022)'s study, natural resources conflict involves multiple actors whose response to extractive community grievances determines whether issues in the extractive sector will translate into conflict. In Hamid et al. (2022)'s finding, conflict ensues and is prolonged in extractive sectors when actors (extractors) (oil multinational cooperation, government and affected communities) choose repression as a response to various grievances (Ross, M. L., 2001; Paine, 2016). Hamid et al. (2022)'s approach to studying the interconnection between natural resources shows that the reaction stage often determines whether grievances will be translated into a conflictual situation or not.

Natural Resources and Conflicts in Africa: Cases Survey

Natural resources have been the centre of multiples communal, state-level and inter-state conflicts in Africa. To understand some case studies of resource conflicts in Africa, the chapter analysis is based on interrogating conflicts under various natural resources. Natural resources examined in this section include land, solid minerals, oil and petroleum, and water resources. Oil in Africa has also been a major source of conflict. This is evident in major oil-producing Africa countries including Nigeria, Libya, Algeria, Angola, Sudan, Cameroon, Ghana and Chad among others. In Africa, there is hardly any oil-rich state not facing oil-based resources issues. Abiodun (2007) contends that oil resource conflicts in Africa emanate from 'controversies over the ownership of oil-extractive sites; disagreements over the management of oil revenues; crises arising from extractors mode of exploration and protests oil-bearing communities against extractors damages and insensitivity to oil-bearing communities'. The Nigeria's Niger Delta is an excellent case study. Today, the region is described as ungovernable owing to various records of conflicts in the region. Resource conflicts in the Niger Delta region emanate from resource control and revenue management to the activities and exploration of oil multinational cooperation leading to environmental degradation, oil spillages and the absence of sustainable Cooperate Social Responsibility from oil multinational cooperation among others.

The Niger Delta region thus is characterised by armed struggle championed by hundreds of oil-ethnic militias and armed groups (Gilbert, 2010: 52; Yemisi, 2020). In the annual NNPC Statistical Bulletin cited by Onuoha et al. (2021), there are 2,753 cases of vandalisation in 2006; 1,937 in 2007; and 1,801 in 2016. Also, during the implementation of the Presidential Amnesty Programme for the Niger Delta militants, which spanned between 6 August and 4 October 2009, 26,808 militants surrendered their arms and ammunition. In 2018, there were also recorded violent incidents resulting in loss of life and source of livelihood. Natural resources conflict has also led to the proliferation of Small Arms and Light Weapons (SALW) in the region. In the course of the Niger Delta Amnesty Programme SALW recovered to include: 2760 assorted guns, 287,445 ammunitions of different calibre, 18 gunboats, 763 dynamites, 1090 dynamite caps, 3,155 magazines and several other military accessories, such as dynamite cables, bullet-proof jackets and jack-knives (Abazie-Humphrey, 2016: 143).

In Angola, the immediate post-independence period was characterised by crises of nation-building. The second phase of the Angola crisis began in 1992 involving the Movement for the Liberation of Angola (MPLA) and the National Union for the Total Independence of Angola (UNITA) (Abiodun 2007). The crisis has been described as a resource war because of the role of the natural resources in the financing, prolongation and complexities of the peace process. Two major resources contributed to the Angola crisis, namely oil and diamond. In Angola, the MPLA government controlled most of the oil-extractive sites and used the revenue from oil to finance the war and procure weapons used to fight the UNITA rebels. On the other hand, UNITA's access to diamond sites played an important role war financing the procurement of weapons (Abiodun 2007).

In Sudan, the governance of the oil region and control of oil revenue have also been major issues in the country's crisis. Despite the role of the African Union and the Intergovernmental Authority on Development (IGAD) in bringing the civil war to a moment of peace in 2010, the dispute over natural resources has led to the resuscitation of crises in the region. Sudan is the sixth major oil producer in Africa. Oil revenue accounted for more than 93% of Sudan's exports and 50% of domestic revenue in 2009. The control of oil-rich regions of the Bentiu region, South Kordofan, Adar and Heglig has been a major source of conflict. Sudan conflict has led to the death of approximately 500,000 people. After a moment of relative peace between 2005 and 2010, another wave of conflict over the oil-rich region of Abyei located along the South-North border has been a major source of conflict between the North and South Sudanese government. Oil exploration and control in Equatorial Guinea and Congo-Brazzaville have contributed to the political turmoil experienced in both countries.

Solid minerals in African countries have also been a major source of natural resource conflict. Abiodun (2007) notes that resource conflicts emanating from solid minerals often emanated from disputes over ownership of solid mineral extractive sites; various political, economic and environmental grievances against extractors of mineral resources. Solid mineral resources have been the major factor in conflicts in Liberia, Sierra Leone and the Democratic Republic of Congo (DRC). In Liberia, iron and diamonds were major drivers of the conflict, especially the second phase of the Liberian conflict between 1999 and 2004, which involved two armed groups, the Liberians United for Reconciliation and Democracy (LURD) and the Movement for Democracy in Liberia (MODEL). In Liberia, the control of timber was also an important cause of conflict. Richards (2001: 65) conceptualised conflict over timber as a 'forest war'. In Sierra Leone, control of diamond extractive sites and access to diamond trading opportunities was an important cause and driver of the civil war that rocked the country between 1991 and 2002. The Revolutionary United Front—a small contingent of guerrillas—financed the war through revenues derived from the control of the main diamond mines (Abiodun, 2007: 115–116). Solid mineral resource conflict in DR Congo is another evident case. DR Congo is blessed with numerous mineral deposits. The DRC conflict was fuelled by solid materials such as diamonds, coltan, gold and timber (Olanrewaju et al., 2020). In the case of Sierra Leone and DR Congo, the extractors' failure to provide a sustainable natural resources governance mechanism further prolonged the conflicts. Diamond extracted by the group has also fueled the conflict in Angola and the finance of UNITA.

Several studies on resource conflict in Africa have focused on wars emanating from oil and solid mineral, it is significant to state that oil and solid mineral resources conflicts cannot chronicle the entire story of resource conflicts in Africa. Resource conflicts also emanate from land and water resources. Land as a natural resource has been linked to several conflicts in Africa. Widespread conflicts over land stem from disputes over ownership (extremely complicated when such land bears mineral or oil resources) and boundary disputes. Apart from hundreds of communal land and boundary disputes in almost African countries, there are inter-state land disputes. A most cited example is the conflict between Nigeria and Cameroon over the Bakassi Peninsula. The conflict brought the two countries to an offensive stage until the matter was resolved at the International Court of Justice (ICJ) in 2003. Another case of land dispute is the Namibia and Botswana dispute over the Kasikili (Namibians) and Sedudu (Botswana) (Abiodun 2007). The dispute was also resolved at the International Court of Justice in 2001. The consistent crises emanating from land, especially in terms of the border, led to the AU Border Program in 2007.

Like oil and solid minerals, water in Africa has also been linked to conflicts. The most referenced case in Africa in contemporary times is the ongoing grand Ethiopian Dam construction which has brought tension between Egypt and Ethiopia over water resources from the River Nile. In 2011, Ethiopia launched the construction of the Grand Ethiopian Renaissance Dam (GERD) which when completed will become the eighth largest dam in the world. Although the dam was considered a major economic breakthrough in Ethiopia, the government of Egypt has considered it a threat to its national economy. Given that the Nile River flows through Ethiopia, the filling of the dam was affecting the downstream flow and use by other riparian states. Egypt has championed this dam construction conflict with 90 per cent dependent on its war from the Nile. Also, environmental and climatic conditions in Africa have been linked to conflicts in Africa. African countries like Nigeria, Ghana, Mali, Central African Republic, Ethiopia, Tanzania and Uganda have a record of farmers-herders conflicts.

The outcomes of natural resources conflict in Africa have continuously affected the growth and development of African states. Conflicts caused and fuelled by natural resources have led to succession, civil wars and communal disputes in African states (Collier and Hoeffler, 1998, 2002, 2005; Ross, 2004). In Nigeria, there have been a series of secession crises emanating from the resource-rich region of the Niger Delta. Also, the mineral-rich province of Katanga in DR Congo with the extraction of copper (Larmer and Kennes, 2019) and the Cabinda region are vivid cases. Also, Ross (2004) states that Sudan's division into the northern and southern regions can be linked to the discovery and availability of rich oil deposits central to South Sudan's economic potential. Also, host communities experienced the negative impact of resource extraction and conflict. In the Nigeria's Niger Delta region, resource conflicts have contributed to the growth of insecurity in the region. In the Niger Delta regions, kidnapping of oil workers and expatriates, oil bunkering, illegal exploration and sale of black markets crude oil, and the bombing of oil pipelines characterised the region. Hence, it is referred to as an ungovernable space. Resource conflict has also led to the death of thousands in the affected states. The crises attached to resource conflict have also led to the loss of livelihoods. In conflicted areas, peasants cannot engage themselves in farming especially when such a region is rich in mineral or oil resources which have led to resource war between various actors involved. The citizens, thus, migrate given the insecurity that characterised the region.

Table 1.1 Civil Wars linked to natural resource wealth in Africa 1990–present

Countries	*Period of conflict*	*Resources*
Angola	1975–2003	Oil, diamond
Central African Republic	2012–2016	Oil, Uranium, diamonds
Democratic Republic of Congo	1960–1965; 1996–1997; 1998–now	Copper, diamonds, gold, cobalt and coltan
Liberia	1986–1996	Timber, diamonds, iron, rubber, gold
Sudan	1985–2005	Oil
Sierra Leone	1991–2000	Diamonds
South Sudan	2018–	Oil

Source Ross M (2001) and Lwanda (2003)

Similar impacts are felt in the Angolan oil provinces of Cabinda (Table 1.1).

Silencing the Guns and Architecture of Accountability in Africa Resource Conflict

Given the complexities and challenges attached to African countries' extractive sectors, there has been a cacophony of voices on the need for the African governments to institute adequate and sustainable resources governance mechanisms. Alstine (2014: 22) conceptualised resource governance as 'rules established to shape how extractive sectors contribute to sustainable growth and development and poverty alleviation within host countries'. Resource governance efforts have been pursued from various standpoints, including oil sector reform and the push for transparency and accountability towards efficient resource allocation, have received significant attention. Hanson et al. (2014: 3) also contend that resource governance involves a 'comprehensive political process, involving myriad stakeholders'. According to Hanson et al. (2014: 3), natural resource governance encompasses the framework of rules, institutions and practices regulating the natural resource value chain and the extent to which key principles of transparency, openness, accountability, fairness and environmental sustainability are observed in the extraction of, movement of and receipts from natural resources.

At the continental level, the African Union, in line with the organization's mission and objective, has continued to initiate and implement policies to address conflicts arising from the resource. African Union Agenda 2063 incorporates the need to address all sources of conflict on the continent. Termed 'Silencing the Guns', under this framework, the African Union anticipates that by 2020, 'guns would be silent on the continent'. Put differently, all conflicts and wars would be brought to an end (AU Commission, 2063, 2015). However, while the organisation has made considerable progress in this regards, conflict emerging from natural resources remains a clog in the wheel of peace and security in Africa. In addressing natural resource conflict, there have been considerable approaches towards providing adequate natural resource governance. Through the African Peace and Security Architecture (APSA), AU has promoted a sustainable degree of peace and security necessary for sustainable development. Through APSA, AU has intervened and introduced peace initiatives in resource conflict states such as South Sudan, Ethiopia, Gambia, Sudan, Zimbabwe, DRC, Somalia and Burundi. Other peace and security initiatives working closely with APSA include the Continental Early Warning System (CEWS), the African Standby Force (ASF), the Panel of the Wise and the Peace Fund, among others. Regional organisations in Africa such as the Economic Community of West African States (ECOWAS) and its security arm—ECOWAS Monitoring Group, IGAD and South Africa Development Commission (SADC), among others—are contributing significantly to ensuring member states have a degree of sustainability in their extractive sectors to challenge and change the narratives of the resource curse.

The AU is also making significant progress in ensuring that the government of African states pursues sustainable resource governance. The African Mining Vision is an important step in this regard. The African Mining Vision (AMV) was adopted in February 2009 at the African Union Summit in Addis Ababa. AMV focused on increasing transparent, equitable and optimal exploitation of solid mineral resources in Africa (Gavin, 2020). The vision thrust also stresses the need to utilise solid mineral revenue for the development of African countries. In order 'to provide strategic operational support for the Vision and its Action Plan', the African Minerals Development Centre was established. Also, to domesticate the AMV at the country level, the Country Mining Vision (CMV) was established and requires member states to align their national objectives with the ideas underpinning the tenets (Africa Union Commission 2009, African Union Commission, 2015).

As part of the effort to reform the African extractive sector, visionary leadership and strong resource institutions has been considered important in the quest for sustainable resource governance. Drawing Hamid et al. (2022)'s study on the interconnections between inequality, grievances and conflict shows that leaders' response to extracting communities' grievances is an important determinant of resource conflicts. Governance indexes are either inadequate or unavailable in most African resource-rich countries with a history of resource conflict. Hence, these states have always been ranked among the failed states. The rate of corruption in the extractive sectors further complicates leadership crises. Resources-rich countries have been associated with high corruption. Many resource-rich countries have elites who pursue 'spoils politics', rent-seeking, state capture and self-enrichment, thus strengthening authoritarianism; most countries are likely to remain dependent on their extractive industries for decades to come (Gapa, 2020: 679). Okolo and Wright, for example, show that the political elites engaged in massive corruption arrogantly and flamboyantly displayed their wealth through high society parties and the purchase of limousines and jets while ignoring the devastating poverty and suffering around them (1994: 132). Also, the absence of strong institutions to guide the rule of access, revenue allocation and use has contributed to the resource curse argument. Hence, borne out of Africa extractive sector leadership crises, corruption and weak institutions, that the question of transparency and accountability become the point of debate.

To ensure transparency and accountability in Africa's extractive sector, the role of non-governmental organisations (civil societies) cannot be underestimated. African countries are increasingly subscribing to different transparency and accountability-focused institutions. Among these institutions include Revenue Watch Institute (RWI), Extractive Industries Transparency Initiative (EITI), Publish What You Pay (PWYP), the Kimberley Process Certification Scheme (KPCS), BudgiT and the Oil Revenue Tracking Initiative (ORTI). Among this organisation, the Extractive Industries Transparency Initiative (EITI) activities have been more pronounced. As of 31 October 2018, eighteen (18) out of twenty-four (24) implementing African countries have been validated under EITI standards. Extractive Industry Transparency Initiative (EITI) was launched in 2003 and is an organisation which upholds global standards of 'transparency' and 'accountability' in the Extractive Industries of mineral resources-rich states. To ensure that resource wealth translates into development, resource-rich countries are taking steps to reform their laws to address new contexts and challenges, including national and international demands for increased scrutiny and transparency in the extractive industry sector. Several governments are employing the platform of EITI and other extractive civil societies to promote transparency and accountability in their extractive sector.

Nigeria, Liberia, Ghana, Sierra Leone, the Republic of Congo and Mali have implemented the EITI standard. The implementation of EITI standards in Nigeria (2007) and Liberia (2009) led to the establishment Nigeria Extractive Industries Transparency Initiative (NEITI) (Yemisi 2021) and Liberia Extractive Industries Transparency Initiative (LEITI) Act. These institutions and their Act provide for disclosure of licenses, government receipts and revenues from extractive sectors. Also, Sierra Leone established the Sierra Leone EITI Multi-Stakeholder Group (SLEITI MSG) under the EITI implementation of resource transparency. Apart from EITI, other civil societies and non-governmental organisation are contributing significantly to resource transparency in Africa. For instance, in Angola, the Acção para o Desenvolvimento Rural e Ambiental (ADRA) has significantly contributed to ensuring transparency in Angola's extractive industries. The policy of 'substantive transparency has shaped ADRA activities'. In 2011, ADRA analysed Angola's state revenue and budget for effective distribution of revenue and utilisation. Revenue Watch Institute (2013) also notes that African countries are reforming their extractive sector laws to promote transparency, accountability and sustainable growth and development.

Conclusion

The chapter provides an overview of resource conflict and governance in Africa. Globally, African countries are rich in abundant renewable and non-renewable natural resources. However, despite these resources, African countries have continued to struggle with economic growth and development, crises of nation-building and incessant conflict arising from the abundance, governance and utilisation of revenues realised from the extractive sector. The chapter adopted the greed and grievances theory to understand the intricacies of resource conflict in Africa. Drawing from scholars' positions on the greed and grievances theory, the chapter holds that both greed and grievances have contributed significantly to the natural resources conflict in Africa. In addition, the chapter provides a nexus between natural resources and conflict in African cases. In African extractive sectors, institutions such as EITI, and PWYP are contributing significantly to the new wave of sustainable resource governance in African countries. To the study, natural resources played an important role in causing conflict, prolongation and crises. The chapter also draws on various country case studies including Nigeria, Sierra Leone, Liberia, DR, Congo, Central African Republic, Angola, Algeria and Libya among others to explain the prevalence of natural resources conflict and resource curse in Africa's extractive sector. In conclusion, the chapter examines the role of the African Union and issues of transparency and accountability in resource governance in Africa.

Bibliography

Abazie-Humphrey, M.I. (2016). The Nigerian Home-Grown DDR Programme—Its Impacts on Empowering the Niger Delta Ex-Militants. In Oswald, Ú., Brauch, H.G., Eréndira, S., Oswald, S., Bennett, J., eds. *Regional Ecological Challenges for Peace in Africa, the Middle East, Latin America and Asia Pacific*, Switzerland: Springer Publishers.

Abiodun, A. (2007). *Natural Resources and Conflict in Africa: The Tragedy of Endowment*, University of Rochester Press.

Africa Union Commission, (2009). Africa Mining Vision. Available at: https://au.int/sites/default/files/documents/30995-doc-africa_mining_vision_english_1.pdf

African Union Commission, (2015). Agenda 2063, The Africa We Want, A Shared Strategic Framework for Inclusive Growth and Sustainable Development First Ten-Year Implementation Plan 2014–2023.

Akpan, O. (2003). Tragedy at Midday: Oil and Underdevelopment of Nigeria. In Akpan, O.E., ed. *The Art and Science of Politics: Essays in Honour of Alhaji Ghali Umar Na'Abba*, Port Harcourt: Footsteps Publications.

Alexis, H. (2020). Natural Resource Abundance: A Hidden Drag on Africa's Development? In Samuel, O., Toyin, F., ed. *The Palgrave Handbook of African Political Economy*, Palgrave Macmillan, 699–724.

Auty, R.M. (1993). *Sustaining Development in Mineral Economies: The Resource Curse Thesis*, London/New York: Routledge.

Auty, R.M. (2001). *Resource Abundance and Economic Development. UNU/WIDER Studies in Development Economics*, Oxford: Oxford University Press.

Auty, R.M., Gelb, A. (1986). Oil Windfalls in a Small Parliamentary Democracy: Their Impact on Trinidad and Tobago. *World Development* 14(9): 1161–1175.

Ayee, J. (2014). The Status of Natural Resource Management in Africa: Capacity Development Challenges and Opportunities. In Hanson, K. T., Alessandro, C. D., Owusu, F., ed. *Managing Africa's Natural Resources*, London: Palgrave Macmillan, 15–38.

Beevers, M.D. (2019). *Peacebuilding and Natural Resource Governance After Armed Conflict: Sierra Leone and Liberia*, Palgrave Macmillan.

Cederman, L.E., Kristian, S.G., Halvard, B. (2013). *Inequality, Grievances and Civil War*. New York: Cambridge University Press.

Cederman, L.E., Kristian S.G., Julian, W. (2017). Predicting the Decline of Ethnic Conflict: Was Gurr Right and for the Right Reasons? *Journal of Peace Research* 54: 262–274

Clayton, G. (2016). Oil, Relative Strength and Civil War Mediation. *Cooperation and Conflict* 51(3): 325–344.

Collier, P. (2000). Doing well out of war: An economic perspective. In Berdal, M. R., Malone, D., ed., *Greed & grievance: Economic agendas in Civil Wars*, Lynne Rienner Publishers, 91–112.

Collier, P., Hoeffler, A. (1998). On Economic Causes of Civil War. *Oxford Economic Papers* 50(4): 563–573.

Collier, P., Hoeffler, A. (2002). On the Incidence of Civil War in Africa, *Journal of Conflict Resolution* 46(1): 13–28.

Collier, P., Hoeffler, A. (2004). Greed and Grievance in Civil War. *Oxford Economic Papers* 56(4): 563–595.

Collier, P., Hoeffler, A. (2005). Resource Rents, Governance, and Conflict. *Journal of Conflict Resolution* 49(4): 625–633.

Collier, P., Nicholas S., eds. (2005). *Understanding Civil War: Evidence and Analysis*. Vol. 1 & 2, Washington, DC: The World Bank.

Coser, L.A. (1956). *The Functions of Social Conflict York*, New York: U.S.A.

Elbadawi, I., Sambanis, N. (2000). *How Much War Will We See? Estimating the Incidence of Civil War in 161 Countries*, Washington, DC: World Bank.

Emmanuel, S.A. (2022). The Effect of the EITI Process on Transparency and Accountability in Sierra Leone's Extractive Industry. In Emmanuel, S.A., ed. *Freedom of Information Law and Good Governance the Curse of Corruption in Sierra Leone*, Palgrave Macmillan, 293–364.

Eyene, O., Reeta, C.T. (2021). *The Political Economy of Natural Resource Funds*. Palgrave Macmillan.

FAO. (2000). *Conflict and Natural Resource Management*, Rome, Italy: Food and Agricultural Organization.

Fearon, J.D., Laitin, D.D. (2003). Ethnicity, Insurgency, and Civil War. *American Political Science Review* 97: 75–90.

Forstater, M., Zadek, S., Guang, Y., Yu, K., Hong, C.X., Geo, M. (2010). Corporate Responsibility in African Development: Insights from an Emerging Dialogue, Chinese Academy of Social Sciences, *Working Paper of the Corporate Social Responsibility Initiative*, No. 60 (October).

Frankel, J.A. (2010). *The Natural Resource Curse: A Survey* (No. w15836), Cambridge, MA: National Bureau of Economic Research.

Gapa, A. (2020). Natural Resources and African Economies: Turning Liability to Asset. In Samuel, O., Toyin, F., ed. *The Palgrave Handbook of African Political Economy*, Palgrave Macmillan, 679–698.

Gavin, H. (2020). The Africa Mining Vision: A Manifesto for More Inclusive Extractive Industry-Led Development? *Canadian Journal of Development Studies/Revue canadienne d'études du développement* 41(3): 417–431.

Gelb, A. (1988). *Oil Windfalls: Blessing or Curse?* Washington, DC: The World Bank.

Gilbert, L.D. (2010). Youth Militancy, Amnesty and Security in the Niger Delta Region of Nigeria. In Ojakorotu, V., Gilbert, L.D., ed. *Checkmating the Resurgence of Oil Violence in the Niger Delta of Nigeria*, L.A.P Lambert Academic Publishing AF. & CO. 2010, 52.

Global Witness. (2003). *The Usual Suspects: Liberia's Weapons and Mercenaries in Côte d'Ivoire and Sierra Leone*, London: Global Witness. http://www.globalwitness.org/reports/download.php/00068.pdf.

Hamid, E.A., Cederman, L.E., eds. (2022). *Natural Resources, Inequality and Conflict*, Palgrave Macmillan, 11–36.

Hamid, E.A., Cederman, L.E., Yaron, A.W. (2022). Mineral Resources and Conflict: An Analytical Overview. In Hamid, E.A., Cederman, L.E., ed. *Natural Resources, Inequality and Conflict*, Palgrave Macmillan.

Hanson, K.T., Owusu, F., D'Alessandro, C. (2014). Toward a coordinated approach to natural resource management in Africa. *Managing Africa's Natural Resources*, London: Palgrave Macmillan, 1–14.

Homer-Dixon, T.F. (1994). Environmental Scarcities and Violent Conflict: Evidence from Cases. *International Security* 19(1): 5. https://doi.org/10.2307/2539147

Jesse, S.O. (2020). Natural Resources and African Economies: Asset or Liability? In Samuel, O.O., Toyin, F., ed. *The Palgrave Handbook of African Political Economy*, Palgrave Macmillan, 667–678.

Karl, T.L. (1999). The Perils of the Petro-State: Reflections on the Paradox of Plenty. *Journal of International Affairs* 53(1): 31–48.

Kiiza, J., Bategeka, L., Ssewanyana, S. (2011). Righting Resource-Curse Wrongs in Uganda: The Political Economy of Oil Discovery and the Management of Popular Expectations Published in Mawazo. *The Journal of Humanities and Social Sciences, Makerere University* 10(3): 183–203, September.

Hanson, K. T., Owusu, F., & D'Alessandro, C. (2014). Toward a coordinated approach to natural resource management in Africa. In Managing Africa's Natural Resources (pp. 1-14). Palgrave Macmillan, London.

Koubi, V., Gabriele, S., Tobias, B., Thomas, B. (2014). Do Natural Resources Matter for Interstate and Intrastate Armed Conflict? *Journal of Peace Research* 51(2): 227–243.

Kyem, P.A.K. (2021). *Managing Natural Resource Conflicts with Participatory Mapping and PGIS Applications*. Springer.

Larmer, M., Kennes, E. (2019). Katanga's Secessionism in the Democratic Republic of Congo. In de Vries, L., Englebert, P., Schomerus, M., ed. *Secessionism in African Politics: Aspiration, Grievance, Performance, Disenchantment*, Springer International Publishing.

Larry, A.S. (2007). Seeing the Forest for the Trees: Tropical Forests, the State and Violent Conflict in Africa. In De Jong, W., Donoven, D., Abe, K.I., ed. *Extreme Conflict and Tropical Forests*, Springer, 93–116.

Lujala, P., Gleditsch, N.P., Gilmore, E. (2005). A Diamond Curse? Civil War and a Lootable Resource. *Journal of Conflict Resolution* 49(4): 538–562.

Lwanda, G. (2003). Conflict diamonds and the African resource curse: Peacemaking. *Conflict Trends* (4): 20–24.

Madubuko, C.C. (2015). *Oil Exploration and Youth Unrest in the Niger Delta: A Study in the Rise and Impacts of Socio-Cultural Group Insurgency in Nigeria, 1956–2014*. Unpublished PhD Thesis. University of New England, Armidale.

Mildner, S.-A., Lauster, G., Wodni, W. (2011). Scarcity and Abundance Revisited: A Literature Review on Natural Resources and conflict. *International Journal of Conflict and Violence (IJCV)* 5(1): 155–172.

Mukoro, A. (2010). Governance Failure, Civil Societies and the Niger Delta. In Ojakorotu, V., ed. *Anatomy of the Niger Delta: Causes, Consequences and Opportunities for Peace*, London: Transaction Publishers.

Natural Resource Governance Institute. (2017). 2017 Resource Governance Index. Available at: https://resourcegovernance.org/sites/default/files/documents/2017-resource-governance-index.pdf

Odewumi, S.G., Patrick, O.E. (2005). World Natural Resources and conflict, in Transformations. In Abolade, A., eds. *International Relations since 1945*. A-Triads Associates Educational publishers and printers.

Okoli, A.C., Uhembe, C.A. (2015). Crisis of Natural Resource Governance in Nigeria's Extractive Industry: Examining the Phenomenon of Artisanal Mining/Quarrying. *Global Journal of Human-Social Science: F Political Science* 15(7).

Okolo, J.E., Wright, S. (1994). Nigeria. The Political Economy of Foreign Policy in ECOWAS. Shaw, T.M., Okolo, J.E., eds. 125–146. New York: St. Martin's Press.

Olanrewaju, F.J. (2017). The AU's Progress and Achievements in the Realms of Peace and Security. *India Quarterly* 73(4): 1–17.

Olanrewaju, F.O., Segun, J., Adekunle, O. (2020). Natural Resources, Conflict and Security Challenges in Africa. *India Quarterly*, 1–17.

Omotola, S.J. (2010). Niger Delta Technical Committee (NDTC) and the Niger Delta Question. In Ojakorotu, V., ed. *Anatomy of the Niger Delta: Causes, Consequences and Opportunities for Peace*, London: Transaction Publishers.

Onuoha, F.C., Okafor, J.C., Femi-Adedayo, O.O. (2021). Nigeria: Militancy, Insurgency and the Proliferation of Small Arms and Light Weapon. In Tar, U., Onwurah, C.P., ed. *The Palgrave Handbook of Small Arms and Conflicts in Africa*, Palgrave Macmillan, 762–763.

Otoabasi, A., Umoh, U.E. (2021). "Resource Curse" and "Resource Wars" and the Proliferation of Small Arms. In Usman, A.T., Onwurah, C.P., ed. *Africa in the Palgrave Handbook of Small Arms and Conflicts in Africa*, 245–264.

Paine, J. (2016). Rethinking the 'Resource Curse': How Oil Wealth Prevents Center-Seeking Civil Wars. *International Organization* 70: 727–761.

Revenue Watch Institute. (2013). 2013 Resource Governance Index: A Measure of Transparency and Accountability in the Oil, Gas and Mining Sector. Available at: https://anti-corruption.org/wpcontent/uploads/2013/09/rgi_2013_Eng.pdf

Richards, P. (2001). Are "Forest" Wars in Africa Resource Conflicts? The Case of Sierra Leone. In Peluso, N.L., Watts, M., ed. *Violent Environments*, Cornell: Cornell University Press, 65–82.

Ross, M. (1999). The Political Economy of the Resource Curse. *World Politics* 51(2): 297–332.

Ross, M. (2001). How does natural resource wealth influence civil war? *University of California at Los Angeles Political Science Department, Los Angeles*. Available online at: http://www.eireview.org/.Processed

Ross, M.L. (2001). Does Oil Hinder Democrac.? *World Politics* 53(3): 325–361.

Ross, M. L. (2004b). How Do Natural Resources Influence Civil War? Evidence from Thirteen Cases. *International Organisation* 58(1): 35–67.

Ross, M.L. (2015). What Have We Learned About the Resource Curse? *Annual Review of Political Science* 18: 239–259.

Ruben D.K. (2007). Greed or Grievance in West Africa's Forest Wars? In De Jong, W., Donovan, D., Abe, K.I, ed. *Extreme Conflict and Tropical Forests*, Springer, 37–56.

Salah, J.O. (2020). Natural Resources and African Economies: Asset or Liability? In Samuel, O., Toyin, F., ed. *The Palgrave Handbook of African Political Economy*, Palgrave Macmillan, 667–678.

Schellens, M.K., Diemer, A. (2020). Natural Resource Conflicts: Definition and Three Frameworks to Aid Analysis. In Leal Filho, W. et al., ed. *Partnerships for the Goals, Encyclopedia of the UN Sustainable Development Goals*, Springer Nature Switzerland.

SIPRI Yearbook. (2000). Stockholm International Peace Research Institute, Stockholm.

Transparency International. (2021). *Nigeria: Corruption Perceptions Index*, Berlin: Transparency International Secretariat.

The Fund for Peace. (2015). Failed States Index, 2015. Available at: www.fundforpeace.org

Umoh, U.E. (2010). The Crisis of Abundance and the Challenge of Nation Building in Nigeria. Paper Presentation in the Department of History and International Studies, University of Uyo, Nigeria.

UNO. (2012). Toolkit and Guidance for Preventing and Managing Land and Natural Resources Conflict. United Nations Plaza, Rm. 2084 New York, USA.

Van Alstine, J. (2014). Transparency in energy governance: The extractive industries transparency initiative and publish what you pay campaign. *Transparency in Global Environmental Governance: Critical Perspectives*, 249–270.

Ojakorotu, V. (2018). Resource Control and Conflict in Africa. In Samuel, O.O., Toyin, F., ed. *The Palgrave Handbook of African Politics, Governance and Development*, Palgrave Macmillan, 367–386.

Yemisi O.I. (2020). Elite Corruption and Youth Militancy in Nigeria: Case of Niger Delta Crisis. *Journal of African Problems & Solutions* 2(2): 11–28.

Yemisi, O.I. (2021). Nigeria Extractive Industry Transparency Initiative (NEITI), Resource Transparency and Niger Delta Crisis (2004–2019). In Chukwuma, O. Lemuel, O., ed. *History and the Niger Delta: Oil Politics and Culture*, Kaduna: Pyla-Mak Publishers Limited.

CHAPTER 2

The Place of Mineral Resource Conflicts in Critical Security Analysis in Africa

Chukwuemeka Nwosu

Introduction

The main thesis here is to take a cursory survey of how mineral resources in Africa have continuously been a source of conflict, with particular reference to countries like Nigeria with in the era of crude oil discovery the abundant natural resources in the Gulf of Guinea and the plethora of mineral resources in South Africa which resulted in the economics of apartheid: European wealth and African poverty. As earlier stated, the chapter will discuss energy security and human insecurity as high point of critical security analysis.

Over the recent decades, government officials, analysts and academics alike have identified mineral resource deposits in Africa as a source of growing conflicts, affecting countries like Nigeria, Gulf of Guinea and Southern African States with settler colonies for the benefit of the white

C. Nwosu (✉)
Department of History and International Studies, Imo State University, Owerri, Nigeria
e-mail: barrchukwuemekanwosu@yahoo.com

K. J. Ani (ed.), *Resource Conflict and Environmental Relations in Africa*,
https://doi.org/10.1007/978-981-19-7343-7_2

minority Boers, as well as the Portuguese. The Niger Delta is one of Africa's richest regions, blessed with enormous human and varied material resources (Alagoa, 1980; Ikime, 1980; Law, 1991; Wangbu, 2005). Diverse forms of violence overlap in this urban armed conflict, not only politically-motivated armed conflict but also ethically influenced. Nonetheless, the significant consequences of the range of violence perpetrated within urban conflicts have not however, been acknowledged in analyses of Niger Delta armed conflict (Ani et al., 2018, 2021; Okeke-Ogbuafor et al., 2019).

In recent times, the urban armed conflict in the region has worsened due to the pervasive presence of government force and the ethnic militia groups. These delinquent gangs have reorganized under the control or influence of paramilitaries or the guerrillas (This Day, Lagos, February 24, 2005).

Nigeria and the Era of Crude Oil

On Sunday, 15 January 1956, the Anglo Dutch group, Shell D'Archy, discovered crude oil in commercial quantities in the creek-side village of Oloibiri. This seeming breakthrough, which also held so much promise and great prospects for the sustainable development of the Niger Delta, marked an epoch in the history of the region (Idemudia and Ite, 2006: 391). Consequent upon the discovery of oil in the Niger Delta region, it initiated a plethora of challenges in the wake of that development. Subsequent upon the discovery of oil in the Niger Delta area, Western oil prospecting companies start to make concerted effort towards getting exploration as well as prospecting licenses from the Nigerian government. Thereafter, oil was, subsequently, discovered in diverse parts of the Niger Delta area, and by February 1958, Nigeria became an oil exporter with a production level of 6,000 barrels per day (Ibeanu, 1999). Consequent upon the boom in oil revenue in Nigeria which tallied with the centralization of political powers. The space called "Niger Delta" has been defined by the Niger Delta Commission Act, as the region which includes Abia, Akwa-Ibom, Bayelsa, Cross River, Delta, Edo, Imo, Ondo and Rivers States. Mitee argued that as oil was discovered in commercial quantity in the Niger Delta, the region gradually became seen and expressed in terms of an oil-producing area of the country, not necessarily in an area geographically classified as Delta. The huge revenues generated have not reflected in the lives of the majority in most communities, from the era of crude oil boom till date.

In the light of the foregoing, the country became the largest petroleum producers in Africa and the sixth in the world (Odoemene, 2011). Furthermore, since the early 1990s, the petroleum sector has accounted for more than 15% of the country's Gross Domestic Product (GPD), while oil exports have accounted for over 95% of total export earnings and about 75% of government revenue (Balouga, 2009: 8). Besides, five decades and a half of oil exploitation have transformed the wetland into an industrial wasteland (Uyigue & Ogbeibu, nd: 2). The imprint is about 7,200 kilometres of pipelines, 159 oil fields, and 275 flow stations, with have flares visible day and night from miles away. With regard to our area of study, the nature of oil politics is indeed convoluted. In this respect, Alamieyeseigha (2005: 9) contended that:

> The kismet of states are resolved by the outcome of oil industry operations and it is not only volatile but adversely affect the lives of people globally. Oil promotes the factories of the industrialized nations and supply revenue that facilitates oil export to implement goal-oriented state and economic development programme. The absence of oil would have had devastating effect on the lives of people in particular and economic growth and development all over the world. With respect to political and diplomatic strategies, oil has become a paramount factor for various governments and a vital factor in state policy. Oil symbolizes ruthlessness of the big business moguls whose primary aim is to make their pecuniary gains.

In yet another genre, Omitola (2012: 252–270) contended that the exploitation of crude oil continues unabated without due cognizance to the views and aspirations of the oil-bearing communities by both the oil multinationals and the Nigerian government which by virtue of Petroleum Decree of 1969, Offshore Decree 1971 and Land Use Decree 1978 received the largest percentage of the oil receipt. Undoubtedly, the decrees have their various dimensions as well as provisions designed to dominate the people's interest by the oil companies and government who are supposed to be the custodians of the environment both terrestrial and aquatic habitats. On the basis of archival sources relevant to this study, it was discovered that the historical roles of the federal government, and multinational oil companies in the petroleum industry especially as it relates the exploration and explanation of oil in the Niger Delta with the concomitant consequences on the people in the region has been a major driver of crisis.

Furthermore, this development compromised the neutrality of the government in mediating in matters affecting the oil companies and the host communities. What is more, whenever the multinationals are making huge profit, usually it translates into more income for the federal government of Nigeria. Moreover, there is obviously a strong alliance of interest between state officials and the oil companies. Often times, most state officials and frontline politicians have vested interest in the petroleum enterprise. However, this state of affairs very much incapacitates the state from intervening on behalf of the host communities in enforcing internationally laid down regulations binding oil companies. With respect to establishing the legal basis of the federal government ownership of petroleum mineral resources, it is instructive that both the municipal and international laws recognize the concept of ownership of natural resources which petroleum deposits constitute a part thereof. Again, it is indeed instructive that the mode and procedure of ownership vary from one country to another depending on the historical experience as well as development strategies of the countries involved. As earlier stated, often times, most petroleum-producing countries, owing to their historical and colonial experience, petroleum is vested exclusively in the state. Among the developing nations, Mexico was in fact the first to declare that oil production and deposits in the ground belong to the state exclusively. It was against this background that European and American oil companies were nationalized in 1938.

Significantly, the African petroleum-producing states of Algeria, Libya, Egypt, Gabon as well as Nigeria belong to or rather subscribe to this arrangement. For instance, in Nigeria, diverse legislations dating to the colonial period vested the right of ownership of petroleum deposits and other natural resources in the state exclusively while keeping the constituent units federating the state in abeyance. The colonial government Mineral Acts of 1946 and 1958 vested the entire property and control of all minerals and mineral oils, in, under or upon any land in Nigeria and all rivers, streams and water courses throughout Nigeria in the British Crown. Subsequently, the 1963 Republican Constitution of Nigeria vests the federal government with the exclusive power to legislate on mines and mineral oils including oil fields, oil mining, geological survey and natural gas. Before the emergence of Minerals Act of 1946 and 1958, as earlier stated, there was the Minerals Ordinance of 1914 preceding the act. The ordinance granted the right of oil prospecting and exploration to Britain. Accordingly, this was the basis upon which shell BP was granted the sole licence for oil exploration in Nigeria. This paved the way for other oil companies such as Mobil Exxon, Gulf, Agip, Safrap (ELF), Texaco and others to come into oil prospecting and exploration in Nigeria. The oil companies, at the early stage, maintained a 50–50 sharing formula with the government and thus, had no direct involvement in the oil exploration.

However, the federal government in 1969 annulled the 1914 Minerals Ordinance and the Minerals Act of 1946 and 1958, respectively, and effectively transferred the ownership of oil to the state. It also set up an Oil Corporation in 1971 and entered into joint venture agreements with oil companies operating in Nigeria (International Institute for Democracy and Electoral Assistance: Democracy in Nigeria, 2000: 242). The proximate and likely environmental consequence of the place of mineral resource endowment is that the Niger Delta region has become highly insecured for both the indigenes and the oil companies, as militant insurgencies had remained a continuum for conflict in the region. Consequently, young people in the Niger Delta region are now exposed to cultism, armed banditry and illegal use of light and heavy arms. With the proliferation of arms, most of which are sophisticated than the ones used by the regular police, and the ability of the government to provide security as one of its statutory role is virtually difficult in the region.

These militias, private thugs and government forces have been witnessed in full blown conflict areas like the 1999 genocide in Odi and the continuous raids by the Nigerian military on villages and communities populated by innocent civilians. Thus, it is reported that thousands of innocent civilians, especially women, children, pregnant women and the aged were killed in the attack. Furthermore, several others numbering over 30,000 were trapped in the bush, swamps and mangrove forest where they were hiding. Besides, the government forces routinely commit abuses against the civilians and hire out their services in conflict and after conflict from one community to the other, drawing their power from the "barrel of the gun" (arms) (Sha'aba, 1998).

The Place of Mineral Resource Conflicts in the Gulf of Guinea and Critical Security Analysis

The status of the Gulf of Guinea states today reflects their colonial heritage and abundant natural resources thereby recasting the theory of "paradox of plenty" and "resource curse". Today, about 4.9 million barrels per day come from the Gulf of Guinea, and overall, the Gulf of Guinea could be home to over 50 billion barrels of crude oil. Undoubtedly, manifold and considerable discoveries are still being made in Ghana as well as the Island state of SaoTome, which analysts speculate have a large reserve mineral deposit of crude oil. With respect to Equatorial Guinea, the country is still at loggerheads with Gabon over the Corisco Bay, as well as other islands, which it occupied in 1972, thought to have undisclosed oil and gas deposits. Against the background of the strategic interest that the Gulf of Guinea now commands, with regard to contestations over mineral resource ownership between states and minorities as well as aggrieved groups within resource-rich states, the threat of insecurity cannot be overemphasized given the linkages between resources and conflicts. In the region, the new security challenges are basically spear-headed by the so-called militants as well as mercenaries otherwise referred to in this study as resource insurgents. These militant gangs and resource insurgents have prevented the state from meeting international energy requirement more especially in terms of prices and security of suppliers. With respect to security in the Gulf of Guinea, it is pertinent to state inter alia according to the United Nations Convention on Law of the Sea III (UNCLOS III), and it allows coastal states to claim a 200 nautical mile (nm) Exclusive Economic Zone (EEZ) out of which 12 nm from the baseline is regarded as territorial waters while an additional 12 nm in which a state continues to enforce its laws is the "contiguous" zone (United Nations). There is no gainsaying the fact that the mineral resource laden-rich states of the Gulf of Guinea have been regions of continuous conflict especially between Guinea and Gabon whose conflict has been a function of internal and external cross-border contretemps and dissension (Anyika et al., 2022).

Moreover, the mineral resource skirmishes in the Gulf of Guinea have been fuelled by freedom fighters, opposition forces, and oppressed as well as marginalized nationals and between local regimes. These forms of conflicts have been complicated and exacerbated by the interplay of external influence driven by geopolitics and economic interest of actors (Mane, 2005). Furthermore, the major causal factor of inter-state or cross-border conflicts in the Gulf of Guinea has been the availability of abundant natural resources (Shaxson, 2007: 4); in this respect, it is manifest that inter-state security instability in the Gulf of Guinea can be glanced from the point of view of claims to as well as control of territorial boundaries and their resource deposits. These claims and counter claims have arisen among the states because of the singular factor that oil was found in the gulf region of two or more states, hence the intractable conflict. Oftentimes, the existence of oil fields in areas where borderlines may not be challenged, but when deposits stretch across the border in uncertain quantity so that drilling from one country may negatively affect the amount of oil available for exploration by its neighbours, conflict arises (Shaxson, 2007: 4).

The fact still remains incontrovertible that offshore oil rights have remained the bone of contention among states of Gulf of Guinea and which in turn, has escalated to unrestrained armed conflict as a means of regulating who owns what and as a means of regulating incessant competitive claims to boundary disputes consequent upon the existence of huge mineral deposits. For a stable and secured Gulf of Guinea, there is the need to specify in unmistakable terms that borderlines between countries, exchange of seismological data, additional drilling to determine the stretch of oil field or early agreements on how to share proceeds in the event of overlapping oil discoveries are indeed significant measure expedient for conflict prevention as well as ensuring continuity of oil exploration in a stable and peaceful Gulf of Guinea.

Mineral Resource Deposits in South Africa and the Emergence of Apartheid

Under the apartheid, the white minority regime deprived the African black majority the dignity of their human rights and liberty. The apartheid rule denotes white settler colony, inequality, system of imperialism, neocolonialism, exploitation of their natural resources, which culminated in the enthronement of racial discrimination, segregatory and obnoxious laws that separated Africans from the Afrikaners (one born in South Africa but of Dutch descent) in their aboriginal homeland for the benefit of the white minority rule by the Boers in South Africa (Seshibedi, 2022). Economic development in South Africa was European wealth and African poverty. The predominant characteristics of the South African economic system is the total dependence on African labour. In 1652, this was the real state of affairs when Van Riebeech landed at Table Bay and proceeded to enslave or to marry the indigenous, mostly Nama population. And it is true today where Africans out number Europeans by a ratio of 10:1 in mining, by almost 3:1 in manufacture and 4.5:1 in construction.

In fact, from about 1840, wool production was the country's principal export commodity, until 1869, when mineral resources were discovered in large quantity. In this regards, it was the discovery of minerals that gradually transformed the country from an agriculture-based economy to a mining-based one. In mining, for example, European/African wage differentials were 11.7:1 in 1911, 17.6:1 in 1966 and 20.3:1 in 1971 (Seshibedi, 2022). The discovery of a diamond field at Kimberly, in 1867, marked the beginning of a fundamental change of South Africa from a rural to an industrial economy. Suddenly, South Africa became a rich country. By 1871, the value of diamond exports stood at €16,000,000 per year (Barkindo et al., 1994: 154). Kimberly soon became an important mining and commercial centre. In manufacturing, the ratios were 5.1:1 in 1966 and had risen to 5.85:1 in 1971 (Seshibedi, 2022: 33). In the political economy of South Africa, Raph Horwitz quotes a government appointed commission of enquiry which found that African mine wages had decreased by nearly a third between 1896 and 1913 (Horwitz, 1958: 176).

At Natal and the Cape, the diamond industry was prosperous while Transvaal also prospered on gold mining. In 1866 in Witwatersrand, large deposits of fold were discovered and this area was known to be the richest gold deposits in the world. Like diamond, this of course resulted in a gold rush, prosperity, success and bankruptcy. Consequently, it gave a Phillip to the development of new industrial centres as well as of urban communities, such as well as Johannesburg which turned out to be the wealthiest as well as the largest. The growth of some shanty towns in the mining areas was a function of the mining revolution. There was rapid migration to Johannesburg from every part of the country, so that by the close of the century, its population had risen to 166,000. Between workers and between companies, there was a great competition in the gold industry. The outcome of this was the transformation of Transvaal into a modern industrial state, with Witwatersrand as its centre. The gold industry accounted for 97 per cent of Transvaal's export in 1896. Raph Horwitz, who studied the contribution of gold to the South African economy, showed that in most of the years between 1929 and 1963 (excluding the war years 1940–1945), gold sales paid for more half of South Africa's total imports (Horwitz, 1958: 295).

In addition, one other thing that led to economic development of South Africa was the discovery of coal in large quantities in Natal as well as the Cape Colony. The discovery of coal made a valuable contribution to the advancement of industrialization. Indeed, coal became an important source of fuel for the mining industry. Not only that it provided job opportunities for many people but was a valuable source of wealth.

Energy Security and Human Insecurity as High Point of Critical Security Analysis

Often times almost all powerful states in world politics, with the exception of Canada, the UK and Russia, require large volumes of import oil to sustain the demand from its domestic economies. Countries like USA, India and China need to import over half of their oil requirements, while members of the G8, like France, Germany, Italy as well as Japan, are almost entirely reliant on foreign oil. Furthermore, this reliance is set to increase, as increased demand from powerful states is not matched by rise in domestic production. By 2030, the shortfall between consumption and production for the core powers—the extent to which they are reliant upon imports—is set almost to double. From the foregoing, this fact ensures that controlling the conditions under which this resource is produced, exported and delivered to consumers has become a key strategic concern for powerful states. Against this backdrop, in the post-colonial period, where formal notions of imperial control no longer frame North–South relations, political, economic and also military intervention in oil-rich regions by the world's core powers has continued to play itself out of the foreground. Moreover, in particular, the stability as well as friendly orientation of key oil-producing states and regions is a paramount concern for strategists, and foreign and security policies have most times reflected this fact. In regions where conflict is often endemic like the Gulf of Guinea in Africa, for instance, and where there exists a range of forces seeking to challenge existing social orders, and therefore, potentially endanger the flow of oil under conditions favourable to the major consumers, these powers have often acted to support those governmental and non-governmental forces considered "friendly" or favourable to their interest. However, billions of dollars of economic and military assistance have been granted to oil-rich regimes by the core powers, often in direct competition with one another for influence. And this is the energy-security nexus in critical security analysis.

Oil-rich zones are often some of the most unstable politically of all the regions in the Global South. Dutch disease—whereby substantial oil incomes drive up exchange rates, slowing overall growth and "hollowing out" non-oil sectors—affects many oil-rich economies. Thus, in parallel, these regions tend to have a set of political instabilities that have the potential to exacerbate existing conflicts and generate new ones. Joseph Stiglitz (2003) has contended that control over natural resource wealth provides leaders with little incentive to share power and gives leaders the means with which to buy legitimate rather than earning it through elections. Dictatorial and authoritarian state forms can be more easily maintained and continued in oil-rich regions, against the background that centralization of wealth works to insulate the ruling strata from popular pressure to reform. Invariably, the prevalence of non-democratic governance can be seen across the oil-rich Caspian Region, Middle East and West Africa, where the power of corrupt dictatorships is considerably based upon the huge wealth generated via the energy sector.

Also, the reduction of legitimate political space for most of the population, in addition to often-vast inequalities in wealth distribution, as the oil income is retained within a small circle of economic and political elites, can easily breed domestic unrest. A wide variety of social and political forces, across the oil-rich South, have arisen to challenge the current distribution of power, as well as the condition under which energy stocks are released onto international markets. However, often times most of these adopt peaceful means of protest, but increasingly these have been matched by armed campaigns against the prevailing order, as groups turn to violence in a bid to achieve their objectives. Besides, attacks on energy infrastructure and foreign oil expatriates have increased, and these are often dotted with wider insurgencies for greater autonomy and control over natural resources. Indeed, the ideological base supporting these movements is largely dependent on a particular case, ranging from leftist groups in Colombia, to ethno-nationalist groups in the Niger Delta of Nigeria, to al-Qaeda-affiliated groups in Saudi Arabia. The absence of stability in this context refers to the absence of challenge to the status quo, and the pursuit of this objective has severe ramifications for human security in the regions. Thus, operating through the aegis of "counter-insurgency or counter terrorism", local security forces often engage in repeated human rights violations in order to subvert threat.

Conclusion

The chapter has attempted to examine the place of mineral resource conflicts in critical security analysis in Africa. It took a cursory survey of how mineral resources in Africa have continuously been a source of conflict, with particular reference to Nigeria within the era of crude oil discovery in the Niger Delta region; the abundant natural resources in the Gulf of Guinea with the concomitant conflict and insecurity; and the plethora of mineral resources in South Africa and how it leads to the emergence of Apartheid: European wealth and African poverty. The chapter also discussed energy security and human insecurity as high point of critical security analysis. The chapter concludes on the note that the place of mineral resource in Africa instead of brining the desired economic growth and development to the continent, it was replete with conflict and cataclysmic upheaval that resulted in the death of a sizable proportion of the populace and ultimately, a source of insecurity. The chapter recommends that there is the need to stipulate clear borderlines between countries, exchange of seismological information, additional drilling to confirm the stretch of an oil field or early agreements on how to share proceeds in case of overlapping boundary oil discoveries which are significant steps for conflict prevention and ensuring continuity of oil and other mineral exploration devoid of conflict and insecurity in the Niger Delta region and also a secured Gulf of Guinea.

References

Alagoa, E. J. (1980), "Peoples of the Cross River Valley and the Eastern Niger Delta", in Ikime Obaro, (ed.), Groundwork of Nigerian History Ibadan: Historical' Society of Nigeria and Heinemann Educational Books.

Alamieyeseigha, D. S. P. (2005), "The Niger Delta Crises: Yesterday, Today and Tomorrow". Paper presented at the Institute of African Studies, University of Ibadan, Ibadan, Nigeria.

Ani, K. J., Oko Otu, C. & Ojakorotu, V. (2021), The Quest for the Attainment of Relative Peace in the Niger Delta, *African Renaissance,* 18(4): 55–70.

Ani, K. J., Nnanwube E. F. & Ojakorotu V. (2018), "Agriculture, Oil Resource Curse and Conflict: An Assessment of Nigerian Development Quagmire, *African Renaissance,* 15(3): 49–66.

Anyika, V. O., Ojakorotu, V. & Ani, K. J. (2022), Piracy in the Gulf of Guinea-Trends, Causes, Effects and the Way Forward, *African Journal of Development Studies,* 5–20.

Balouga J. (2009), "The Niger Delta: Defusing the Time Bomb". First Quarter, International Association for Energy Economics.

Barkindo, B., Omolewa, M., & Babalola, G. (1994), Africa and the Wide World 3: Africa since the Scramble. Ikeja, Lagos: Longman Nigeria, Plc.

Horwitz, R. (1958), The Political Economy of South Africa. New York: Praegar.

Ibeanu, O. (1999), "Insurgents, Civil Society and Democracy in Nigeria: Ogoni Encounters with the State, 1990–1998". Research Report for ICSAG Programme of the Centre for Research and Documentation (CRD), Kano.

Idemudia, U. & Ite, U. E. (2006), "Demystifying the Niger Delta Conflict: Towards an Integrated Explanation". *Review of African Political Economy (ROAPE),* 33(109): 391–406.

Ikime, O. (1980), "The Peoples and Kingdoms of the Delta Province", in Ikime Obaro, (ed.), Groundwork of Nigerian History, Ibadan: Historical Society of Nigeria and Heinemann Educational Books.

International Institute for Democracy and Electoral Assistance; Democracy in Nigeria (Stockholm, 2000).

Law, R. (1991), The Slave Coast of West Africa 1550–1750: The Impact of the Atlantic Slave Trade on an African Society. Oxford: Clarendon Press.

Mane, O. D. (2005), Emergence of the Gulf of Guinea in the Global economy: Prospects and Challenges. IMF Working Paper, Office of the Executive Director-Africa, (WP/05/235).

Odoemene, A. (2011), "Social Consequences of Environmental Change in the Niger Delta of Nigeria", *Journal of Sustainable Development (JSD),* 4(2): 1–10.

Okeke-Ogbuafor, N., Ani, K. J. & Gray T. (2019), "Two Approaches to Conflict Resolution and their Applicability to Ogoniland, Nigeria", *Journal of Global South Studies,* 36(1):164–185.

Omitola, B. O. (2012), "The Struggle for the Nigerian Soul: Niger Delta Debacle", *Journal of Alternative Perspectives in the Social Sciences,* 5(1): 252–270.

Patrick, F. Wilmot. (1980), Apartheid and African Liberation Ile-Ife: University of Ife press Ltd.

Seshibedi S. S. (2022), The Nexus between Petroleum Energy Security and South Africa's Foreign Policy, Dissertation, Masters of Social Science in Political Science, University of Fort Hare, South Africa.

Sha'aba, R. A. (1998), MOSOP and the Ogoni Struggle, in Omotoye Olorede et al., (eds.), Ken Saro-Wiwa and the Crises of the Nigerian State, Lagos: CDHR.
Shaxson, N. (2007), Poisoned Wells: The Dirty Politics of African Oil New York: Pal Grave Macmillan.
Stiglitz, J. (2003), 'Foreword', in Svetlana Tsalik, Caspian Oil Windfalls: Who Will Benefit?, New York: Caspian Revenue Watch, Open Society Institute.
This Day, Lagos, February 24, 2005.
Udechukwu, U., & Okolie-Osemene, J. (2015), "Complexion of the Petroleum Industry: Rethinking the Roles of Government and Oil Companies in Niger Delta Communities, in Yinusa Kehinde Salami et al., (eds.), Nationalism and Economic Justice in Nigeria, Ile-Ife: Obafemi Awolowo University Press.
United Nations, United Nations Convention on the Law of the Sea III. (Online) Available at www.un.org.
Uyigue, E. & Agho, M. (2007), "Coping with Climate Change and Environmental Degradation in the Niger Delta of Southern Nigeria Benin: Community Research and Development and Development Centre (CREDC).
Wangbu, J. (2005), Niger Delta: Rich Region, Poor People, Enugu: Snaap Press.

CHAPTER 3

Theoretical Assessment of the Roles of Diamond in the Sierra Leone's Civil War

Timothy Chibuike Anyanwu and Emmanuel Metu Egbule

Introduction

Sierra Leone, like many African countries, has witnessed series of conflicts since her independence. It is unfortunate to note that in a country like Sierra Leone that can boast of such rich mineral deposits as diamonds, titanium ore, bauxite, iron ore, gold, and chromite, there is limited resource to sustain the need of the masses. The question becomes: Does it mean that the mineral resources in this Island country were not sufficient to provide the needs of the nations? Could it be said that the mineral resources were rather a curse than a blessing? Why exactly was the alluvial diamond a catalyst and sustainer of the Sierra Leone's civil war? Can it be justified to assert that large endowments of natural resources, especially the alluvial diamond deposits, have been a curse for Sierra Leone as they are for many other countries that have found themselves

T. C. Anyanwu (✉) · E. M. Egbule
Department of History and Strategic Studies, Alex Ekwueme Federal University, Ebonyi, Nigeria
e-mail: chibyktimothy@gmail.com

K. J. Ani (ed.), *Resource Conflict and Environmental Relations in Africa*, https://doi.org/10.1007/978-981-19-7343-7_3

embroiled in wars over abundant resources? This research uses qualitative research design based in historical studies to answer the foregoing questions. The aim is to use make theoretical explanations of the conflict through building a link between the conflict and the mineral resources of the country. The study therefore employed two theories as veritable tool to explain that the conflict was caused and sustain with the alluvial diamond that was in large deposit in the country.

Historical Overview

Sierra Leone was a name given by the Portuguese who explored the coastland from 1461. It is presently used to refer to an independent nation in West Africa, bounded on the north and east by Guinea, on the southeast by Liberia, and on the southwest and west by the Atlantic Ocean. The total area of the country is 71,740 sq km (27,699 sq mi). Freetown is the capital and largest city (Encarta, 2009). Historically, the country came into being in 1787 when the British government repatriated ex-slaves during the abolition era. After the 1772, when freedom was promised to any slave escaping to Britain, many blacks fled from the American colonies, and from 1786, British philanthropists organized their settlement on the Sierra Leone coast (Uwechue, 1976). Following the American war of independence that ended in 1782, many ex-slaves, including demobilized black soldiers, blacks from Nova Scotia and Jamaica returned to Sierra Leone as settlers to occupy the massive coastal land purchased from local chiefs and developed for the settlement purposes (Uwechue, 1976).

From the early days of its settlement, Sierra Leone started having conflicts between the settlers and the aboriginals. By the time the country gained her independence on April 27, 1961, the conflicts took another dimension such that six years after independence, there was a military coup in 1967 that ousted the government of Siaka Stevens and Sir Henry Lightfoot-Boston of the All People's Congress who were the Prime Minister and Governor General, respectively. Martial law was proclaimed, and in the riots that followed, four people were killed. Soon after, a group of young army officer arrested more top leaders of the country, suspended the constitution, banned political parties, and invited Lieutenant-Colonel Andrew Juxon-Smith to head a military government, under the National Reconstruction Council (NRC) (Uwechue, 1976). On April 18, the Juxon-Smith-led government was overthrown and replaced with the

National Interim Council (NIC) which was formed with the objective of returning the country to civilian rule (Uwechue, 1976).

After Sierra Leone was declared a republic on April 19, 1971, Stevens was sworn in as President with Mr. C.A. Kamara-Taylor doubling as both the Minister of Finance and Vice President. On July 30, 1974, Kamara's home was attacked in what seemed like an attempted coup. About sixty-five people suspected to have involved in the attempted coup were detained. In September, fifteen were tried and sentenced to death by hanging. Nine soldiers were also court martialed for their roles in the crises (Uwechue, 1976). Sierra Leone became a one-party state in 1978 after a new constitution was introduced thereby making the APC the only legal party. Same year, Stevens was sworn in for a seven-year term in office. The economy of the nation has started suffering some setback because of many factors, including the poor export process that could not offshoot the import costs. This led to the declaration of state of economic emergency in 1987 by the government of Major General Joseph Saidu Momoh.

The introduction of one-party system in Sierra Leone transported the conflict in the region into another level. Powlick (2005) observed that the various antigovernment and oppositions groups in Sierra Leone saw the APC government as a common enemy that must be fought. To these groups, the APC government was a corrupt clientalist regime. Powlick (2005) and Abdullah (1998) argued that the three rebellious movements: the Revolutionary United Front (RUF), the two military juntas; the National Provisional Ruling Council (NPRC); and the Armed Forces Revolutionary Council (AFRC) were all made up of largely young people in their twenties at most (although Sankoh, the leader of the RUF, was much older), were the product of a post-colonial political culture bereft of a formally articulated radical alternative to single party rule. But by 1990–1991, a full fledge civil war broke out when Foday Sankoh, a formal army corporal, hijacked unorganized movement of young boys who were gathering in Freetown after the institution of fees for government schools, observed Powlick (2005). Abdullah (1998), Gershoni, (1997), Murphy (2003), Peters and Richards (1998), Richards (1996a, b), and UNAMSIL (2005) were all quoted in Powlick (2005) to have agreed that it was through hijacking this group that an army of children, both boys and girls who fought the civil war, were gotten. These children were used as both combatant and noncombatant soldiers. While majority of the boys either fought or worked in diamond mines, the girls served in such other purposes as sexual and domestic labor. Furthermore, threats of rape, torture, and murder were employed by the RUF in "recruiting" child soldiers into their fold. As a way of training, the child soldiers passed through obnoxious indoctrination rituals, such as injecting them with cocaine. Once children were indoctrinated into the RUF, they were often forced to lead raids against their own villages as tests of their loyalty. This process ran through the period of war in Sierra Leone.

Theoretical Framework

There is no gainsaying that the application of theories to acquire, understand, interpret, modify, or explain both humanistic and scientific studies is generally ideal and accepted. This is so because certain modern scholarship emphasizes the use of theoretical framework to lay the foundation and shape the direction of research studies, observed (Alozie, 2013). But even in the face of the foregoing, it is germane to stress here that many niches of scholarship are either lacking a suitable theoretical application or are being suffocated or limited to few available ones. Some of such gray areas lacking massive availabilities of theories include studies on conflicts and mineral resources. This is so because according to Amaechi (2015), some of these fields are evolving; thus, they are lacking a universally accepted theoretical framework. This has posed a great challenge to scholarship and in some cases. To Amaechi (2015), in Africa, the situation is worse as could be seen from the deplorable experiences of the continent where some violent conflicts have been tagged "intractable" in order to cover up the failure of the existing approaches.

There is also the challenge associated with the study of human behavior because of the dynamic nature of man that is caused by both nature and nurture. Mbalisi (2015) and Teseror (1992) on this noted that a study of human relations presents a number of theoretical and conceptual issues among scholars, particularly, with regard to its nature and evolution as a human phenomenon; for instance, "the question of what inter-group relations is and how it has been viewed in human societies over time." Notwithstanding the foregoing, there exist some theories that can be used to explain the Sierra Leone's conflict as it concerns this study. Such available theories include the Human Needs Theory and the Theory of Resource Abundance.

Human Needs Theory

Human Needs Theory in a nutshell explains that people embark on conflicts when they feel that their basic needs are threatened. It argues that once people are able to secure their needs, they tend to be peaceful. There is no gainsaying that this theory is a veritable tool to explain why people go into conflicts. Looking at human needs, one believes the Says Law that they (human needs) are insatiable (Baumol, 1977). By extension, the insatiability of these needs explains why many conflicts are intractably endless (Ani, 2017). This is so because once one need is attained, another emerges. Thus, when the most fundamental needs of man (e.g., food) are met, others become salient. This is therefore to say that as long as humans keep having needs to satisfy, conflicts will remain.

The atmosphere in Sierra Leone from the onset was obviously a serious threat to the personal needs of a great percentage of the masses. For instance, insecurity was mounting alongside scarcity of food and rural underdevelopment as the years passed. The crises bedeviling the nation were compounded by economic recession and food-shortages in rural areas in the 1980s and early 1990s. With profits from state resources channeled into the pockets of the ruling coastal elite, the rural south-eastern areas, traditionally strong-holds of the Sierra Leone People's Party (SLPP), remained neglected and under-developed. Immediately prior to the outbreak of the war, these areas were severely hit by food-shortages and high unemployment. The promises of food, assess to diamond mines, protections, and so on made the masses to queue into the activities of the rebel groups. Most times, child soldiers were also used to plunder villages to get food and other important necessities. Another dimension of threat to basic human need in Sierra Leone was seen in the educational sector. Right to education of individuals is not negotiable, and this fact was understood by the youths of the country. It was on the foregoing ground that when they perceived that this basic right was about being taken away from them through the government's increment of school fees under a deplorable learning condition, there was a wild crisis by the students. It was this crisis in a form of protest that was hijacked and turned into a full blown civil war. This is therefore to state that the negligence of such human needs as food, shelter, employment, education, and so on served as both remote and immediate causes of the Sierra Leone's conflict.

Resource Abundance Theory

Looking at the above-discussed theory of human needs, it becomes paradoxical to state that in a nation like Sierra Leone where there are abundance mineral resources; people could be suffering from hunger and other related basic necessities of life. At this point, it surfaces to add that availability of resources in a given area does not guarantee availability of food, security, employment, shelter, clothing, eradication of hunger, and so on (Ani, & Ojakorotu, 2018; Ani et al., 2019). A situation where resources are either poorly or mismanaged, there is every tendency that hunger and starvation will set in. Sierra Leone was a typical example of the foregoing sentence.

One of the major reasons peace is preferred to conflict is because conflict is expensive to execute. The cost of acquiring arms, maintaining an army, executing a war, and so on can only be carried out when and where there is availability of resources for such purposes. The resource abundance theory of war holds that war can only be an option over peace only when the two parties involved have abundance of resources at their disposal and are willing to dispense such in executing wars. It should be noted that the availability of abundance resources can operate in two major ways: while on the first instance, the warring parties may be fighting to secure and be in sole possession of the resource. In some cases, the resource in question may be deposited in the rebel's territory. In such case, conflicts may arise because of a perceived mismanagement of the resources by the government or uneven employment or distribution. In such circumstance, a group of people may rise to challenge the status quo (Ani, 2021). Another dimension is in the use of such resources to execute wars. Here, either the both parties have access to the resource, or in some cases, the rebel group has unwarranted access to the resource. In this case, they can easily exchange them with weapons and other things they need to execute the war.

The latter case is highly determined by the nature of the mineral resource involved; this thrives well when the resource is easily lootable. Such resources like crude oil, alluvial diamond, and so on fall into this category of lootable mineral. Unlike kimberlite diamonds found in concentrated mines, alluvial diamonds are found in diffuse riverbeds; this makes it easy for it to be looted in large quantity. This makes the mineral resources play two roles in the conflicts in Sierra Leone: (1) it is the reason for the wars as the various warring groups fight to be in control of the diamond deposit, and (2) it facilitates the conflict by providing revenues used to purchase arms and provision armies.

The foregoing was the case with Sierra Leone during the civil war. The nature of the diamond in Sierra Leone made it very easy to be mined to support the war by both the rebel and the government parts. This is made possible because unlike other types that are concentrated in large deposits, the alluvial diamonds are scattered in riverbeds and the ground. Consequently, mining them was made much easier with the help of little or no technology. Manual labor by unskilled miners thus can serve as an efficient force to extract a good quantity of the alluvial diamond in matter of days by merely sifting through gravel—gravel from river banks, from river beds, and from small pits—and an individual miner can unearth several carats a day worth of rough diamonds (Powlick, 2005).

Conclusion

There is no doubt that the war in Sierra Leone was caused by such other factors as political instability, unemployment, hunger, and so on. The role of diamond cannot be overemphasized. The presence of alluvial diamond in a large quantity in the country was rather a course than a blessing. It further contravened the greenwar theory which maintains that war generally comes out of poverty and that people prefer to fight because of grievance over the lack of availability of natural resources. For instance, in arid climates, access to water is often the object of serious and potential violent conflicts. This study therefore theorized that the greenwar theory is not generally applicable in all war situations. An examination of the war in Sierra Leone rather proved the ineffectiveness of the theory because there was an availability of resources.

Consequently, this research has succeeded in using the Human Needs Theory to explain that the war erupted the time it did because basic necessities of life were lacking in Sierra Leone even when there was abundance of resources. This among other things was caused by mismanagement of the resources as evidence abound that the government, instead of properly using the mineral judiciously to run the affairs of the state, rather used them to settle some political allies. This made the mines to be in hands of private individuals who overlord themselves on the peasants. By the time the war ensued, it is obvious that diamond was used by the both sides to sustain it. For instance, the rebel group created international network that had diamond at the hub. The activities of Charles Taylor of Liberia and his link with the Sierra Leone's rebel group remain pronounced. With time, it was suspected that same rebels also had links with the Al Qaeda and American televangelist Pat Robertson. With such links, the use of finances realized from diamond was more of a multiplier in the war. Thus, while a good number of member of the rebel were combatants, the rest served as miners of diamond to maintain steady supply of the resource for the execution of the war. This therefore means that the abundance of resources in Sierra Leone was not only among the causes of the war, it further serviced the war on the both parts of the warring parties.

References

Abdullah, I. (June 1998),"Bush Path to Destruction: The Origin and Character of the Revolutionary United Front/Sierra Leone". *The Journal of Modern African Studies,* 35(2): 203–235.

Alozie, B. C. (September 2013), British Conquest and Administration of Ngwaland,1892–1960. Unpublished M.A. thesis. University of Nigeria, Nsukka.

Amaechi, C. M. (2015), *Umuada and Traditional Peacebuilding in Igboland, Nigeria, 1900–2010.* Unpublished Ph.D., Department of History and International Studies, University of Nigeria, November, 2015.

Ani, K. J. (2017), "Sustainable Peacebuilding Strategies for the Management of Ezza Conflicts in Nigeria and the Barolong Land Disputes in South Africa", PhD thesis Submitted to North West University, South Africa

Ani, K. J. (2021), Political Economy of Resource, Human Security and Environmental Conflicts in Africa: A Concluding Remark in Kelechi Johnmary Ani, Victor Ojakorotu & Kelvin Bribena (Eds) *Political Economy of Resource, Human Security and Environmental Conflicts in Africa,* London: Palgrave Macmillan, 297–306

Ani K. J., Ojakorotu V., & Uwizeyimana, D. E. (2019), "Resource and Environmental Insecurity in the Lake Chad Region", *Journal of Reviews on Global Economics,* 8: 1617–1621.

Ani, K. J., & Ojakorotu, V. (December 2018), Aqua Conflict, Resource Conflict, Resource Curse and the Challenge of International Cooperation Among African States, *African Renaissance,* Special Issue: 27–42.

Baumol, W. (1977), Say's (at Least) Eight Laws, or What Say and James Mill May Really Have Meant, *Economica,* 44(2): 145–161.

Freetown. (2008), Microsoft® Encarta® 2009 [DVD]. Redmond, WA: Microsoft Corporation.

Gershoni, Y. (1997), "War without End and an End to a War: The Prolonged Wars in Liberia and Sierra Leone." *African Studies Review,* 40(3): 55–76.

Mbalisi C. N. (April 2015), Inter-Group Relations of Mbano in Imo State, Nigeria and its Neighbors, 1906–2006. A Ph.D., Dissertation Submitted to the Department of History and International Studies, University of Nigeria, Nsukka.

Murphy, W. P. (2003), "Military Patrimonialism and Child Soldier Clientalism in the Liberian and Sierra Leonean Civil Wars" *African Studies Review*, 46(2): 61–87.

Peters, K. & Paul, R. (1998), "'Why We Fight': Voices of Youth Combatants in Sierra Leone" Africa, *Journal of the International African Institute,* 68(2): 183–210.

Powlick, K. M. (2005), Natural Resources and Conflict: Diamonds in Sierra Leone. http://www.sierra-leone.org/aerial.html.

Richards, P. (1996a), *Fighting for the Rain Forest: War, Youth and Resources in Sierra Leone.* Oxford: The International African Institute.

Richards, P. (1996b), *Fighting for the Rainforest- War, Youth & Resources*, in Sierra Leone Oxford: James Currey.

Teseror, T. (1992), *Tiv and Their Neighbours*, Jos: Pilha Printing Press, pp. 10–11.

UN Mission in Sierra Leone. (Accessed October 2005), "Sierra Leone-UNAMSIL-Background" URL: http://www.un.org/Depts/dpko/missions/unamsil/background.html.

Uwechue, R. (1976), Africa Year Book and Who's Who 1977, London: Africa Journal Limited.

CHAPTER 4

Deepening the Trajectory of Local Autonomy in Nigerian Niger Delta Peace-Building Process

Ikemefuna Taire Paul Okudolo and Victor Ojakorotu

Prologue: The Context of Peace in the Niger Delta

The oil wealth of the Niger Delta region of Nigeria has caused the area to be a theatre of violence induced by disagreements of how oil proceeds are shared (Garuba et al., 2012). The region recurrently experiences protests, demonstrations, insurgencies and also militancy over perceived depravities from the zone's crude oil endowment. The recourse to violence and many times unsportsmanlike pursuits by self-interested stakeholders, with each not minding to indulge in inhuman and unethical practices to actualize their parochial desires, have practically become a norm. The key players in the Niger Delta oil parlance are together the state and non-state actors. These key stakeholders usually engage in unwholesome practices

I. T. P. Okudolo (✉) · V. Ojakorotu
North West University, Mafikeng, South Africa
e-mail: ikemefunapaul@yahoo.com

K. J. Ani (ed.), *Resource Conflict and Environmental Relations in Africa*,
https://doi.org/10.1007/978-981-19-7343-7_4

at times in the bid to protect their interests through the various activities they engage in to derive gain from the region's crude oil endowment. Ordinarily, the state actors in Nigeria's oil and gas business comprise the federal, state and local governments, with the local government purportedly meant to play a prominent role in sustaining peaceful interrelations in the crude oil governance system with other actors because of its closeness to the main source of action (Khemani, 2001). On the non-state actors' divide are the natives of oil-producing communities, the oil multinational corporations, indigenous oil companies, civil society advocacy organizations and interested parties in the international community space and the oil-bearing community peoples.

The absence of mutual interactions, particularly between the Nigerian state represented by the federal and state governments and multinational oil corporations, on the one hand, and the indigenes of, as well as residents in oil-bearing communities, on the other side, largely has produced skirmishes that threaten peace of the Niger Delta. Amid misunderstandings over alleged undermining of the interest of particularly the oil-producing communities, sustainable peace and development continue to evade the people of the Niger Delta. Hence, Maphosa's (2012) supposition that where poor natural resources governance exists, producing disgruntled feelings in one or some of the parties in the crude oil matrix, conflicts, wars and civil strife, tends to follow. Citing examples of South Africa, Nigeria, Democratic Republic of Congo and Angola, Maphosa (2012) notes that natural resources correlated clashes in oil-rich African and other developing nations lead to degenerate lifespan in oil-rich communities, and cause huge death tolls from the conflicts. He further notes that conflict situations resultant from apparent objections and disagreements over sharing procedures from natural resources rents tend to aggravate the problem of internally displaced persons and refugees; negate rural-urban migration; and oftentimes compel the international community to treat as a pariah where such crises-prone inclinations linger.

It is well-known that the people of the Niger Delta contribute to make peace to elude the region too. They do this more often than not by mostly having resort to violent protests and in the last decade to full-blown militancy as a form of political communication. However, these forms of expressions, Imobighe (2004) as well as a CISLAC commissioned report (n.d.: 4), describe the agitations of the Niger Delta people as genuine given the poor state of public infrastructure, youth unemployment, poverty, squalor and generally poor living conditions of the region viz-a-viz its contribution to Nigeria's national wealth. Quantum number of newspaper reports, public opinions cum comments and public outcries express a gargantuan scale of ongoing fleecing of oil proceeds from the region at the detriment of the region's human security.

The Niger Delta region has been described as the greatest contributor to Nigeria's wealth because of the area's crude oil reserves that is exported for financial returns deposited as part of the country's commonwealth (Azigbo, 2008). It is almost indisputable as records show that 80% of Nigeria's revenues from trading with international partners come from crude oil extraction from the communities in the Niger Delta region (Ifeka, 2001; Babatunde, 2010; Bribena, 2011; Ikelegbe, 2012). Imobighe (2004) notes that 95% of export receipts as well as 90% of Nigeria's foreign exchange earnings are generated from the region. Naturally, the resource potential of the region was to be a source of attraction to the governments of Nigeria, transnational oil corporations (TNOC), indigenous oil and gas enterprises as well as every other enterprise that crude oil's significance touches. Crude oil exploration naturally has a multiplier consequence to every other business venture because of its value chain effect.

Where oil business exists, even the canteen/restaurant operator, horticulturist, barber, fisherman, smallholder farmer and other agri-businesses, etc., are expectedly bound to experience a level of boom in patronage. It is obvious then that the people of the Niger Delta would have expectations of a kind of reward to their lives and sustenance from the oil resource that is extracted from the region. The expectation of such reward in the people's minds ordinarily is supposed to go beyond the federal government's statutory grants, subventions and allocations; the corporate social responsibilities of multinational oil companies and both state and local governments' constitutional obligations as codified in the Concurrent Legislative List and the Fourth Schedule of the 1999 Constitution (cf. The 1999 Constitution of the Federal Republic of Nigeria & Fundamental Rights (Enforcement Procedure) Rules with Amendments, 2011).

Chiefly to the Niger Delta areas, amongst other important benefits, is the issue of functional and adequate public infrastructure, youth employment and vibrancy of the local economies. A region that constitutes the provider of the mainstay of an economy ought to possess public utilities equivalent of what obtains in advanced social systems and not experience massive psycho-social alienation from the state due to seeming marginalization. Youths from such areas ought to be gainfully employed, or at least get engaged in one form of productive activity in line with oil extraction and exploration optimally. Potable water, good road networks, modern shelters and well-equipped educational and health institutions, amongst other necessary social services for ideal standard of living to be enjoyed, ought not to be scarce in host communities, where crude oil ventures go on like in the Niger Delta. But, as Bribena's (2011) study has shown, there exists a correlation between the high rates of agitation in the Niger Delta with the abject state of public infrastructure of the region. According to Bribena (2011), the neglect of the region especially in terms of inadequate public infrastructure has resulted in the Niger Delta region to have extraordinary prevalence of HIV/AIDS and rise in irredentism. Existence of too many micro-militia gangs exemplify the rise of irredentism in the region. Also, the massive untoward degradation of the human and environmental rights of the citizens are outcomes of the poor state of public infrastructure in the Niger Delta. Other fallouts of the decadent infrastructure in the Niger Delta from Bribena's (2011: 28–34) research are low diversification of the local economy, agricultural land and marine life depletion, citizens' hopelessness in terms of poor living standards, brutish existence, absence of longevity, and frustration, high unemployment and poverty rates. Also evident, as byproducts of absent public utilities in the Niger Delta areas in Nigeria are high rural-urban drift, uncomfortable rural settlement as well as enabled 'environmental refugeesm'.

According to Onu (2003), environmental refugeesm is a developing concept that attempts to comprehend resource curse debacle in regions like the Niger Delta. The concept connotes displacement of people from their traditional homeland as inevitability due to the devastation of their abodes by activities related to oil exploration, exploitation and extraction. Furthermore, Onu (2003) asserts that environmental refugeesm in the Niger Delta area has caused population expansion in urban settlement due to massive drifts of 60% rural youths and 40% able family breadwinners from oil-producing communities to urban centres of their states. In the Niger Delta of Nigeria, aggravated inter- and intra-ethnic cum communal crises over struggles for arable land or lucrative fishing spots are as a result of environmental refugeesm. It is empirically true that Nigeria's Niger Delta communities experience high rate of internal displacement of people or refugee's inflow seeking safe havens for survival. Records indicate that refugee upsurge in nearby oil-rich areas is large because of the deflated aboriginal economic activities and destruction of ecosystems of their native lands from oil and gas unearthing (Bribena, 2011; Babatunde, 2010).

By and large, the picture of deprivation and poverty painted from the forgoing discussion is bound to perpetuate disaffection in the people of any oil-producing area. Hence, the thinking of Omeje (2005) that claims of unwarranted vandalism of oil pipelines and sabotage of oil investments belonging of TNOC (transnational oil corporation) in the Niger Delta should be characterized as spurious antics. The allegations brought against the Nigerian state and TNOC as par the plight of the people, by especially Niger Delta activists and environmental protection advocacy groups, carry substantial weight. The position of this article is that where a people suffer amid plenty that is known to them, a common course of agitation would be protests, demonstration, and militancy.

A psycho-traumatized people that feel pushed to the extreme, insurgency then becomes inevitable. One easy means to denigrate human security of a people is to extract wealth from their locale while at the same time shortchanging them of their fortune and in the process destroy their ecosystem. It is to be noted that security issue has radically shifted away from the traditional notion of security as par using military and paramilitary apparatuses (Hussein et al., 2004). Security in scholarships nowadays is conceived more in terms of people's security and centred on the security of the human being as against securing borders, lives and properties with military tactics. The United Nations Development Programme (UNDP) 2030 Agenda places the eradication of conditions that bring about want, illness, slavery and violent disagreements as fundamental for sustainable human security. Meanwhile, in the Niger Delta situation, the very conditions that undermine human security are what exist following the business of exploiting the region's oil resource.

A plausible deduction to be made out of a Niger Delta peoples' agitation is that oil resource governance of the country is dysfunctional. Every recourse to violent agitations as a remedy of their condition by the Niger Delta people is most likely as a consequence of governance failures, especially of the grassroots government closest to the oil-bearing host communities (Okudolo et al., 2019). In order words, tenacious presence of human insecurity in the region ordinarily reflects more than ever on the perverted local tendency and conditions of local lives, and this represents in significant ways the absence of good local governance as well.

Nigeria, no doubt, consented to the UNDP's 1994 global Human Development Report (HDR) which specified seven elements of human security that must exist for people to flourish: environmental, food, health, community, political, economic and personal security. This UNDP's 1994 HDR to Gomez and Gasper (n.d.: 2) can be summarized thus: 'freedom from want and freedom from fear'. Empirically, one need not pursue to validate the hypothesis that the absence of these human security elements in the governance system, structure and process of the upstream and downstream crude oil extraction activities in oil-bearing communities of the Niger Delta as it affects local lives would unavoidably end in disharmony. An understanding of the nexus between Nigeria's local governance as par building sustainable peace in the Niger Delta experience is worth, therefore, the interrogation.

According to the Organization for Economic Co-operation and Development (OECD), natural resources like crude oil are endowments of nature that should portend economic benefits to the well-being of those they are entrusted to (OECD, 2013). Owing to this, the 2008 Uppsala Conflict Data Program (UCDP) notes that conflict that flow from resource mismanagement characteristically producing armed struggles consequential to not less than twenty-five interrelated demise of lives within a year, says much about contestations of a bitter kind (UCDP 2008 Annual Report). Where conflict arises over resource endowment governance, it is an indication that the governance and management mechanisms in place are steeply fraught with illegitimacy.

Indeed, the condition of life in the Niger Delta resonates the UCDP 2008 Annual Report and what Tim Jackson, a professor of sustainable development, termed 'prosperity without growth'. In truth, where growth empirically eludes an arena of obvious prosperity arouses a fast-gravitating situation into human insecurity (Jackson, 2017). Therefore, the hypothetical assumption worth exploring by this article is that owing to the absence or ineffectiveness of local autonomy, as the supposed nearest governance protectionist mechanism for oil-producing communities against apparent wrongs, and therefore peace-building and peacekeeping, the ready remedy to right off any perceived infraction against such people becomes violent agitations that inescapably overtime come to be dialectically instructive as a form of political communication. Certainly, borrowing Held and McGrew's (2003: 1) charge for greater understanding of the undercurrents of how glocalization transfused into globalization, interrogating the vitality that local autonomy portends to consolidate peace in the Niger Delta 'has become more, rather than less, urgent intellectual and political task'. Importantly then, the need to understudy how local area governance and local governmental operations, structure, administration and management interrelates with stakeholders in the oil sector, and particularly with oil-producing host communities, to otherwise help to build sustainable peace in the Niger Delta will be less difficult to appreciate.

Illuminating Local Autonomy

As a scholarly terminology, local autonomy denotes both an adjective and a noun. But, its identity is mutually inclusive no matter the figure of speech used to pinpoint the concept in research. As an adjective, synonyms like local independence, grassroots autonomy, local government autonomy and local government independence can be substituted for local autonomy. Conceived in this sense, local autonomy in one word refers to freedom or liberty. It speaks, therefore, to the liberty or freedom of the local community organizations through their local governments or local authorities (including traditional and customary authorities) to exercise rule over affairs affecting them. In an extreme sense of conceptualization of the term as an adjective, local autonomy means the ability of a local jurisdiction and all its apparatuses of governance to be self-governing (Udoh, n.d.). One unique notion that revolves around every attempt to theorize local autonomy in the literature is self-determination or self-government. Although self-determination varies society-to-society, the traces of it is identified as one interrogates subjects like grassroots development, grassroots political participatory, local election, local economy, local lives, decentralization and local government/governance, local authorities or traditional authority both as in theory and as in practice. Chiefly, the adjectival connotation of the concept of local autonomy comes out very invigorated in a discourse on fiscal federalism as regards revenues and tax relations of local government authorities with other tiers of government (Okudolo, 2018; Okudolo et al., 2018).

As a noun, local autonomy has more to do with the grassroots governance, local area administration, rural-urban local governments and local authorities. For this reason, local autonomy will refer to local government authorities encompassing only governmental structures with the power to make and enforce public laws. It is in the light of this that the United Nations (UN) sees local autonomy as referring to the political structure of local government and other public authorities operating within the local government area. It is as a result of this that the UN's Public Administration Department defines local government as a political division of a nation that is constituted by law and has substantial control of local affairs including the power to impose taxes or exact labour for prescribed purposes (cited from Onah, 2004). On the whole, local government is the least tier of government that oversees the provision of public utilities within urban-rural local council areas and manages jurisdictional affairs of the rural local government parts of a country in particular. It is the nearby governmental political structure to the grassroots and its proximity is very visible to rural people, grassroots dwellers, community people and inhabitants in towns. By deduction, local government can be interchangeably used for local autonomy and vice versa for our purpose here.

On the surface, unlike many concepts in politics, governance and the social sciences in general, broadly looking at local autonomy, it seems not to suffer from conceptual vagueness or nuance, and its notion is not nebulous, uncertain or ambiguous (Free Dictionary.com by Farlex; Casasnovas et al., 2009). But scholars like Clark (1984), Frug (1980), Dworkin (1972), Clark and Dear (1984) and Putman (1983) argue to the contrary that conceptual unison of what local autonomy is has been achieved. Putman (1983), for instance, holds that the term local autonomy is not innately generic because it is ever known to be subjected to political manoeuvring which differs in many respects from one society to another. But clearly and as a matter of fact, in most discussions on the concept, consensus abound that local autonomy is about self-governing and self-government of local/municipal areas, local public institutions or corporations or local organizations. Local autonomy as a process actually relates to the rule within locally based non-state actors too such as town unions, traditional institutions, community development associations (CDAs), civil society organizations and other grassroots social organizations, like youth groups, age-grade association, farmers' unions/cooperatives, thrift societies, women groups and market associations (Adams, 2019). That is to say that local autonomy relates to everything about local affairs particularly in all matters associated with social interactions between people whether in the public or private domains.

One notion that stands out, therefore, in illuminating local autonomy is decentralization. It is when decentralization is debated within the confines of devolution, delegation or deconcentration that ideas like grass-roots administration, local government and local governance or local autonomy mainly surfaces. In the main, decentralization or decentralized governance is opposed to centralization or centralized governance, and it refers to the transfer of powers, duties, responsibilities and functions with the power of fiscal allocation and expenditure from the central/national/federal government to subnational and local authorities (Okudolo, 2018). In such context from the above definition, decentralization will likewise relate to self-governance of state regimes and state-owned corporations as well as the self-rule of local groups and political organizations (Wekwete, 2007). However, more often than not, scholars make reference to local administration more in the decentralization theory. Hence, Rondinelli (1981), as well as Ukertor's (2009) assertion that local government is well-known to function by decentralization either by devolution or deconcentration or delegation.

Aside this, it needs to be stressed from the outset that the nature of decentralization leading to local autonomy in each society differs in degree and substance. Several authors allude to this view (Adams, 2019; Mintrom, 1997; Oates, 1999). Stressing how decentralization cause local autonomy to differ between societies, Adams (2019) for instance, quoting Justice Louise Brandeis, concurs that 'one of the happy incidents of the federal system that a single courageous state [applicable to country and state/provinces] may, if the citizens choose, serve as a laboratory; and try novel social and economic experience [add degree of local freedom] without risk to the rest of the country'. Therefore, local autonomy is subject to the vagaries of the internal play of forces, such as politics, intergovernmental relations, governance, mutual ethnic interactions or the vibrancy of local participation in the policymaking circle of every society.

A discussion of federalism, therefore, evokes in a sense the concept of local autonomy too going by the foregoing quote from Adams (2019). The theory of federalism essentially denotes governmental autonomy and, of course, areas of governmental coordination (Watts, 1999). Hence, the concept of intergovernmental relations too which also is generic to federalism in many respects provides illumination to the concept of local autonomy (Okudolo, 2017). According to Wright (1980), the notion of intergovernmental relations underscores the concept of local autonomy in federalism and, therefore, goes to emphasize the federal paradigm's theoretic core-point as a matrix of decision-making amongst independent levels of government. That is, the federal, state and local governments are supposedly autonomous tiers according to the theory of federalism. This implies that where local authorities are designated as inferior or subordinate organs in the intergovernmental relations scheme with the higher tiers is not conterminous with the federal theory itself (Wright, 1983). In the same way, and reasoning along this line, local government autonomy ought to be prominent and should play significant roles in oil resource governance of any nation, and also be visible to mitigate contradictions to building peaceful livelihoods in oil-producing communities.

What Then Is Local Autonomy in Our Context?

The concept of local autonomy needs to be operationalized in the context of the article. Simply put, local autonomy relates to the latitude of free will to exercise power that is permissible to local government as a tier to exert pressure, set rules of conduct within its borders and independently enact institutions and agencies to execute agreed rules of engagement for the oil and gas business under their jurisdictions that compliment rather than is mutually exclusive to federal and state legislations. By our abovementioned operationalized definition, local autonomy speaks to, and in a way recognizes hierarchy of governance in the process to achieve sustainable peace in the Niger Delta of Nigeria, but not as a substance of a subordinated governmental administration. Unfortunately, in practice, local governments hardly ever make input to natural resource governance or collection of crude oil resource rents directly under their noses because *ab initio* they are largely marginalized by the higher tiers in the scheme in Nigeria (Asoya, 2010). As a matter of fact, against the backdrop of the threats to peace in the Niger Delta areas, Maloba's (2015) contention holds water that the South African Constitution, like the Nigerian 1999 Constitution and constitutions of every other developing political system, did not make to institute developmentally inclined local administration systems but one merely just disposed to delivery local social services and utilities.

The foregoing operationalization of local autonomy has several implications. One amongst others is that the above definition of local autonomy can be expressed using different orientations. And, the point needs to be made that actually these various perspectives all offer value to expressing the usefulness of local autonomy in mitigating oil resource contradictions that distance peace in oil-bearing communities. Clearly, and in spite of these numerous conceptual bearings, one good thing at least is that these perspectives are not competing against each other. In fact, the views regarding local autonomy's role in resource extraction are compatible. Hence, the various scholarly perspectives find relevancy in our endeavour here and in every attempt to examine what local autonomy means and portends for crude oil business administration globally.

A legalist approach for instance, scholars whose bias is public law, will view local autonomy within the broad spectrum of the public laws that codify the rights and benefits that local governments exercise in crude oil exploration for instance within their domains (Shipan & Volden, 2006; Arellano-Yanguas & Mejia-Acosta, 2014; Shafritz & Russell, 2003). Such a perspective will stress the independence or otherwise adored by local government authorities within the oil public policies. Those that make reference to the monthly allocations to oil-producing local governments in Nigeria from the Federation Account as par the constitutionally codified 13% derivation ratio make sense from a public law perception.

As a matter of fact, Section 162(2) directs that revenue sharing allocation proposal of the Revenue Mobilisation Allocation and Fiscal Commission, an agency under the Presidency, shall be subject to the legislation of the National Assembly. The subsection 162(2) further avers that to determine the eventual revenue allocation sharing formula, the National Assembly must put into consideration allocation variables and principles such as derivation from natural resources like crude oil, population, internal revenue of subnational government entities, equality of states, terrain cum land mass and density of inhabitants. The aforesaid Section 162(2) concludes with that caveat that whatever sharing formula is agreed upon, it must resonate at least thirteen percent (13%) of revenues derived from natural resources extraction accruing to the Federation Account. The Section 162(3) provided that revenues from the Federation Account shall be shared between the three tiers of government (i.e. Federal-State-Local government) based on the prescribed legislation as agreed to by the Senate and House of Representatives of Nigeria. Whereas the Section 162(5) codified the principle that the credit of the local government councils from the Federation Account should be distributed to them through a joint account operated by the states and their local governments on sharing rations prescribed by the national parliament of the country and as implemented by the Revenue Mobilisation Allocation and Fiscal Commission (see 1999 Constitution of Nigeria).

In this vein, local autonomy will be conceived according to the dictate of public policies and the fundamental law of the land. Those who engage the concept from this perspective are fond to cite articles, sections and provisos in public documents, as well as dwell on such notions as rule of law and constitutionality of actions taken by government and other stakeholders in the process of crude oil revenue extraction and sharing. For example, ample studies question the efficacy of Nigeria's fiscal federalism formula from the main revenue earner, crude oil, to local government where the 'real politik' of resource curse is felt. At present, the revenue distribution formula of Nigeria assigns 48.5, 24, and 20% of revenues to the federal-state-local governments, respectively, with the remainder 7.5% shared on basis of derivation to oil-producing areas par state, as stabilization fund to needy states and to the Federal Capital Territory area of Nigeria (Khemani, 2001).

A functional approach will be chiefly focused on the duties allotted to local autonomy more by the fundamental law of the land. Those that dwell on the functional perspective or approach (cf. Bwengye, 2018; United Nations, 2004) will usually make reference to codified functions of local government as linked to issues surrounding development, especially from natural resources extraction, and what local government actually does in that respect. Nigerian Civil society groups, especially the environmental protection advocacy ones, and policy analysts in recent times strongly condemn the non-inclusion of local governments to make good their latent and manifest functions (cf. George, 1988) against the backdrop of the deteriorating damage to the ecosystem of oil-producing local areas which they continue to suffer (Khemani, 2001). The thrust nowadays seems to be advocating fresh initiatives that would engage greater local community involvement in monitoring activities in crude oil upstream and downstream operations. Thus, researches that dwell on this approach ably interrogate the vitality that local autonomy offers to manage resource extraction grievances or environmental abuses by oil companies. The functional approach, from an intellectual point of view, tends to align with the structure-functionalism theory.

On manifest functions, for instance, the duty of local government as enshrined in the Fourth Schedule of the 1999 Constitution on economic development of the area suffices. The opening phraseology of that Section 1(a) of the 1999 Constitution specifies the important function of Nigerian local governments to include contemplation of recommendations to be tendered through the joint state-local government economic planning board or any commission at the state level charged with commercial viability cum economic development of the state. It should be noted that whatever recommendation is proposed to the board or commission must be to the effect of touching on the jurisdiction of the local council authority within its State.

More significantly, the crux of this article is the latent functions actually being performed by local autonomy in mitigating challenges to sustainable peace in the Niger Delta flowing from the language of the foregoing constitutional obligation. We posit *ab initio* that the article's primary intervention is such as to propose avenues to deepen performance of the latent functions that local government should play to abate oil resource grievances in the Niger Delta areas of Nigeria.

An organizational or systemic approach on its part derives insight from the Eastonian Systems Theory (see Anifowose, 1999). Essential to this approach is an understanding of how inputs in the form of grievances, demands, complaints and actual protests by indigenes of oil-producing communities are managed by local authorities, especially local government. These inputs, when animated, become empirical elements in the political system requiring to be addressed. The organization structure already in place, including the sum total of federal and state legislative powers, statutes and roles, is, therefore, expected to react to the inputs by way of corrective policies, programmes and projects. The results of implemented policies, programmes and projects are what constitute outputs, while the unintended results which may generate or not generate further demands constitute the outcomes. Accordingly, the organizational or systemic approach suggests that crude oil governance resolves around an input-process-output-feedback mechanics. The pertinent conceptual question, therefore, of this approach is at what stage and in which point is local autonomy most treasured as an organizational setting in the political economy system of oil governance in Nigeria. As a progressive paradigm shift, Vasquez (2016) and Arellano-Yanguas and Mejia-Acosta (2014) note that increasingly in recent times more and more studies concede that local autonomy's impact in oil and gas business offer positive feedbacks to push further overall efficiency and effectiveness of the sector.

Lastly, the intergovernmental relations approach represents a fusion of all the other approaches. However, this approach emphasizes predominantly the constitutional configuration of powers, responsibilities and duties of all the tiers in the entire process of crude oil governance, administration and management. Accordingly, this approach highlights how the norms of federalism align with the notion of decentralization or as McGrew (2003) prefers to see it as the notion of 'confederalism' to address cooperative and coordinate functionality of all the tiers devoid of a complex of hierarchical subordination in the oil and gas sector. This implies the need to eschew hierarchical schedules of responsibilities and duties that heightens dysfunctional governance of the oil sector. Rather, this school by deduction advocates the pursuit of the best possible option to advance peace in the Niger Delta even if it will require allowing local government to participate in federal and state legislative competency arenas in the oil sector. Such a strategy, it is believed, can be an all-encompassing ambition for the sector to quickly settle discords.

While the Exclusive Legislative List of the 1999 Constitution itemizes mines and minerals including oil fields, oil mining, geological surveys and natural gas under it, the Concurrent Legislative List 17(b) provides for 'the regulation of ownership and control of business enterprises throughout the Federation for the purpose of promoting, encouraging or facilitating such ownership and control by citizens of Nigeria'. Presupposing, therefore, Item 17(b) of the Concurrent Legislative List can be construed as that a state's House of Assembly can make laws to regulate oil business within its domain. But local government role in Nigeria's oil and gas sector as codified is snuffed of any iota of autonomy from the outset and by the use of the phrase: 'conferred on'. For instance, Section 4.2(b) of the Fourth Schedule, Function of Local Government states:

> 2a The function of a local government council shall include participation of such council in the Government of a State as respect to the following matters-
>
> 2b the development of agriculture and natural resources, other than the exploitation of materials...and such other functions as may be conferred on a local government council by the House of Assembly of the State.

The foregoing review of perspectives or approaches to contextualizing what local autonomy indicates in the paper conforms to Vasquez's (2016) orthodoxy. Vasquez's orthodoxy goes thus: greater successful and equitable and fair distribution of rents from hydrocarbon assets like crude oil amongst stakeholders and near absence of cacophony over oil rents administration is correlated to and a function of the more policy roles and involvement of local autonomy in the sector. Explaining further, Vasquez believes that no matter how one chooses to see it, local autonomy in the long run serves as a potent apparatus to improve transparency and discussions in the delivery of crude oil rents to government and dwellers in oil-rich localities, and thereby safeguarding optimum benefit of oil-producing communities from their natural resource.

Theorizing Local Autonomy to Our Context

Intellectualizing a concept like local autonomy within the ambit of our treatise is obviously a necessity if we are to achieve tangible contribution to abate the oil governance crises confronting the Niger Delta peoples. To intellectualize, according to the Cambridge English Dictionary, is to reflect or deliberate on an issue devoid of sentiment, bias, prejudice or belief. Of course, as is obvious, the abject failure to translate the oil wealth of the region into concrete utilitarian value is enough to stimulate anger let alone scientific inquiry. Hence, the advocacy to intellectualize this discourse by exploring some theories itself becomes a worthy venture. This is because such knowledge helps to disentangle biases and resentment to enable a dispassionate examination of this topic of currency to peaceful existence of the Niger Delta people in a more methodical way.

These two normative theories: theory of federalism and the models of intergovernmental relations with local government are very pronounced in the burgeoning scholarships on local autonomy. In its classical sense, federalism is understood as a compact or contract or agreement to remain under one overarching government while at the same time assigning some measure of independence between two levels of government: the federal/centre/central/national government and the federating state/lander/provincial/regional governments. Local government is not recognized as a tier of government within the broad genus of classical federalism theory (Okudolo, 2017). Hence, Kenneth Wheare (1963) and other such classical federalist scholars characterize federalism as shared sovereignty between a national/federal government and some semi-autonomous units of government. A notion Watts (1999) conceived as the shared-rule and self-rule arrangement between federal-state layers of government.

But with the manifestations of the welfare state and the developmentalist state, and the necessities of a trajectory and dialectics of development, classical federalism theory naturally had to mutate. The view of the sociological school of thought on federalism as championed by William Livingston and Willian Riker portrays the radical transformations that classical federalism just has to undergo. Federalism's sociological vision holds that a federal system is defined more by its sociological realities, positing that every federal nation shifts from time to time between being organic, cooperative or coordinative (Sawer, 1969). The also means that federalism's traditional view of two levels of government has to transmute in line with the demands of erecting the welfare state as par human security, and bringing about developmentalism as par good governance and effective delivery of good life to citizens.

In its current appearance, therefore, and in the sense of a post-modern liberal federalism theory, federalism is more concerned with addressing governance issues beyond the two classical structure of government. That is, today's federalism more and more recognizes governmental autonomy to lower tiers of governments beside the federal and state governments as long as it stands as a potent mechanism of resolving the sociological complications and realities of society. It is in this light that Watts (1999) stressed that local government in federations today is increasingly becoming more autonomous as a way to enhance effective and efficient governmental service delivery. Elaigwu (2007) quoting the Indian jurist, Justice Ranjit Sarkaria, captures the post-modern liberal orthodoxy of federalism a la contextualizing local autonomy to our context:

> The classical concept of federation which envisaged two parallel government of coordinate jurisdiction, operating in isolation from each other in watertight compartment is nowhere a functional reality now. With the emergence of the welfare state, the traditional theory of federalism completely lost its ground. After the First World War, it became very much a myth even in the old Federations... By the middle of the twentieth century, federalism had come to be understood as a dynamic process of cooperation and shared action between two or more levels of government with increasing interdependence and centrist trends.

Cawson and Saunders' (1983) dual-state thesis supports the post-modern orthodoxy of federalism. They argue that practical reality which has befallen on classical federalism is by virtue that structural power diversification and decentralization to the least tier of government addresses better governance issues in contemporary federal societies. The dual-state thesis posits that local government encores all the paraphernalia of a society that apply to the federal and state governments and consequently should be treated accordingly. Roberts' (1997) reading of the dual-state thesis is that as long as local government jurisdictions have territory, government and population, they should be properly suited and given requisite prerogative to administer their jurisdiction. Theorists like Duncan and Goodwin (1988) and Stoker (1988) nevertheless criticize the dual-state thesis. They hold, respectively, that societies where rigid variance exists between local autonomy's ideology for governance, such as in oil sector administration and that of the higher tiers, cannot function properly and that the dual-state thesis fails to appreciate that local government exists by, and in turn influences to shape the overarching State's environment of public administration that persists (Roberts, 1997). But what these criticisms fail to acknowledge is that the dual-state thesis did not envisage any iota of full sovereignty from its interpretation of local autonomy. Implying that its notion of local autonomy is one whereby local government for instance should have power to modify—in a supportive and not in a contradictory way—federal or state policy for oil administration within its borders as it suits its administration. Meaning that local government that co-exists within a political state under the shared-rule vision of federalism ought to equally enjoy requisite measure of the self-rule aspect of the federal theory that higher tiers relish. However, the dual-state thesis concedes that a somewhat basis of asymmetrical power should be between the higher tiers and local governments, but such unevenness of legislative competency should not be to the detriment of local governments' capacity to manage social pressures and disorders they face.

Post-modern interpretation of the functional model of intergovernmental relations with local government too could be said to emerge simultaneously with the drastic paradigmatic changes the federal theory underwent. Ayoade (1988) highlights six levels of intergovernmental relations that are prevalent in federalisms: federal-state relations, federal-state-local relations, federal-local relations, inter-state relations, state-local relations and inter-local-local relations. Similarly, Bello-Imam (1990) discerns these levels of relations which to him are ubiquitous in a federal polity: National-State Government Relations, National-State-Local Government Relations, National-local Government Relations, Inter-State Government relations, State-Local Government Relations and Inter-Local Governments relations. Nigerian scholars examining the concrete practice of intergovernmental relations such as Bello-Imam (1990) and Usman and Erunke (2012) identify three predominant models that operate: principal-agent, functional dualism and partnership models.

On their part, Shafritz and Russell (2003) argue that federal societies move within time and space between cooperative, organic and coordinative intergovernmental relations, noting from their research that cooperative intergovernmental relations are the real essence of federalism. By this thinking, Shafritz and Russell (2003) seem to suggest that Bello-Imam's partnership model—a model which is a synonym of cooperative federalism—is best for federations in managing policy challenges. In their support of the above view, Yahaya (1989) and Vasquez (2016) postulate that the partnership model, which stresses cooperate interdependence and inter-coordination amongst governments in solving social challenges, can best maximize and accelerate national development, especially where local governments enjoy requisite power and capacity to cope with socio-economic upheavals within its area. Yahaya (1989), therefore, concedes that local autonomy is most valuable to address grassroots social problems that are close by to them like such that is confronting oil-producing communities in the Niger Delta.

Take Shafritz and Russell's (2003: 132) description of intergovernmental relations as model of cooperating and interacting agents working jointly to address common social problems, rather than subordination or conflicting or sometimes hostile governments pursuing dissimilar or differing ends. Therefore, the above characterization of the theoretic shifts in federalism empirically not only foreshadowed changes in the thinking on intergovernmental relations but actually help fashion it (Okudolo, 2018; Okudolo et al., 2018). To a degree, alongside the fundamental shifts in the structural application of federalism *a la* development, occurs the search for suitable models of intergovernmental relations society-qua-society. All in the quest to facilitate coherent governance between the higher tiers with local government to the benefit of the management of social tensions of society. This search, for a better serviceable model, therefore, is geared towards the discovery of the best possible method for intergovernmental relations to effectively mitigate problems of good governance. Thus, intergovernmental relations theorizing for the best model that can deliver peace-building for instance will, therefore, occupy the epicentre of academic discourse and the arena of social policymaking engineering as regards absence of peace in oil-producing Niger Delta localities.

Intellectualizing Local Autonomy in Crude Oil Resource Governance of Nigeria

Given thus that our two normative theories are intertwined, we, therefore, needed to unpack them to illuminate their eclectic application in this article. Nigeria is a federal system consisting of a federal government, 36 state governments and 774 local government authorities (see 1999 Constitution). Amongst the federating states of Nigeria, nine coastline adorned states constitute the regions referred to as the Niger Delta states. These states are Delta, Edo, Rivers, Cross Rivers, Abia, Imo, Akwa-Ibom, Ondo and Bayelsa states. Put together, these states have about 185 local government authorities out of the 774 constitutionally specified ones. The locality referred to as the Niger Delta area of Nigeria by public gazette covers an area of about 70,000 km^2 or 27,000 square miles, covering close to 7.5% land area.

In official quarters, the oil and gas sector of Nigeria is subdivided into two business sectors: upstream and downstream. Activities covering excavation, exploration, mining, drilling and search for crude oil fall under the upstream sub-sector. The ventures regarding refinement and processing of crude oil, its trading/sale/dealing and supply/distribution/dissemination come under downstream. It should be noted that this article does concede to Monday et al.'s (2016: 207) view that deregulation of the downstream oil sector governance is a more controversial one in Nigeria. But, and more specifically, the roots of the problems bedevilling peace in the Niger Delta springs from the upstream sector and sinks into the downstream, and that both sectors sink Nigeria generally into far down catastrophic, detrimental and damaging dimensions. Even the likes of Okoko (1991), Ifeka (2001), Bribena (2011), and Omeje (2005) all believe that activities surrounding the crude oil upstream have imposing direct bearing on environmental toxicity and degraded livelihoods thus constituting a core cause of intense co-habitation squabbles of the other stakeholders with mostly the oil-producing people at the victim end of the rung.

The connotation that can be drawn from the earlier cited legislative competency areas from the Exclusive, Concurrent and Fourth Schedule of the 1999 Constitution of Nigeria displays wholly the absence of local autonomy in oil resource governance of Nigeria. Grasped entirely, the federal 1999 Constitution of Nigeria preconceived *ab initio* the absence of local governmental authorities and local-based organizations' active participation in every stake or ability to negotiate the dovetailing conditions upon their lives from oil resource upstream and downstream processes. Whereas the deliberative processes in the oil upstream and downstream sectors that condition peacebuilding is most felt at the grassroots domain of local government than the other higher strata of governance. Ordinarily, therefore, Nigeria's post-modern federal and intergovernmental relations practical orthodoxy ought to embrace shifts towards integrating local government policy interconnections, and local peculiarities of each oil-bearing local community in the decision process to facilitate peace. In a way, the article's advocacy proves as correct the hypothesis that a glaring absence of local autonomy in Nigeria's oil governance worsens the acrimony in the Niger Delta in concord with the acknowledgement below:

> ... Principle 4 [i.e. consent] recognizes that a commitment to equal worth and personal responsibility requires a noncoercive process in and through which people [i.e. local autonomy] can pursue and negotiate their interconnections, interdependence, and difference. Interlocking lives, projects, and communities require forms of deliberative procedures and decision-making that take account of each person's [i.e. each of federal-state-local government] equal interest in such processes. The principle of consent constitutes the basis of collective agreement and governance. When coercion and force take the place of deliberative and consensual mechanisms, discussion is halted and conflict settlements are typically made in favour of sectional interests. Against this, the idea of self-determining agency must acknowledge that, if it is to be equally effective for all, people [i.e. local autonomy] should be able to participate on a free and equal basis in a process in which their consent (or lack of it) can be registered in the government of their collective affair [i.e. crude oil revenues]. (cited from Held, 2003: 517)

Local Autonomy and Corporate Social Responsibility

Ikelegbe (2008, 2012) is of the view that strengthening corporate social responsibility (CSR) in the Niger Delta of Nigeria is a sure way for sustainable peace-building for the region. CSR, understood as when oil companies voluntarily integrate social and environmental concerns in their businesses, is today a consequence of globalization (Held, 2003). CSR in the oil and gas sector has not only assumed a global phenomenon; it is today considered a global best practice in the environment of crude oil exploration and exploitation (Ikelegbe, 2008). Ikelegbe (2012: 111) further states that CSR implies that multinational oil corporations in Nigeria for instance 'move beyond charity principle into accepting obligation to contribute to the less fortunate and consider the needs and interests of affected groups, persons or communities resulting from their enterprise activities'. Proximity of local authorities to grassroots needs, aspirations and infrastructural lags, especially of oil-producing communities of Nigeria, then the efficacy of CSR in the Niger Delta thus seems largely dependent on the ability of local autonomy to marshal it.

CSR, one way or the other, is unfortunately not properly integrated and thoroughly infused in the upstream and downstream public policies of Nigeria and in the country's oil governance stratagem to realize energy security (Ikelegbe, 2012; CISLAC, n.d.). For instance, Ikelegbe (2012) holds that goals encapsulated in such policies like the 2007 Nigeria Extractive Industries Transparency Initiative (NEITI), the 2012 Extractive Industries Transparency Initiative (EITI) and the Local Content Policy for Nigeria's oil industry did not properly cater for nor define the necessity of CSR. Thus, Garuba et al. (2012: 4) supposition that EITI's failure to adequately delineate CSR in the document could account for the poor environmental assessment report of the Ogoni oil-rich land as indicated in the 2011 United Nations Environmental Programme (UNEP) assessment. The little inadequate intricacy to CRS in the EITI may not be far from accounting for this unfortunate assessment outcome.

Even more worrisome than the poor attention to CSR as a key public policy insertion in the Niger Delta peace process is the glaring absence of local autonomy connection with CSR to mitigate resource curse. Beautiful as the proposed Petroleum Industry Bill (PIB) that is yet to be passed into law looks, one futuristic lacuna it is likely to suffer is the lack of recognition of local autonomy's latent potential to best galvanize CSR for peace-building. In its current outlook, the PIB's goal amongst others aims to fashion out an enabling business environment for oil sector operators to enhance exploitation and exploration of crude oil and optimize domestic oil and gas supplies. According to Nairaland Forum online (May 20, 2013), the PIB also strives to captivate foreign direct investment, improve government's oil revenue generation form profit-driven oil entities and deregulate and liberalize the oil sector. PIB also seeks to build well-organized and operative regulatory agencies, stimulate local content in the oil industry, and facilitate health, safety and the environmental security from crude oil exploration.

Although the PIB is said to seemingly strive for social justice and provides for economic emoluments to oil-bearing communities (Nairaland Forum online, May 20, 2013), it practically overlooked how best to sustain this social justice. PIB's failure to demarcate the place of local autonomy to achieve equity and fairness in the distribution of CRS is a critical missing link to PIB's ability to produce lasting peace in the Niger Delta. Without doubt, the local governments covering oil-producing communities know best the challenges of their local economies. Local governments better appreciate the public utilities that oil corporations in their CSR engagement can provide to bring succour to the community dwellers. Local autonomy is best positioned amongst the three tiers to gauge the social, infrastructural, economic, political and even necessities to enhance the physical outlook of their jurisdictions. Hence, in the event that CSR is to contribute optimally to the Niger Delta peace process, local autonomy cannot but be part and parcel of the planning, formulation, execution, evaluation and feedback process on its outcomes.

Local Autonomy and Civil Society Engagement

Bwengye's (2018) study shows that local government collaboration with civil society organizations or what can be captured as both informal and formal non-state actors has been effective in the implementation of decentralist programmes across all policy areas. To our context, in support of Bwengye's (2018: 149) thesis, these non-state actors encompass a broad gamut of social groupings inclusive of non-governmental, private voluntary, community-based and peoples' organizations, making up the formal category. The informal categorized civil society organizations are 'civic clubs and professional associations that operate outside the confines of the state and the market' (ibid.: 149). Permissible too it will be to include community age-grade, youth and women associations as belonging to the informal civil society classification because of the important asset they represent as non-state actors in governance. In strengthening the management of peace in the Niger Delta, local autonomy involvement with civil society has been manifestly felt. It is such teamwork that accounted substantially for whatever success may have been made on the Amnesty Programme of the late President Musa Yar'adua.

The advocacy against the environmental devastation of the Niger Delta is one area that civil society collaboration with local government can be better effectual (Allen, 2010). It is a known fact that environmental activists persistently call out the oil spillage and other bad environmental conducts of multinational oil giants. Civil society too has been commendable in the area of engaging with the international community on the plight of the oil-rich Niger Delta. Unfortunately, very insignificant scholarships, commissioned projects, as well as policy analysts, discern the richness to be gained in the area of peace-building in the Niger Delta with greater collaborations between civil society and local government. Various studies lay credence to the landmark achievements in the social, political and economic lives of citizens through combined partnerships between non-state actors and local autonomy (World Bank, 1996; Amin, 1997; United Nations, 2004). In Namibia, for example, realization of the value of civil society-local autonomy partnerships enabled CSO/LGs Joint Planning to be incorporated as part of the 2005 National Planning Commission statute (cited from Bwengye, 2018). Nigeria ought to emulate the Namibian policy thrusts for CSO/LGs Joint Collaboration as part and parcel of her oil governance measure to curtail restiveness in the Niger Delta. Egli and Zurcher (2007: 13) reveal how civil societies' analytic, applied and expository studies in Tanzania aid human capacity development of local government staff to alleviate socio-economic, political and environmental problems of the locale. In consonance with Ghaus-Pasha's (2004) research, this article contends that future success of the post-Amnesty Programme of Yar'Adua as a tool for sustainable peace in the Niger Delta depends tremendously on stronger partnerships of local autonomy with locally operating non-state actors.

Comparative experience, therefore, of CSO/LGs conglomeration in the management of socio-economic life-threatening problems as is the Niger Delta predicament should not be belittled. The activities of environmental protection advocacy groups in Nigeria working closely with local governments can add to effective monitoring of oil spillage and every other ecology-damaging action related to oil excavation. Even the eradication of organized pipeline vandalism and illegal oil bunkering which amounts to loss of over 10% of daily crude oil output (Human Rights Watch, 2002), and Shell's estimation of bunkered oil from SPDC sites of 5,000 bpd and 25,000 bpd from the Western Division and Nigeria, respectively (Human Rights Watch, 2003), can be halted through stronger LG/CSO collaboration. In the view of Ehigiator (2003), organized crude oil bunkering deteriorates the peace of the Niger Delta. In order words, the promotion of CSO/LGs alliances with security forces can help sustain a range of surveillance, monitoring and information exchange in addressing this scourge. More importantly, the non-governmental stakeholders at the grassroots of Nigeria are the best bastion for exposing inefficiency in local governance which ultimately impacts on peace-building.

Local Autonomy and Community Engagement

The sense of community engagement according to Australia's East Gippsland Shire Council Community Engagement Policy (2017) is all about the role of local government as facilitator of participatory governance. The document describes community engagement 'as a range of opportunities for public involvement in the council decision-making, relationship building and community capacity building'. The document goes further to stress that 'community engagement is achieved when the community is and feels part of a process' (East Gippsland Shire Council Community Engagement Policy, 2017: 3). Sound good governance paradigm dictates that local autonomy, particularly in grievance-prone conditions, should be imaginatively deployed to mitigate violence, insurgency and militancy (Bwengye, 2018). The role of Nigerian local governments in oil-rich localities in fostering people participation in a situation of human insecurity like what obtains in the Niger Delta, therefore, has become salient. Given that Fitzgerald et al.'s (2016) research found that community engagement does impact significantly in shaping public policy successes. Because of this, local autonomy should be viewed as a necessary science and technology by policymakers in Nigeria's oil sector administration for sustaining sanity in its operations (Mukwevho & Nkuna, 2018).

Again, by implication, the process of outlining how crude oil excavations and exploration happen, as well as delineating the downstream structure, should involve the local government in oil-bearing areas.

Because local governments are the closest level of government to victims of oil spillage and other environmental hazards from oil exploration, they can better foster what Surowiecki (2004) sees as collective wisdom for policymakers to not only nurture constant policy-knowledge but overcome policy uncertainties. Being the grassroots organ of government, the potential of local government to aggregate the gains from community engagement and participation is obvious. One obvious advantage from community engagement in relation local autonomy in peace-building in devastated oil-rich communities is that they can express their displeasures over governance through local elections. Local polls are avenues community engagement charge at and speak to political authorities at the higher tiers that are not addressing forms of economic, social or political grievances (Mukwevho & Nkuna, 2018). The principle of the 'paradox of poverty amid wealth' that Thovoethin and Yusuf (2010) alluded to in their publication can be used to explain why Niger Delta communities lilted more to one political party and leaning in the first 10 years of the Fourth Republic from 1999. It is obvious that poor community engagement so deployed in the Niger Delta in relation to the striving for local autonomy's presence in oil sector's administration sustains the rancorous existence of the people. And this goes to explain why almost all electoral positions in these communities went to a particular political party as an expression of the continuing perceived disgust of the people's situation from their indirect contribution to Nigeria's benefaction.

Local Organizations and Sustainable Peace

The inclusion of non-state organizations such as town unions, community development associations (CDAs), market women groups, etc. builds on the UN principle of evolving a set of tenets that help sustain peace-building. The one-time UN Secretary-General, Boutros Boutros-Ghali in his 1992 report now popularly entitled: An Agenda for Peace, considered peace-building by means of 'an action to identify and support structures which will tend to strengthen and solidify peace in order to avoid a relapse into conflict' (cited from Curtis, 2012). As their studies indicate, Curtis (2012) and Hutton (2014) agree that peace-building symbolizes utilization of potential organizations and ideas projected to circumvent deterioration of outcomes accustomed to or addicted to feud and contradicts peacekeeping. Based on this thinking, grassroots organizations like youth groups, grassroots politically inclined associations and even Niger

Delta cultural festivals make-up forms of local mechanisms that can help to raise peaceful socio-economic and political existence. The Nigerian Bulletin (May 29, 2016) identifies 10 cultural festivals in the Niger Delta that aid to sustain peaceful living in the Niger Delta. They are the Niger Delta festival for arts and culture, the Ijaw nation's Boat Regatta Festival, the Iweji Festival for thanksgiving for bountiful crop harvests, and the Awankere Juju festival. Others are the Ine/Ekensu festival in celebration of peace, the Ikwerre/Kalabari festival, the Okrika festivals of the Rivers people, the Ukwatta festival to usher in the planting season, the Adane-Okpe festival and the Okiroro/Okere festival in honour of ancestors for life and prosperity.

The potential of these local organizations to uplift peacetime in the Niger Delta from the ruins of oil resource curse cannot be underrated. If not for anything, these local mechanisms help to curtail socio-psychological traumas and anger being experienced and expressed by the Niger Delta people as a result of the devastation of their environment, livelihoods and lives, and also because of perceived shortchanging of their oil wealth by the federal-state governments and multinational oil corporations. The success of national agencies like OMPADEC (oil mineral producing board), NDDB (Niger Delta development board), NDDC (Niger Delta development commission), etc. greatly depends on local autonomy's and local organization's avid engagement and collaborations. After all, local government has units under it that cater for various social services, including cultural and social events. A good example say the granting of bursaries and scholarships to indigent undergraduates/postgraduate candidates from oil-producing areas by OMPADEC, NDDB, NDDC or the Ministry of Niger Delta affairs created under President Musa Yar'Adua in 2008. We believe that local autonomy and local organizations are very vital for the success of such a project because they readily can provide authentic data on worthy candidates than the state or federal government to assume. It can be argued that the non-constructive engagement of local government and other local non-state actors in the Amnesty Programme to eradicate militancy in the Niger Delta, as implemented from the Musa Yar'Adua/Goodluck Jonathan administration, can be attributed to the policy's intangible success. In truth, the scepticism about the Amnesty Policy and its accompanying uncertainty stems from the elusiveness of the policy's implementation that seem distance to local organization and their local authorities (Thovoethin & Yusuf, 2010).

The value of traditional institutions, as a subset of local organizations, to peaceful existence in the Niger Delta should not be undervalued too. Incorporation of Niger Delta traditional rulers in peace-building will help to boost condemnation of militancy in the region and also to curb kidnapping, vandalism, insurgency and youth restiveness in general (Oluho, 2014). Late President Musa Yar'Adua's policy advocacy to entrench a constitutional role for traditional institution aligns with the notion of democratic pragmatism and organic democracy (George, 2010). Democratic pragmatism and organic democracy *a la* enshrinement of constitutional duties for customary authorities according to George (2010: 4) does not compromise or contradict the principles of democracy, but instead is a facilitator of grassroots democracy. Traditional institution in the Niger Delta has been instrumental as a medium of conflict resolution, peace-building, peacekeeping and supportive of public programmes aimed at appeasing the angered people in collaboration with higher political and bureaucratic authorities (Mohammed et al., 2014). It can be inferred that Ojakorotu (2008, 2009) supports the view that traditional authority, amongst other local organizations as well, is helpful to the course of late Ken Saro Wiwa's advocacies over the plight of the Niger Delta people, as well as support to restrain the criminalization of the people's alleged accusation of marginalization against the Nigerian state. Accordingly, considerable policy structures should be instituted for the utilization of traditional chiefs of the region by the federal-state-local governments in the implementation of peace-building and peacekeeping measures.

Epilogue: Incorporating Local Autonomy as Framework in the Niger Delta's Peace-Building

There are evidently scanty literatures cum researches that probe local autonomy's worth for oil governance in Nigeria and even globally. And this state of scholarship is worrisome. Classical federalism and traditional intergovernmental relations theorists are likely to challenge what this article aims to propose, stimulate and establish and also deepen. The schools' argument can be couched thus: the generic concept of federalism and intergovernmental relations posits that local governments are infra-sovereign entities deriving their existence at the behest of not a federal fundamental grundnorm but a quasi-extra-legal constitutional rule more often of the federating states/provinces/regions. Nonetheless, post-modern liberal and radical thinking about efficiency of governance and effectiveness of service delivery to citizens' dictate that the supposition of these traditional-classical thoughts ought to alter in the face of their aptitude as a problem-solving modicum. This fresh insight that this article advocates is exactly what the notion of bottom-up federalism underscores (Gamkhar & Pickerill, 2012; Shipan & Volden, 2006; Vasquez, 2016; Dellavalle, 2017). By designation, bottom-up federalism implies that local circumstances can and do in fact through either a snowball or pressure value effect condition policies of the higher tiers (Shipan & Volden, 2006). Another version holds that bottom-up legitimacy is very fundamental to the understanding that true sovereignty lies with the voting populace whom are most qualified to decide their fortune and resides mainly in the grassroots (Dellavalle, 2017: 19). Likewise, the practicality of bottom-up legitimacy constitutes a form of cosmopolitanism that reverberate the view upheld by Held (2003: 514) that the outlook of globalization is equally provoked by happening from the grassroots to upper realms of governance as from national levels downwards alone.

In other words, the condition of peace in the Niger Delta region resonates first from the local and then beyond the local to the subnational state level, into the national, thereby contributing its quota to shape globalization. As a consequence of feeling the brunt of complaints of citizens in oil-producing Niger Delta communities by virtue of nearness, it becomes obviously unrealistic to sophisticatedly exclude local autonomy formally and informally as a change agent as reading peace-building. This stylish disconnection has long persisted in Nigeria's oil governance structure and history continues to beckon on the nation and reminding its policymakers of the necessity to alter this trend. Specifically, to peace-building process in Nigeria's Niger Delta region, local autonomy will serve as a framework to advance progress on these fronts.

Improver cum provider of oversight feedback data on activities of stakeholders in the Niger Delta oil terrain that sustain enslaving local economies of the region. Facilitator of cooperative development planning and economic advancement of the region so as not to allow an enclave kind of market to prevail, but rather to promote integration of Niger Delta local economies to the broader state-national macroeconomic infrastructure.

Promoter of local initiatives and ventures that sustain local content around the crude oil extractive business as a profound source of revenue making and employment for oil-rich community dwellers. Regulator of corporate social responsibility as a corrective panacea to address governments' failures in the areas of transformation of the physical outlock of the Niger Delta and provide modern and functional public infrastructure, public utilities and social services that will raise longevity and living conditions of the region's people. Promoter of mechanisms that guarantee social justice to the people living in oil-producing localities; raise their standard of living and distance them from frustration and other psychological traumas that instigates militancy, insurgency and even suicide that derive from experiencing poverty while surrounded by wealth.

Collaborator with federal-state government, civil society and security agencies to uphold transparency, probity and accountability of multinational oil businesses, elected officials at the higher tiers and public administrators charged with crude oil governance administration in Nigeria to ensure that oil-rich communities where excavation and exploration go on are not shortchanged. Facilitator of regular meets between local organizations and other stakeholders via a committee approach to share experiences, discuss new innovations, jointly address common problems and promote participatory oil governance as a link to promoting democratization of Nigeria.

Insurer that oil revenues are incorporated into local government budgetary needs for the developmental schedules of their jurisdictions in tandem with each locality's contribution to the Federation Account and not at variant with the extant revenue sharing public policies of Nigeria. Advancer of the drive towards greater autonomy for local authorities in the intergovernmental relations scheme to utilize their oil revenues specifically for the peculiar needs of the locale, as well as promote the customary, traditional and cultural identity of the people within the dictum of 'one Nigeria'. Cooperator of and with the federal and oil-producing state governments to ensure that crude oil revenues are expended such that sustainable peace reigns in the Niger Delta.

References

Adams, B. E. (2019). "Decentralization Policy Experimentation in Education: The Consequences of Enhancing Local Autonomy in California", in *Publius: The Journal of Federalism*, online pjz006, https://doi.org/10.1093/publius/pjz006.

Allen, F. (2010). *Implementation of the Oil-Related Environmental Policy in Nigeria: Government Inertia and Conflict in the Niger Delta*. Online Published Doctor of Philosophy Thesis, University of Kwazulu-Natal, South Africa. Retrieved on May 22, 2019, from researchspace.ukzn.ac.za/xmlui/bitstream/handle/10413/1190/Allen_F.pdf?...1.

Amin, R. (1997). *Development Strategies and Socio-Democratic Impact of Non-Governmental Organizations*. Dhaka: University Press.

Anifowose, R. (1999). "Approaches and Methods to the Study of Politics", in R. Anifowose & E. Enemuo (eds) *Elements of Politics*. Lagos: Sam Iroanusi Publication.

Arellano-Yanguas, J. & Mejia-Acosta, A. (2014). *Extractive Industries, Revenue Allocation and Local Politics*. Geneva: United Nations Research Institute for Social Development.

Asoya, S. I. (2010). *The Impact of Oil Spillage on Agricultural Production: A Case Study of Ibeno Local Government Area, Akwa-Ibom State, Nigeria*. Published Online Masters Degree Thesis in Disaster Risk Management, University of Free State, Bloemfontein, South Africa. Retrieved on May 13, 2019, from https://www.ufs.ac.za/docs/librariesprovider22/disaster...training.../2264.pdf?....

Ayoade, J. A. (1988). *Intergovernmental Relations in Nigeria*. Ibadan: NISER Publication.

Azigbo, O. (2008). "Paying Lip Service to the Niger Delta Development", in *Vanguard Newspaper*, February 18, 2008, p. 18.

Babatunde, A. (2010). "Environmental Conflict and the Politics of Oil–Bearing Areas of Nigeria's Niger Delta", in *Peace and Conflict Review*, 5(1), pp. 1–12.

Bello-Imam, I. B. (1990). "Intergovernmental Relations with Particular Focus on the Financial Aspect", in I. B. Bello-Imam (ed) *Local Government Finance in Nigeria*. Ibadan: NISER Publication, pp. 243–254.

Bribena, E. K. (2011). *Nigeria, Oil and Gas Exploration and the Niger Delta Question: A Study in Corporate Social Responsibility*. Online Published PhD Thesis of the North West University, Mafikeng Campus, South Africa. Retrieved on April 23, 2019, from https://dspace.nwu.ac.za/handle/10394/16024.

Bwengye, S. G. (2018). "Monitoring the Role of Local Government in Implementing Decentralisation Policy Reforms: An International Perspective", in *Journal of Public Administration*, 53(2), pp. 142–154.

Casasnovas, G. L., McDavid, D. & Costa-Font, J. (2009). "Decentralization and Management Autonomy?", in *International Public Management Review*, 10(2), pp. 103–118. Retrieved on April 25, 2019, from journals.sfu.ca/ipmr/index.php/ipmr/article/viewFile/71/71.

Cawson, A., & Saunders, P. (1983). "Corporatism, Competitive Politics and Class Striggles", in R. King (ed) *Capital and Politics*. Routledge.

Civil Society Legislative Advocacy Centre (CISLAC). (n.d.). *The Oil Subsidy Regime and De-Regulation Policy in the Downstream Sector*. A Publication of CISLAC, supported by Oxfam Novid.

Clark, G. L. (1984). "A Theory of Local Autonomy", in *Annals of the Association of American Geographers*, 74(2), pp. 195–208. Retrieved from https://doi.org/10.1111/j.1467-8306.1984.tb01448.x.

Clark, G. L. & Dear, M. (1984). *State Apparatus: Structure and Language of Legitimation*. London and Winchester, MA: George Allen & Unwin.

Curtis, D. (2012). "The Contested Politics of Peacebuilding in Africa", in D. Curtis & G. A. Dzinesa (eds) *Peacebuilding, Power and Politics in Africa*. Cambridge Centre of African Studies Series ebook Article, pp. 1–28. Retrieved on May 16, 2019, from https://muse.jhu.edu/chapter/733548.

Dellavalle, S. (2017). ""Top-Down" vs. "Bottom-Up": A Dichotomy of Paradigms for the Legitimation of Public Policy in the EU", in *Perspectives on Federalism*, 9(2), pp. 18–46. Retrieved on May 25, 2019, from www.on-federalism.eu/attachments/258_download.pdf.

Duncan, S. & Goodwin, M. (1988). *The Local State and Uneven Development Behind Local Government Crisis*. London: Cambridge Policy Press.

Dworkin, R. (1972). "Social Rules and Legal Theory", in *Yale Law Journal*, 81, pp. 855–90. Retrieved from digitalcommons.law.yale.edu/ylj/vol81/iss5/3/.

East Gippsland Shire Council Community Engagement Policy. (2017). Community Engagement Policy. Retrieved on May 20, 2019, from https://www.eastgippsland.vic.gov.au/.../policies/community_engagement_policy_201...

Egli, W. & Zurcher, D. (2007). *The Role of Civil Society in Decentralisation and Alleviating Poverty: An Exploratory Case Study from Tanzania*. Zurich: Swiss Institute of Technology.

Ehigiator, K. (2003). "Oil Smugglers Accused of Fueling Warri Crisis", in *Vanguard Newspaper*, August 21, 2003.

Elaigwu, J. I. (2007). *Fiscal Federalism in Nigeria: Facing the Challenges of the Future*. Adonis & Abbey Pub Limited.

Fitzgerald, C., McCarthy, S., Carton, F., Connor, Y. O., Lynch L. & Adam, F. (2016). "Citizen Participation in Decision-Making: Can One Make a Difference?" *Journal of Decision Systems*, 25(S1), pp. 248–260.

Free Dictionary.com by Farlex. (n.d.). "Autonomous Behaviour". Retrieved from https://www.thefreedictionary.com/Autonomous+behaviour.

Frug, G. (1980). "The City as a Legal Concept", in *Harvard Law Review*, 93, pp. 1057–1154. Retrieved from iglp.law.harvard.edu/.../gerald-e-frug-the-city-as-a-legal-concept-936-harvard-law-re....

Gamkhar, S. & Pickerill, M (2012). "The State of American Federalism 2011–2012: A Fend for Yourself and Activist Form of Bottom-Up Federalism", in *Publius: The Journal of Federalism*. USA: Oxford University Press.

Garuba, D., Abutudu, M. & Banwo, K. (2012). "Introduction: The Challenge of Sustainable Nigeria's EITI Compliant Status", in M. Abutudu, D. Garuba & K. Banwo (eds) *Beyond Compliance: Deepening the Quality Assurance Mechanism of the EITI Process in Nigeria*. Abuja: A Publication of Civil Society Legislative Advocacy Centre (CISLAC), with support from Oxfam Novib.

George, R. (1988). *Contemporary Sociological Theory* (Second Edition). New York: McGraw-Hill Publishers.

George, K. (2010). "Traditional Leadership and Local Government Interface Program", in *Learning Brief No. 1, AFESIS*. Retrieved on May 23, 2019, from afesis.org.za/...content/.../Traitional_Leadership_and_Municipal_Interface_Learning_....

Ghaus-Pasha, A. (2004). The Role of Civil Society Organisations in Governance. A Paper Presented at the 6th Global Forum on *Reinventing Government: Towards Participatory and Transparent Governance*. Seoul, Republic of Korea, May 24–27.

Gomez, O. A. & Gasper, D. (n.d.). *Human Security: A Thematic Guidance Note for Regional and National Human Development Report Teams*. Publication of the United Nations Development Programme Human Development Report Office, Retrieved on April 24, 2019, from hdr.undp.org/sites/default/files/human/security/guidance/note/r-nhdrs.pdf.

Harsch, E. (2007). "Conflict Resources: From 'Curse' to Blessing", in *Africa Renewal: African News and Analysis from the United Nations Online*. Retrieved on May 10, 2019, from https://www.un.org/africarenewal/magazine/.../conflict-resources-'curse'-blessing.

Held, D. (2003). "Cosmopolitanism: Taming Globalization", in D. Held & A. McGrew (eds) *The Global Transformation Reader: An Introduction to the Globalization Debate* (Second Edition). Cambridge: Polity Press.

Held, D. & McGrew, A. (2003). "The Great Globalization Debate: An Introduction", in D. Held & A. McGrew (eds) *The Global Transformation Reader: An Introduction to the Globalization Debate* (Second Edition). Cambridge: Polity Press.

Human Rights Watch. (2002). "The Niger Delta: No Democratic Dividend", in *Human Rights Watch Short Report*, October, pp. 27–28.

Human Rights Watch. (2003). *Human Rights Watch World Report 2003 Events of 2002*. Retrieved on May 23, 2019, from https://www.hrw.org/legacy/wr2k3/.

Hussein, K., Gnisci, D. & Wanjiru, J. (2004). *Security and Human Security: An Overview of Concepts and Initiatives—What Implications for Africa?* Issues Paper, OECD and OCDE Publication.

Hutton, L. (2014). "Internal and External Dilemmas of Peacebuilding in Africa", in *Institute for Security Studies (ISS)*, Paper 25, pp. 1–12. Retrieved on May 20, 2019, from https://www.africaportal.org/documents/11344/Paper250.pdf.

Ifeka, C. (2001). "Oil, NGOs and Youths: Struggles for Resource Control in the Niger Delta", in *Review of African Political Economy*, No. 87, pp. 99–140.

Ikelegbe, A. (2008). *Interrogating a Crisis of Corporate Governance and Its Interface with Conflict: The Case of Multinational Oil Companies and the Conflicts in the Niger Delta.* Proceedings of International conference on the Nigerian State, Oil Industry and the Niger Delta, Department of Political Science, Niger Delta University, Amasoma and the Center for Applied Environmental Research, University of Missouri, Kansas City.

Ikelegbe, A. (2012). "Corporate Social Responsibility Spending: An Important but Neglected Entity in the NEITI Audit", in M. Abutudu, D. Garuba & K. Banwo (eds) *Beyond Compliance: Deepening the Quality Assurance Mechanism of the EITI Process in Nigeria.* Abuja: A Publication of Civil Society Legislative Advocacy Centre (CISLAC), with support from Oxfam Novib.

Imobighe, T. A. (2004). "Conflict in Niger Delta: A Unique Case or a "Model" for Future Conflicts in Other Oil-Producing Countries?", in R. Traub-Merz & D. Yates (eds) *Oil Policy in the Gulf of Guinea: Security & Conflict, Economic Growth, Social Development.* Friedrich-Ebert Foundation, Division for International Publication.

Jackson, T. (2017). *Prosperity Without Growth: Foundations for the Economy of Tomorrow* (Second Edition). London and New York: Routledge Taylor & Francis Group.

Khemani, S. (2001). *Fiscal Federalism and Service Delivery in Nigeria: The Roles of States and Local Governments.* Paper Prepared for the Nigerian PER Steering Committee for the World Bank, July 24, pp. 1–16. Retrieved on May 15, 2019, from www1.worldbank.org/publicsector/decentralization/ ../FiscalFedReport.pdf.

Maloba, D. M. (2015). *Monitoring Good Governance in South African Local Government and Its Implication for Institutional Development and Service Delivery: A Case Study of the Sub-Councils and Councillor Support Department.* Online Published Master of Public Administration Degree Thesis, University of Western Cape. Retrieved on May 13, 2019, from https://etd.uwc.ac.za/xmlui/bitstream/handle/.../maloba_ds_mpa_ems_2015.pdf?...1....

Maphosa, S. B. (2012). "Natural Resources and Conflict: Unlocking the Economic Dimension of Peace-Building in Africa", in *Policy Brief: Africa*

Institute of South Africa (Africa.Org, Portal Online, No. 74, March). Retrieved on May 9, 2019, from https://www.africaportal.org/publications/natural-resources-and-conflict-unlocking-the-economic-dimension-of-peace-building-in-africa/.

McGrew, A. (2003). "Models of Transnational Democracy", in D. Held & A. McGrew (eds) *The Global Transformation Reader: An Introduction to the Globalization Debate* (Second Edition). Cambridge: Polity Press.

Mintrom, M. (1997). "Policy Entrepreneurs and the Diffusion of Innovations", in *Journal of Political Science*, 41(3), pp. 738–770.

Mohammed, S. B., Robinson, J. O. & Aliyu, I. H. (2014). "From Conflict to Peace Building and Post Conflict Reconstruction: A Critical Reflection on the Nigeria Niger Delta Amnesty", in *International Letters on Social and Humanities Sciences*, 30, pp. 81–95. Retrieved from https://www.scipress.com/ILSHS.30.81.pdf.

Monday, J. U., Ekperiware, M. C. & Muritala, B. R. (2016). "Downstream Oil Deregulation and Nigerian Economy", in *ECOFORUM*, 5, Issue 1(8), pp. 207–214.

Mukwevho, M. H. & Nkuna, N. (2018). "Are Citizens Reconfiguring Public Participation? A Response to Municipal Re-Democracy by Vuwani Community, Vhembe District in South Africa", in *Journal of Public Administration*, 53(2), pp. 142–154.

Nairaland Forum Online. (May 20, 2013). "Understanding the PIB (Petroleum Industry Bill): Politics". Retrieved on May 23, 2019, from https://www.nairaland.com/1296810/understanding-pib-petroleum-industry-bill.

Nigerian Bulletin. (May 29, 2016). "Niger Delta: 10 Cultural Festivals You Should Attend in the Niger Delta". Retrieved on May 20, 2019, from https://www.nigerianbulletin.com/threads/niger-delta-10-cultural-festivals-you-should-attend-in-the-niger-delta.213065/.

Oates, W. (1999). "An Essay on Fiscal Federalism", in *Journal of Economic Literature*, 37(3), pp. 1120–1149.

OECD. (2013). "Material Resources, Productivity and the Environment: Key Findings". Retrieved on May 6, 2019, from https://www.oecd.org/greengrowth/MATERIAL%20RESOURCES,%20PRODUCTIVI....

Ojakorotu, V. (2008). "Environmental Activism and the Struggles for Justice by the Non-Governmental Organizations in the Niger Delta of Nigeria", in *The International Journal of Regional and Local Studies, United Kingdom*, 4(2), Series 2, Autumn.

Ojakorotu, V. (2009). "Introduction", in V. Ojakorotu (ed) *Fresh Dimensions on the Niger Delta Crisis of Nigeria: Part of the Conflict and Development Series*. South Africa: JAPSS Press Inc.

Okoko, E. (1991). "Women and Environmental Change in the Niger Delta, Nigeria: Evidence from Ibeno", in *Gender, Place and Culture*, 6(4), pp. 373–378.

Okudolo, I. T. P. (2017). *Constitutional Contradictions and Their Implications on State-Local Government Relations in Nigeria, 1999–2015.* Unpublished PhD Thesis of the Department of Political Science, University of Lagos.

Okudolo, I. T. P. (2018). "Local Government Autonomy and Revenue Generation in Nigeria: A Critical Review of the Kaduna State Tax (Codification and Consolidation) Law", in *Ilorin Journal of Administration and Development, Department of Public Administration, Faculty of Management Sciences, University of Ilorin*, 4(2), July, pp. 12–19.

Okudolo, I. T. P., Kifordu, A. A. & Chukwudumebi, C. (2018). "Constitutionalism and the Entrenchment of Local Autonomy in Nigerian Federalism: Delta State as Case Study (1999–2017)", in *Journal of Nation-Building and Policy Studies (JoNPS)*, 2(2), December, pp. 23–43.

Okudolo, I. T. P., Amamkpa, Williams A. & Ani, K. J. (2019). "Towards Sustainable Energy Security and Socio-Economic Betterment of Nigeria: Focus on Challenges and Prospects of Nation Building", in *Journal of Nation Building & Policy Studies*, 3(2), pp. 5–23.

Oluho, C. (2014). "Unmasking Oil Thieves in Nigeria", in *The Tide News Online*. Retrieved from http://www.thetidenewsonline.com/2014/05/12/unmasking-oil-thieves-in-nigeria.

Omeje, K. (2005). "Oil Conflict in Nigeria: Contending Issues and Perspectives of the Local Niger Delta People", in *New Political Economy*, 10(3), pp. 321–334. https://doi.org/10.1080/13563460500204183.

Onah, E. I. (2004). "Federalism and Intergovernmental Relations in the New Democratic Dispensation in Nigeria", in *Nigerian Institute of International Affairs, Nigerian Forum: A Journal of Opinion on World Affairs*, 25(9–10), September–October, pp. 250–259.

Onu, C. H. (2003). "The Oil Rich Niger Delta Region: A Framework for Improved Performance of the Nigerian Regulatory Process", in *Royal Swedish Academy of Science*, p. 78.

Putman, H. (1983). *Realism and Reason: Philosophical Papers* (Vol. 3). Cambridge: Cambridge University Press.

Roberts, N. (1997). *Theories of Local Government and the Nigerian Experience: Discourse or Real Politik.* NISER Monograph Series No. 9.

Rondinelli, D. A. (1981). "Government Decentralisation in Comparative Perspective: Theory and Practice in Developing Countries", in *International Review of Administrative Sciences*, XLVII(2), pp. 137–149.

Sawer, G. (1969). *Modern Federalism.* London: Sage Publishers.

Shafritz, J. M. & Russell, E. W. (2003). *Introducing Public Administration.* New York: Anderson Wesley Longman Inc.

Shipan, C. & Volden, C. (2006). "Bottom-Up Federalism: The Diffusion of Antismoking Policies from U.S. Cities to States", in *American Journal of Political Science*, 50(4), pp. 825–843. Retrieved on May 24, 2019, from https://www.researchgate.net/publication/227605062_Bottom-Up_Federalism_The_Diffusion_of_Antismoking_Policies_from_US_Cities_to_States.

Stoker, G. (1988). *The Politics of Local Government*. London: Alllen and Unwin.

Surowiecki, J. (2004). *The Wisdom of Crowds: Why the Many are Smarter Than the Few and How Collective Wisdom Shapes Business, Economics, Society and Nations*. New York, NY: Doubleday.

The 1999 Constitution of the Federal Republic of Nigeria & Fundamental Rights (Enforcement Procedure) Rules with Amendments 2011.

Thovoethin, P. S. & Yusuf, S. A. (2010). "The Nigerian State and Peace Building Mechanics in the Niger Delta Region". E-International Relations Publishing, online publication May 29, 2010. Retrieved on May 21, 2019, from https://www.e-ir.info/2010/11/28/the-nigerian-state-and-peace-building-mechanics-in-the-niger-delta-region/ or https://www.e-ir.info/.../the-nigerian-state-and-peace-building-mechanics-in-the-niger-....

Udoh, N. A. (n.d.). "Local Government Autonomy in Nigeria: Myth or Reality?" Retrieved on April 25, 2019, from ssjcd.org/wp-content/.../LOCAL-GOVERNMENT-AUTONOMY-IN-NIGERIA:pdf.

Ukertor, C. M. (2009). *The Principles and Practice of Federalism and Local Government Autonomy in Nigeria: Reality or Mirage?* Nsukka: Chuka Educational Publisher.

United Nations. (2004). *Decentralization and Poverty Reduction: Africa and Asian Experience*. New York: UN Division for Public Administration and Development Management.

Usman, A. B. & Erunke, C. E. (2012). "State-Local Government Relations in Nigeria's Fourth Republic: An Assessment of the (1999–2010) Experience", in *European Scientific Journal*, 8 (20), September Edition, pp. 162–176.

Vasquez, P. I. (2016). "Four Policy Actions to Improve Local Governance of the Oil and Gas Sector", in *International Development Policy*, online Article 7.1. Retrieved on May 15, 2019, from https://journals.openedition.org/poldev/2227.

Watts, R. L. (1999). *Comparing Federal Systems* (Second Edition). Canada: Queen University Press.

Wekwete, K. (2007). "Strengthening State Performance Through Decentralised Governance", in *African Governance Forum (AGF VII): Building the Capable State in Africa*, Regional Bureau for Africa, New York: U.N. Development Programme Publication, June.

Wheare, K. C. (1963). *Federal Government*. London: Oxford University Press.

World Bank. (1996). *Pursuing Common Goals: Strengthening Relations Between Government and Development NGOs*. Dhaka: University Press.

Wright, D. S. (1980). "Intergovernmental Games: An Approach to Understanding Intergovernmental Relations", in *Southern Review of Public Administration*, 3(4), pp. 388–403.

Wright, D. S. (1983). "Managing the Intergovernmental Scene: The Changing Dramas of Federalism, Intergovernmental Relations and Intergovernmental Management", in W. E. Eddy (ed) *Handbook of Organizational Management*. New York: Marcel Dekker.

Yahaya, A. D. (1989). "Local Government Reforms: The Military Initiative", in P. Ekeh, P. Dele-Cole & G. O. Olusanya (eds) *Nigeria Since Independence: The First 25 Years, Vol. V: Politics and Constitutions.* Nigeria: Heinemann Educational Books.

CHAPTER 5

Fulani Herdsmen and Farmers Conflict Relations in Idomaland 1999–2017

Abutu Freeman Gabriel Adikwuoyi

Introduction

The persistent conflicts and other security challenge in Idomaland in recent times have continued unabated. While the land grapples with factors, such as disagreements among the elite, unemployment, under-employment, poverty and lack of effective government presence resulting in insecurity, another emergent factor that is adding to these challenge is the current activities of Fulani herdsmen who are traversing the entire nooks and crannies of Idomaland in search of pastures for their cattle and perpetuating a lot of atrocities to the properties and lives of the Idoma people with little or no form of reaction from the people either as a result of ignorance of the character traits of these herdsmen or some sought of selfish parochial considerations.

A. F. G. Adikwuoyi (✉)
Department of English, History and International Studies, Admiralty University of Nigeria, Ibusa, Nigeria
e-mail: abutufreeman@gmail.com

K. J. Ani (ed.), *Resource Conflict and Environmental Relations in Africa*,
https://doi.org/10.1007/978-981-19-7343-7_5

Consequently, this paper set out to bring to limelight, the challenges and consequences of these invasions of Idomaland using the activities of these herdsmen in respect to killings/destruction of properties and other social vices which have led to conflicts and insecurity in virtually all part of Nigeria, particularly in Central Nigeria (fondly called the Middle Belt States) including Agatu a district of Idomaland. For a clear understanding of the content of the work, the paper is divided into: Introduction, a brief History of the Idoma and Fulani, Interactions between Idoma and Fulani, Implications/Consequences, Conclusion and recommendations.

Idoma is one among the ten largest ethnic groups in Nigeria scattered into a number of states, such as Nasarawa, Kogi, Enugu, and Cross Rivers respectively.[1] However, the attention of this paper is on the Idoma people of Benue State. According to the 2006 population census, the Idoma people of Benue State numbered about 2,550,000. With this population figure, the directorate of information office of the governor, Benue State Nigeria, declared that Idoma people in Benue State are the second largest ethnic groups in the State. They inhabit an area of about 13,015 kilometers covering: Otukpo, Okpokwu, Ado, Oju, Ohimini, Agatu, Ogbadibo, Obi and Apa local governments with Otukpo as its traditional headquarters. Idomaland is bounded on the north by River Benue on the west by the Tiv speaking people of Benue State, on the south by Nsukka and Abakaliki Igbo speaking people of Enugu and Ebonyi State, respectively, while to the east are the Igala speaking people of Kogi State. Most of the Idoma are inland south of Benue, 72 kilometers east of the confluence with the Niger River.[2]

Historically, the Idoma people are believed to have migrated from the old Kwararafa confederacy to their various locations. Though settling at Apa, Erim's study enables us to follow step by step the settlement of each Idoma group at their present location. Even though the work never told us what led to these dispersals and settlement at different locations as seen today. This paper is of the opinion that the nineteenth-century Fulani Jihad led by Othman Dan Fodio played a significant role in this Idoma dispersal, and intermingling with other ethnic groups in different locations thus making the present Idoma societies heterogeneous in nature.[3]

Historicity of Idoma and Fulani Interactions

Although Fulani are spread all over the continent of Africa given their transhuman animal rearing culture, history has it that this ethnic group originated from the Senegambia part of Africa before spreading to the various parts of the globe including Northern Nigeria where they rose to political ascendancy and prominence through the 1804 Socio-political and economic jihad led by Uhtman Dan Fodio.[4] The quest to push further into central Nigeria (where the Idoma belong) was, however, truncated following the conquest and subjugation of the entire Nigeria in the early twentieth century by the British colonialists. Thus bring to a halt completely, the jihadist movement into most Central Nigeria.[5] There is no clear cut date as to when the Idoma and Fulani met and started interacting. However, the works of scholar, such as Erim, Okwu, Agbo and Colonial Reports among others, point to the fact that one of the major causes of Idoma dispersal from their ancestral Apa after leaving Kwarafa kingdom, was as a result of the Othman Dan Fodio led *Efuonya* (horse war). According to the Colonial anthropological and ethnographical Report on Idoma, the Idoma first settled in Wukari after the destruction of Kwararafa and Apa by the jihadist,[6] this assertion brings to bear the fact that interaction between the Fulani and the Idoma in pre-colonial times was hostile with the Fulani having the upper hands because of their superior military might which made the Idoma to disperse into the various locations particularly the Southern part of the Benue Valley where they are found in large numbers today. With colonization, came a more military might of the British Colonialists who for administrative convenience and plot to keep the people in total submission, created boundaries between the various ethnic groups which Udo in his words captured thus: The fixing of boundaries brought to an end to the practice whereby groups which are powerful enough would forcibly encroach upon the land of neighboring groups.[7] Given this colonial creation, the activities of the Fulani's were mostly restricted to the core Northern parts of Nigeria throughout the Colonial periods with practically nothing to do with the Central Nigeria including Idomaland. With independence in 1960 and the enthronement of freedom of movement and settlement in any part of Nigeria as enshrined in the Constitution of the Federal Republic of Nigeria,[8] coupled with the high level of desertification in most part of Northern Nigeria, increase in populations (both in Human and cattle), the Fulani began a gradual but steady push into the greener and pasture favored Central Nigeria including Idomaland to graze their cattle. It is these aforementioned factors that brought the Idoma into contact with the Fulani again after the initial Othman Dan Fodio's jihad war. This contact and penetration of Idomaland, started from the Northern fringes of Agatu who out of religious affiliation and the initial friendly posture of the Fulani, gave them allowance to graze within areas where crops are not planted. According to an informant:

> The first sets of Fulani that came to our land, were very friendly, they normally come during dry seasons and help in harvesting of our crops before their cattle goes into grazing and leaves immediately in the next farming season when the rains start. As time went by, they began to settle in our mist and even invite their siblings to join them. This was how we interacted with the Fulani people cordially until recently when several incidences of cattle eating our crops were being recorded and when we complain, they claim ignorance while the incident persists. It is this nonchalant attitude of theirs to our source of livelihood, that brought about the hostility that led to conflicts and persistent blood shedding between we (the Agatu) and Fulani[9]

This informant assertion is buttressed by *Wegh* when he submitted with regard to Tiv land that:

> ….the Fulani herdsmen and Tiv farmers had lived peacefully together for several decades. Violent confrontations seemed rare because the herdsmen apparently appreciated their guest status. They normally negotiate their entry into communities through legitimate gate keepers and were allotted grazing and residential spaces. If their cattle strayed and ate up someone's crop, the herdsmen negotiated and paid compensation. Communities on their part ensured that herdsmen who lost their cattle or were assaulted by anyone were fairly treated and compensated. Today, the seemingly orderly and peaceful dispositions of the herdsmen have disappeared. In its place, we now have herdsmen who carry AK47 and other automatic rifles which they have used to kill and maim hundreds of unsuspected farmers and driven them out of their homes[10]

Notwithstanding the ongoing battle between the Fulani and the Idoma stock of Agatu, the Fulani, in their desperate move to graze their cattle at all cost, are moving into other parts of Idomaland where they and their cattle are wreaking havoc to both lives and properties of the Idoma people with little or no concise efforts by the Idoma to stop them. It is on this note that we here point out some of the challenges that this invasion may produce.

The Place of Land Resource and Fulani Herdsmen in Idomaland

Land is almost certainly the foremost resource desired by Man for his daily life. This is because, most human undertakings at various phases are tired to land. Hence, what land means to people, is consequent upon its usage and specifications by them. Given this differentiation, request for and use of land varies from one group to another. However, agricultural activities (particularly farming) conceivably occupy the highest form of complexity of land use.[11] The large quest and use of land by farmers are occasioned by the fact that not all land is capable of supplying crop-specific needed water and nutrients, soil temperature, structure and texture and p-h level are inevitable preconditions for choosing any land for agricultural activities. These preconditions added to the limited nature of land and its manifold use by man makes competition for it among humans increasing difficult.[12] Consequently, there is this strong and continuous battle for its application by mankind since creation. With the increase in human population and activities particularly among agriculturalist and non-agriculturalist, the struggle for ownership and usage added to the threatening change in climate condition, that is making land usage extremely difficult tends to put the battle for land on the rise.[13]

Also, it has been explained that increasing population growth rate has continued to wield great pressure on available land resource with contrasting environmental and socio-economic implications of which Farmers-Herders conflict (our area of concern) has remained the utmost preeminent resource-driven conflict in Nigeria.[14]

The compulsion to produce food of crop and animal, as well as raw materials for industries and export with the aim of meeting the ever-growing demand world over, has steered the escalation of land use. The struggle between these two agricultural land user-groups has oftentimes turned into serious overt and covert led to the display of antagonisms and social abrasions in many parts of Nigeria. The conflicts have confirmed the high potentials to worsen the insecurity and food crisis predominantly in countryside communities within Idomaland where most of the conflicts are confined with echoing costs nationwide.

In discussing the challenges of the presence of the Fulani herdsmen in Idomaland, it is pertinent to note the occupational difference of these two ethnic groups as this will serve as a launching pad for understanding the main theme of this paper. The Idoma, just like most of other ethnic groups of Central Nigeria, are farmers and dealt much with land which they hold in high esteem not just as gifts from God through their ancestors, but also as a source of livelihood which must be protected by all means.[15] The Fulani, on the other hand, are transhumant by nature. Ever since they started their Eastward movement from the Futa Jallon highland in the Senegal as early as the sixteenth century, the Fulani are known to be perpetually "on the wing of season" as they move their livestock in search of suitable grazing areas and watering points. This practice has already become deeply ingrained into their culture, making it difficult for them to be convinced of getting resettled permanently in one place.[16]

Given these occupational differences between the Idoma who are settler/farmers and the transhumance Fulani, it is clear that the two parties cannot live together without conflict which is bound to happen as is being witnessed in Agatu and other parts of the nation. Giving the importance of land to an agrarian society like Idomaland, one is quite surprised to see the high level of nonchalant being perpetrated toward the Fulani incursion into Idomaland. Hence, some of the expected challenges include but not limited to.

Persistent Conflicts

From the analysis of the occupational differentiation of these two ethnic groups, one can clearly see that the two groups have different world view to the issue of territory/land. While the transhumance Fulani see land as a gift of nature to be used by them for grazing of their cattle without any form of hindrance from anybody, the Idoma sees land as a property bequeathed to them by God through their ancestors to be held in custody for future generations. This is beside the use of land as source of their livelihood through farming which was and still is their main occupation. Given these different views, it will only take a matter of time for conflict to breakout between the Fulani and any Idoma community hosting them now. This is because, the push factors that is causing their mass migration into Idomaland are still on hence there is an expectant influx of more Fulani into Idomaland. The consequence of this influx will be contention for farming space and grazing spots which will eventually lead to conflicts as it happened in Agatu between 2013 and 2017.[17]

Lost of Territories/Farmlands

One of the factors that define a Person, Ethnic group or Nation is the area or land mass they occupy. This makes the issue of territory very crucial to all human races including the Idoma people. Being an agrarian society, like most of the other ethnic groups in the Benue Valley, the Idoma people attaché a lots of importance to their land which they cultivate to feed their family and meet other life challenges and therefore will do anything including fighting to protect and preserve it from any encroachment particularly from external invaders. On this note, it is important to point out here that given the antecedents of this Fulani herdsmen claim and occupation of lands in other parts of Benue State and the Nation at large with the aid of their sophisticated weapons, it will be a matter of time for them to do same in Idomaland if their gradual infiltration and quest to enter and live in Idomaland is not stopped on time before it will eventually lead to loss of lands to them (the Fulani) who as at the time of this research, are more sophisticatedly armed than any Idoma community.

Increase in Social Vices

While the killings and maiming of the victims of Fulani herdsmen attacks make headlines in all social media and other sources of information dissemination, one fact of the act that seems to be evading the attention of many reporters and scholars is the involvement of these herdsmen in many social vices such as armed robbery, rape, stealing and kidnapping. Armed with this sophisticated weapons, these herdsmen perpetrate a lot of atrocity against their victims. Many instances abound in Benue state where these herdsmen force themselves on women and rape them in the farm. Also, eyewitness reports indicate where these herdsmen use their weapons to rob unsuspected victims. A case worth mentioning here is an incident that happened along the Makurdi-Nakka-Ankpa expressway which until recently was home to these Fulani herdsmen. According to this informant "we have received information on several occasions that it is the Fulani herdsmen that use to rob on this route. However, I did not believe until when I encountered them myself on 21/05/2013. On this day, we were traveling in a commercial bus from Ankpa to makurdi. when we got to the outskate of Adoka and Nakka boundary where you have the government forest reserve, some group of Fulani men pushed their cattle into the road and forced us to stop. When we did, they brought out their AK47 riffles and asked us to surrender our money and other valuable or die. That was how we were robbed by them to my surprise."[18]

If this informant account and other eyewitness reports are anything to go by, then needless to say that same conditions and situations will be replicated in Idomaland if the same people are allowed to come and settle in Idomaland.

Consequences of Fulani Occupation of Idomaland

Decrease in Population

It is no longer doubtable that the current Fulani herdsmen are well armed with modern warfare weapons such as AK47, chemical weapons which they use in terrorizing any persons or communities that opposes their grazing activities and the killing of any communities or persons who dear them to a fight. Records of numbers of persons killed by these Fulani herdsmen all over the nation need not be mentioned here, however, for emphasis and for the fact that Agatu is also part of Idomaland, it is important to show that within the year 2013 to the later part of 2017, Fulani herdsmen attacks have claimed over 5000 lives in about 100 attacks on various communities in Nigeria. In 2015, over 300 lives were lost to herdsmen attack of Agatu alone.[19] This is not to talk of the unrecorded pockets of killings and destruction of properties in Okpokwu Local Government Area on 23/08/2017, and the recent killing of over 72 and 23 innocent souls including pregnant women and children in both Guma, Logo and Okpokwu local Government Areas of Benue State where Idoma sons and daughters were most of the victims. In a dispensation where Idoma people are being deprived of many socio-economic and political opportunities on the bases of their small size in population,[20] I think the last preventable thing that should happen to the Idoma people is to allow these dreaded Fulani herdsmen to invade and occupy their land for any reason including the planned Cattle Colony or the obnoxious Water Resources Bill being initiated and sponsored by the Federal Executive Council under the supervision of the presidency.

Hunger and Poverty

Idomaland is an agrarian society that is contributing her own quota to the massive food production from Benue state which has earned the State the appellate of the "Food Basket of the Nation."[21] However, if the current surge of invasion of the land is not stopped and it resulted into conflict just like in Agatu and other parts of the State and Nation, the farmers, who depend on their farming activities for substance and livelihood, will be cut off from their farms thus breeding food shortage and hunger in the land. Besides hunger, the little resource that would have been used for survival will be diverted into buying arms to wage these conflicts, treating and burying victims and provide securities within the land. Also because the people's source of income is dependent on the land and their farms, such persistent conflict will cut them off from farming for fears of being attacked leading to preventable poverty impact on the people.

Underdevelopment of the Land

Historically, it has been proven that no land riddled with conflicts can develop since government individual and organization will not be willing to plunge their resource into a conflict-riddled land for fear of such investments being destroyed. Besides this, when conflicts happen, schools are closed down, markets are also closed down. In fact all socio-economic activities that serve as agents for development are all put on hold while the conflicts lasts. Being a land that is already lacking behind in terms of socio-economic and political development, Idomaland should be the last community on planet earth to allow any conflict-prone circumstance such as the Fulani herdsmen invasion to befall them.

Conclusion

This paper has attempted to exhume and bring to limelight the hidden negative impacts of the invasion and gradual occupation of Idomaland by the transhumance Fulani herdsmen and holds that, given the glaring consequence being suffered by our brothers and sisters in Agatu (one of the Local Government Areas of Northern Idomaland and our Tiv neighbors and the entire Middle Belt in the hand of these Fulani herdsmen, it is doubtless to say that allowing these herdsmen into Idomaland with their glaring forceful land acquisition and occupation is simply inviting unintended doom into the land. Given these character traits of the Fulani herdsmen, the paper submits that: Idoma people should arise with all seriousness and stop their incursion now before it's too late for posterity will not forgive us if we mortgage the future of the Idoma child on the alters of Benevolence or selfish parochial interests. On this note, the following recommendations are made.

Recommendations

1. Idoma traditional leaders should stop collecting monies and other gift items from herdsmen in exchange for access to grazing spots as this act have been interpreted by the Fulani's on many occasions to mean mortgaging of the people's land to them (the Fulani).
2. Idoma elite should support (with all vigor) the anti-open grazing law of the Benue state government and also melt out punishment to any Idoma person that goes centrally to this law.
3. Following the threats and perceived genocides committed against our unprepared Tiv neighbors, all the Idoma communities particularly those on the Northern fringes of Agatu and Apa should always be battle ready and defend themselves in case of any assault. From the Fulani herdsmen.
4. Idoma people should not deliberately offend the Fulani herdsmen so as to avoid preventable confrontations.

Notes

1. For details of the dispersal of the Idoma speaking People of Nigeria into the various States of Nigeria, see F. G. A. Abutu. "Elite Conflict and the Challenge of Development in Idomaland 1960–2000", Unpublished PhD Thesis Submitted to Post Graduate School Benue State University Makurdi for the Award of Doctor of Philosophy in History 2019, p. 45.
2. O. Igboaka. *The Alekwu Cult and Its Challenge to the Catholic Church Thrust Towards Inculturation in Idomaland*. Enugu: SNAAP Press Limited, 2007, p. 12.
3. E. O. Erim. *The Idoma Nationalities 1600–1900: Problems of Studying the Origin and Development of Ethnicity*. Enugu Fourth Dimension Publishers, 1981, pp. 34–37.
4. R. A. Adelaye. *Power and Diplomacy in Northern Nigeria: The Sokoto Caliphate and Its Enemies, 1808–1906*. London: Longman Press, 1971, p. 34.

5. R. K. Udo. "Environment and People of Nigeria: A Geographical Introduction to the History of Nigeria", in O. Ikimi (ed), *Ground Work of Nigerian History*. Ibadan: Heinemann Press, 1980, pp. 135–137.
6. Colonial Reports on the Idoma people of the Benue Valley in J. Iyo. "The Origin, Early Migration and Settlement Patterns of the Tiv in the Lower Benue Valley of Nigeria c1475–1900AD", in Y. A. Ochefu et al. (ed), *A History of the People of Benue State*. Aboki Publishers Makurdi, 2007, pp. 37–44. Also see E. O. Erim. *The Idoma Nationalities 1600–1900: Problems of Studying the Origin and Development of Ethnicity*..., 1981, pp. 34–37.
7. R. K. Udo. "Environment and People of Nigeria: A Geographical Introduction to the History of Nigeria"..., p. 137.
8. See the Constitution of the Federal Republic of Nigeria on the access to free movement on Section 2, Subsection 3b of the 1999 Constitution as amended.
9. Ngbedeh Adaoche 67 years farmer, interviewed in Obagaji 12/01/2017.
10. See F. S. Wegh. "Challenge of Fulani Herdsmen Attacks to Tiv Survival and Wellbeing", in A. S. Ihuah (ed), *Herdsmen and Farmers Conflicts in Central Nigeria*. Centre for Research Management Benue State University, 2017, p. 107.
11. See Ani Kelechi Johnmary, Anyika Vincent and Mutambara Emmanuel. "The Impact of Climate Change on Food and Human Security in Nigeria", *International Journal of Climate Change Strategies and Management*, 2022, 14(2): 148–167.
12. See Ani Kelechi Johnmary, Victor Ojakorotu and Uwizeyimana Dominique Emmanuel. "Resource and Environmental Insecurity in the Lake Chad Region", *Journal of Reviews on Global Economics*, 2019 (8): 1617–1621.
13. See Ani Kelechi Johnmary and Uwizeyimana Dominique Emmanuel. "Climate Change and Environmental Conflicts in Nigeria: Focus On Farmer-Herder Crisis in Ebonyi State", *African Journal of Peace and Conflict Studies*, 2022, 11(1): 7–22; Ani Kelechi Johnmary and Uwizeyimana Dominique Emmanuel. "Climate Change, Environment and Armed Conflict in Nigeria", *International Journal of Criminology and Sociology*, 2020, 9: 1–7.
14. See Ani Kelechi Johnmary and Uwizeyimana Dominique Emmanuel. "Climate Change and Changing Environmental Insecurity in the Lake Chad", *Journal of African Union Studies*, 2020, 9(2): 65–88.
15. For more on the Idoma people's attachment to *(Aje) land*, see Nats Agbo, A Short History of Idoma Lagos Nigeria Apaugasma Communication Limited, 2012, p. 121.

16. B. J. Takaya. "Pastoralists and Farmers Conflicts in Central Nigeria: Towards a Holistic Analysis of Causal Factors", in A. S. Ihuah (ed), *Herdsmen and Farmers Conflicts in Central Nigeria*..., p. 1.
17. The mayhems and other atrocities committed against the Agatu section of Idomaland can be seen in a serial of July 2015 report by the Mercy Corp. quoted in N. Bagudu. "The Fulani (Herdsmen) Militant Attack on Communities in Plateau State, Clarifying the Issues and the Way Forward", in A. S. Ihuah (ed), *Herdsmen and Farmers Conflicts in Central Nigeria*..., p. 25.
18. Elaigwu Emaikwu 56 years interviewed in Makurdi on 11/01/2018.
19. This information was collected from the global terrorism index analysis quoted in the forward of the book A. S. Ihuah (ed), *Herdsmen and Farmers Conflicts in Central Nigeria.*
20. For the marginalization of the Idoma people, particularly the denial for Apa State creation, see Nats Agbo, A Short History of Idoma Lagos Nigeria Apaugasma Communication Limited, 2012, p. 161.
21. The appellate "FOOD BASKET OF THE NATION" was adapted by Benue State indigenes following the huge food being produced in the state both for local consumptions and export.

CHAPTER 6

Mineral Riches and Violent Conflicts in Nigeria: An Appraisal of Mining Conflicts in Ebonyi State

Vincent Okwudiba Anyika and Chinyere Samuel Ecoma

Introduction

Conflict has always been a part of every society. It manifests in situations where the activities of individuals or groups are perceived as not being mutually beneficial or are inconsistent with the interest of other individuals or groups. Conflict has multifaceted dynamics as it manifests in every aspect of human relations or interactions at varying magnitude. Conflict is a form of discord, friction or disagreement within, between and among human groups in the society. It typifies a situation characterized by contest of interests, thoughts, values, attitudes, understanding

V. O. Anyika (✉)
Alex Ekwueme Federal University Ndufu-Alike, Abakaliki, Nigeria
e-mail: vinanyika@gmail.com

C. S. Ecoma
Veritas University, Bwari, Nigeria
e-mail: ecomachinyere@yahoo.com

K. J. Ani (ed.), *Resource Conflict and Environmental Relations in Africa*,
https://doi.org/10.1007/978-981-19-7343-7_6

and perception. Violent conflict, on the other hand, is an intense form of conflict that involves at least two parties using physical force to resolve competing claims or interests (Ani et al., 2021). Violent conflict spells catastrophe for the human society as it usually brings about chaos, social disorder, loss of human lives and property, and psychological trauma in the society. It stunts socio-economic development and reverses that course of economic growth in the society.

Violent conflicts have becomes a major clog in the wheel of Africa's socio-economic development as the continent is punctuated with series of violent conflicts. The mining of mineral resources that dot the African geographical span has been a major cause of violent conflicts. The persistent eruption of conflicts in African states has reversed the course of economic growth and social cohesion. Countries like the Democratic Republic of Congo, Liberia, Sierra Leone, Sudan, etc. still live in the nightmare of conflicts that emanated from mining activities. In Nigeria, the evidence that mineral extraction fuels conflict is substantial as conflicts associated with mining activities are gradually increasing in intensity and frequency and have resulted to heavy loss of human lives and property and has taken a heavy toll on the communal peace. For instance, conflicts associated with the mining of gold and other minerals in Zamfara state have constituted major obstacle to peace and stability in the areas. It is estimated that about 5000 persons have been killed in 5 years (Inwalombe, 2019). Conflict gold constitutes a major obstacle to peace and drives the black-market economy in Zamfara (Ogundipe, 2019). It provides a significant source of income to armed non-state actors from the North-West who kill and sexually abuse civilians with impunity and many of these armed group trade gold for weapons and ammunitions (Ogundipe, 2019). Thousands of the indigenous people in the area have left their homes and farming and economic activities have been put to a standstill in most rural areas (Inwalombe 2019). In April 2019, security agencies affirmed that illegal mining of solid minerals was that major driver of violence that had claimed hundreds of lives in Zamfara state in recent months (Inwalombe, 2019). According to authorities, Zamfara state is rich in gold, lead and even rare earth and bandits were killing villagers to take over the land for mining of the minerals (Ogundipe, 2019). The thrust of this paper, however, is not on the Zamfara conflict but on mineral mining-related conflicts in Ebonyi State.

Theoretical Background

The dynamics of conflicts are best understood within the ambit of relevant conflict theories. Such theories serve as explanatory tools that provide fundamental, systematic and analytical framework to the understanding of the causes, characteristics and trajectories of conflicts. There are some contemporary conflict theories that offer explanations to the causes and nature of contests, dissensions, frictions, tensions and other manifestations of disagreements or conflict in human societies as well as their political, social, economic and cultural implications at the individual, communal, state and international levels. Conflict theories by their imbued systematic and analytical nature serve as viable tools for conflict resolution endeavours as they enable issues to be addressed objectively. According to Lumumba-Kasongo (2017, p. 30), "the main questions that most conflict models or theories pose when dealing with conflicts are: (1) why do conflicts occur? (2) How do they occur? (3) Who are the agents and what are their agencies? (4) How are they managed? (5) What resources are used to advance them? (6) What are their intended and non-intended consequences? (7) Can they be prevented both in the short as well as in the long run?" These holistic questions are systematically addressed by some conflict theories though not in the same order. The weakness and strength of a conflict theory are ascertained by observing the extent to which the theory accommodates the basic question relating to conflicts (Lumumba-Kasongo, 2017). The intent of conflict theories as noted by Nillesen and Bulte (2014) is to effectively explain and systematically analyse conflicts in their peculiar contexts; to acquire specific qualitative, quantitative and critical knowledge; and to produce a conceptualized direction for change or policy strategy with reference to conflicts that manifest in a given society. Some contemporary conflict theories that are related to the focus of this paper will be briefly discussed.

Karl Marx's conflict theory serves as the basics of all contemporary conflict theories. The key premise of Karl Marx's conflict theory is that individuals within a society will work to maximize their own wealth and power. Thus, it is the struggle for the maximization of economic interest that brings parties to conflict. In the contemporary period, some conflict theories which are offshoots of Marxism have been espoused by some scholars in their attempts to systematically and analytically explain the nature of conflicts that have characterized modern society. Hirshleifer

(1995) in his attempt to explain the nature of conflict that characterized mineral bearing states advanced the Contest Success Function theory. According to the model, the propensity for conflict is high when one (which may be government) has greater control of oil or mineral resources through its exclusive access to flow of rents than the other group (oil or mineral bearing community) which have limited access. Thus, the group in a disadvantaged position will resort to violence in their contest for greater access to rents. In the contest that ensues, the rentier state often considers that its monopoly of violence has to be enforced through a military action against any resistance to its control over the affected resources and the success of such action will serve to deter future uprising. On the other hand, the winner takes it all posture of the government is equally adopted by the opposing forces, who feel that once they come out victorious from the struggle for resource control or secession for full political control of their enclave, their economic prosperity will be guaranteed. Thus, both parties are motivated by the perceived ends that will come when they emerge victorious from the conflict.

In the contest success paradigm, the nature of government institutions is considered as endogenous variable in every contest because it is inability of such institutions to ensure an optimal re-distribution of rents that accrue from mineral resources that spur agitations. Further, the winner takes it all approach of the elite-dominated government aggravated sentiments that fan the embers of conflicts. In such state, stability will always be threatened because as the economic condition of the disadvantaged group continues to worse, it will reach a point when the people will choose to fight the state at any cost. In the contest success model, interior equilibrium is considered achievable when an optimal re-distribution of resource benefits is institutionalized in the state. Also, the model holds that the intensity of conflict is determined by the economic value allocated to the natural resources being contested; higher resource prices invariably lead to more intense conflicts and vice versa. When the resource price is high, groups will allocate more efforts to the conflict.

Casselli and Coleman (2013) advanced a theoretical approach to resource-based conflicts which they termed ethnic fractionalization model. According to the model ethnic fractionalization is a very significant factor in the resource-conflict nexus. According to the exponents of this model, "the ethnic composition of societies is a vital mediating factor that explains the frequency and intensity of conflicts over resource rents"

(Casselli and Coleman, 2013, p. 23). In explaining how ethnicity interplays with resources to bring about conflicts, the proponents of the model stated that "the geographical location of resource stocks and how these deposit-rich areas map onto the homelands of different ethnic groups are very relevant in the explanation of some conflict dynamics." According to this model, if an ethnic group or a group of people that claim distinct identity dominate a region or feels, they need greater access to resource rents relative to other ethnic groups they may begin to pose serious resistance to the authority of the state; if the group considers that its chances of secession are greater than their chances of winning the battle for greater control of resource rents, such ethnic group may reorganize themselves and wage war for secession from the state. On the other hand, other ethnic groups within the province of resource location could also wage war for greater inclusion if they consider other ethnic groups more advantaged in the re-distribution of resource rents. This was the scenario that led to the Ezza-Ezillo and the Ezillo conflict (Ani, 2017).

The repeated conflict model as espoused by Maxwell and Reuveny (2005) explained why two income maximizing groups engage in repeated conflicts. The model offered profound explanation to the cause of conflicts that emanate in areas where resource location cut across ethnic boundaries. According to the model, 'when groups allocate effort to harvesting from shared renewable resources that are located across their boundaries, a potential nonlinear interaction will emerge between the two groups and they may resort to violence.' A group may resort to fight for greater access to resources if they perceive that the outcome of the war may determine their future position with respect to the contested resources. The incentive for continued prosecution of the violent conflict comes from the perception that the future position of any party to the conflict is dependent on the outcome of current war. Thus, they are motivated to fight even harder so as to have an edge in future conflict. Such decisions give rise to repeated conflicts.

Another approach to the basic conflict model was introduced by Acemoglu, Vindigni and Ticchi (2010). The model provided some explanation to the persistence of civil wars in some mineral bearing states. The model is focused on states with persistent rebel contest of an elite-dominated government. According to the model, a government faced with persistent rebel uprising fuelled by mineral exploitation can choose to invest in a strong military that will have the capacity to crush any rebellion; however, such government has to also consider the risk involved in investing in a strong military as the military at any time may decide to overthrow the elite in power through coup d'état. Hence, the elite-dominated government would have to choose between a weak army and persistent war and a strong army and the risk of a coup (Nillesen and Bulte, 2014, p. 74). When the rents inflow of the elites are not adversely affected by current conflicts, and also when the battle fronts are located in remote mineral bearing areas, the elite may decide to keep condoning persistent conflicts instead of risking its hold to power through military overhaul. Also, condoning persistent conflict may be a strategy by the elite in power to manipulate financial allocations and get greater payoffs. However, when persistent conflicts are at a great cost to the government, the elite in power may decide to crush the rebelling groups once and for all and may resort to the military option by overinvesting in the army through purchase of sophisticated weapons and arms so as to ensure that the state maintains a monopoly of violence. The risk involved here, as earlier stated, is that the overexposure of the military to domestic conflicts will make them thinker that the elite in power are inept in maintaining internal stability and managing resource endowment optimally, thus, they may decide to oust the elite in power through coup so as to have major stake in governance.

The major causes of conflict in sub-Saharan Africa are access and control of land, water resources, mineral resources and the manner of re-distribution of resource rents by rentier states. The conflict in theoretical model of conflict discussed having very significant bearing on the nature and characteristics of conflict that buffet the African continent especially south of the Sahara. In the Ebonyi State mining-related conflict nexus which is the focus of this paper, the Contest Function model and the Repeated Conflict model are considered very relevant in the explanation of its conflict dynamics with respect to mineral resource exploitation.

Mining Conflicts in Ebonyi State

Ebonyi State is richly endowed with mineral resources such as limestone, lead/zinc, granite, galena, glass sand, shale, ball clay, marble, pyrite, refractory clay, gypsum, fluorspar, bentonite, quartz, salt, laterite (Raw Materials Research and Development Council, 2012). The mining of these mineral resources scattered across the state has been associated with pockets of conflict in the state. Since the beginning of mining in Ebonyi State in 1925, conflicts associated with mining have become inevitable

(Elom, 2018). The causes of mining-related conflicts in Ebonyi State can broadly be categorized into three. Some of the conflicts were stimulated or triggered by mining companies in their attempts to undermine other mining interests or companies; some are caused by host communities who felt short-changed or cheated in a mining agreement while others are caused by conflicting communal claims over lands with mineral deposits.

In 2012, the people of Azu-Inyaba where extraction of limestone was going on felt they had an unwanted visitor, Ibeto Cement Limited, which came to the town and installed a multi-million-naira plant. Before the company could settle down for business, the host were up in arms as a result of divisions. Some felt short-changed and they wanted their share of the cake (Ikeh, 2012). Before the company could know what was at stake, the aggrieved party had mobilized and a mob burnt the plant (Ikeh, 2012). That was before it could be put to use. It took the intervention of a former governor, Dr Sam Egwu to get the company another spot, in another town for its business. In February 2015, two mining firms, Ezechuks Standard Link Limited and Jidech Mining Company Limited, operating at Uma-Akpata in Izzi Local Government Area disrupted the peace of the area as they engaged in violent conflict over ownership of a mining site (Uka, 2015). In a bid to forestall the escalation of violence, the Federal Ministry of Mines and Steel Development sealed off the mining site.

Another hotbed of mining-related conflict in Ebonyi State is in the Enyigba-Enyichiri-Alike axis. This conflict is between Enyigba, which belongs to Izzi clan and Enyibichiri-Alike which belongs to Ikwo clan. These communities have been involved in land dispute for about three decades. In July 2018 the two communities the rivalry between the two communities degenerated to violent inter-communal conflict. The recent upsurge and escalation of violence in the area could be linked to the signing of MoU between an indigenous Lead/Zinc mining company, Royal Salt Limited and Enyigba town in 2010. The Royal Salt Company, according to the MoU, would be paying the community an annual rent of 6 million, provide road network, electricity, boreholes at different locations and scholarship to the people as well supply essential services to the Ameri Health Centre. They will also pay the community, youths, women and immediate land owners annual sum of ₦300,000, ₦150,000, ₦100,000 and ₦250,000, respectively, as well as float scholarship fund of ₦500,000 (Ikeh, 2012). The company will also provide the sum of ₦200,000 for school library and laboratory; employ 50% of the unskilled labour force at the mining site and 20% of unskilled labour force from the community at the processing mill (Ikeh, 2012). The Royal Salt Company also agreed to employ 30% of the unskilled/semi-skilled labour force from the community at the mining site as 15 at the processing mill (Ikeh, 2012).

The Enyibichiri-Alike community felt excluded in the deal between the Lead/zinc mining company and Enyigba community despite their claims over some mining sites in the area. Not long after the company began operation, violent confrontations erupted between Enyigba and Enyibichiri-Alike communities leading to huge loss of life and property. In February 2018, youths from Enyigba community allegedly stormed Alike shooting sporadically at the villagers and setting houses ablaze (Eze, 2018). According to premium times report, a two-year-old boy and five others were shot dead. Also, in April 2019 an infant and seven others were shot and burnt to death in a renewed conflict along the Alex Ekwueme Federal University, Ndufu-Alike road, near the border between the two communities. Also, three other persons were attacked and two of them were killed. One of them a woman was the wife of a police officer deployed to Borno State (Eze, 2019). In June 2021, following the resumption of hostilities between the two communities seven children were abducted from Enyigba community (Guardian, June 21, 2021). There is presently fragile peace in the area as armed policemen attached to the mining sites have helped sustain security in the area. The incessant communal clashes between the two communities have often disrupted the peace of the area and constituted serious threat to the lives of the people as well as students and staff of Alex Ekweme Federal University that live and work in the area.

Measures for Addressing Mining Conflicts

Violent conflict is an ill wind that blows no one any good. When such conflicts erupt, it does not only sweep away decades of painstaking development efforts but also creates economic, social and political costs and consequences. The outbreak of violent conflicts reverses every attempt at development. Since the evidence that mineral extraction fuels conflict is substantial, it, therefore, behoves that government and other stakeholders to adopt measures that would forestall that outbreak of conflict at various mining sites that dot Ebonyi State as well as resolve the already existing ones. All traditional and modern approaches to conflict management should be deployed (Ani and Ajaegbo, 2015).

One of the measures for forestalling or mitigate the eruption of mining-related conflicts is by transparency and accountability. A lot of deals between the government, mining companies and host communities are shrouded in secrecy. In some cases, the leadership of the communities do not bring deals they have accepted or entered to the knowledge of the entire community thereby leading to ill feelings, speculations and misinformation that could culminate in violent confrontations. It is also salient for the communities to know the percentage of the revenue that comes to them and how such monies are being disbursed.

Secondly, a measure of regulation should be enforced in the mining the sector to checkmate the activities of illegal miners and to ensure that miscreants and unscrupulous elements do not hijack the sector. This would ensure that the like of what happened in Zamfara is not replicated elsewhere. The activities of miscreants in the mining sector can also endanger the stability of the state, as it did in the Democratic Republic of Congo and Sierra Leone. Furthermore, illegal mining could pose serious environmental consequences to the communities especially in areas where lead is mined (Elom, 2018).

Furthermore, the activities of the mining companies should be brought to public domain. Their contributions to community development should be evaluated from time to time. There should also be a platform for mining companies to meet with their host communities to ensure that both sides live up to their responsibilities. This would help avert the build-up of speculations and misinformation in the host communities and would make the host communities less vulnerable to the antics of political interests that are always out to manoeuvre and manipulate opinions in order to achieve selfish interest through the disruption of communal peace.

Conclusion

Mining-related conflict is another dimension of conflict that is gradually increasing in intensity and frequency in some parts of Nigeria. Such conflicts need to be nipped in the bud to avoid blighting development efforts across the country. As the national economy veers towards the mining sector, adequate measures should be put in place by stakeholders to avert the ugly and horrific experiences of some African countries and to ensure continued economic growth, development, social stability and peaceful coexistence.

In addition to the earlier recommendations, there is this belief among the impoverished of some states such as Ebonyi that the presence of mining companies in their communities would miraculously transform their economic fortunes within a short time. Thus, when they have lived in this illusion for some time without seeing any change, they may take up arms against mining companies. State government should make effort to bring economic growth and development for their people through creation of jobs and attraction of business investments. This will go a long way to empower the people and make them less rent dependent. It was this factor that led to the sabotage and destruction of Ibeto Cement Plant in 2012 in Azu-Inyaba. The government and other stakeholders should make the host communities become aware of their take home in every deal so that they would not have false hope or feel short-changed at any point. Such communities should constantly be informed on the activities of mining companied in their community and forewarned against the antics of mischievous individuals. Also, corruption, greed and neglect on the part of political leadership in such areas should be avoided as the negligence of the welfare of host communities can spur communal resentment that may become violent over time. Where there are established cases of land disputes, the government should wade into the conflict and possibly stop mining activities until such issues are resolved. In the same vein, corporate social responsibilities of mining companies should not be limited to the host communities but should be spread across the surrounding areas to avert the build-up of inter-communal tension and petty jealousy that may undermine peaceful coexistence.

References

Acemoglu, D., Vindigni, A., & Ticchi, D. (2010). Persistent civil wars. *Journal of European Economics Association*, Vol. 8, No. 2, pp. 664–676.

Ani, K. J. (2017). Ezza-Ezillo Conflict and National Implications in Nigeria: The Need for Multi-Dimensional Peace-Building. *Affrika: Journal of Politics, Economics and Society*, Vol. 7, No. 2, pp. 143–159.

Ani, K. J., & Ajaegbo, D. I. (2015). Historical Foundations of Conflict Management and Peace Building Strategies in Nigeria. *Ubuntu: Journal of Conflict and Social Transformation*, Vol. 4, No. 1, pp. 113–133.

Ani, K. J., Onu, C., & Anikelechi, I. G. (2021). Contributions of Interpersonal Conflict Management on Performance of Government Hospitals in Nigeria. *Independent Journal of Management & Production*, Vol. 12, No. 7, pp. 1785–1807.

Casselli, F., & Coleman, W. J. (2013). On the Theory of Ethnic Conflict. *Journal of European Economics Association*, Vol. 11, No. 1, pp. 161–192.

Elom, N. I. (2018). Lead (Pb) Mining in Ebonyi State, Nigeria: Implications for Environmental and Human Health Risk. *International Journal of Environment and Pollution Research*, Vol. 6, No.1, pp. 24–32.

Eze, J. (2018). Six Feared Killed in Ebonyi Boundary Dispute. *Premium Times*, March 4.

Eze, J. (2019). Infant, Seven Others Killed in Ebonyi Communal Crisis. *Premium Times*, April 8.

Hirshleifer, J. (1995). Anarchy and Its Breakdown. *Journal of Political Economy*, Vol. 103, No. 1, pp. 250–270.

Ikeh, I. (2012). Ebonyi Signs Solid Mineral Mining MoU. *NBF News*, October 5.

Inwalombe, D. (2019). Bloody Gold in Zamfara: Threat to Stability or Development Opportunity? *Guardian Newspaper*, 22 April.

Lumumba-Kasongo, T. (2017). *Contemporary Theories of Conflict and Their Social and Political Implications.* Darkar, Senegal: CODESRIA.

Maxwell, J.W., & Reuveny, R. (2005). Continuing Conflict. *Journal of Economic Behaviour Organization*, Vol. 58, No. 1, pp. 30–52.

Nillesen, E., & Bulte, E. (2014). Natural Resources and Violent Conflict. *Annual Review of Resource Economics*, Vol. 6, pp. 69–83.

Ogundipe, S. (2019). While Killings Continued in Zamfara Despite Mining Ban-Nigerian Military. *Daily Times*, July 23.

Raw Materials Research and Development Council. (2012). Mineral Raw Materials in Ebonyi State. www.rmrdc.gov.ng

Uka, F. (2015). Nigeria: Two Firms at War over Ebonyi Mining Site. *Premium Times*, February 16.

CHAPTER 7

Resource Curse and Environmental Conflicts in Angola

Vincent Okwudiba Anyika and Kelechi Johnmary Ani

Introduction

Angola is a classic example of a state where natural resource endowment does not translate to better living standard for the citizens. The country is the second largest producer of crude oil in Africa and has abundant deposits of mineral resources such as iron, manganese, bauxite, uranium, gold, diamond and natural gas. Angola got her independence from Portugal in 1975 after which a long civil war besieged the country. The struggle for control of political power and natural resources was the major factor that precipitated the Angolan conflict. The two parties to the

V. O. Anyika (✉)
Department of History and Strategic Studies, Alex Ekwueme Federal University, Abakaliki, Nigeria
e-mail: vinanyika@gmail.com

K. J. Ani
Department of History and Strategic Studies, Alex Ekwueme Federal University Ndufu-Alike Ikwo, Abakaliki, Nigeria

K. J. Ani (ed.), *Resource Conflict and Environmental Relations in Africa*, https://doi.org/10.1007/978-981-19-7343-7_7

conflict were the two main political parties, Movimento Popular de Libertaçao de Angola (MPLA) and the União Nacional para a Independência Total de Angola (UNITA). The MPLA emerged victorious from the civil war which ended in April 2002 and has continued to hold on to political power and control of oil production. The Angolan Civil War had grave consequences on Angola as it resulted to the death of thousands of her citizens, displacement of its population, destabilization of the production system and destruction of infrastructures (James, 2011). The war period recorded high incidents of infant mortality, prevalence of parasitic and infectious diseases and low life expectancy (James, 2011). In the immediate aftermath of the war, the ruling party in its bid to overcome the economic consequences of the war initiated a policy of economic reconstruction.

Angolan political leaders from the war-time period have misappropriated Angola's oil revenue and have failed to ensure equitable distribution of oil revenue to its populace. Unequal distribution of revenue derived from exploitation of natural resources has characterized Angolan political economy for decades. The factors of corruption and greed among political elites are considered to be at the root of abject poverty that affect significant number of its populace. A few elites in power and their cohorts have been benefiting exclusively from oil revenue and mineral resource exploitation. In 2010, it was revealed that the seven richest persons in Angola were those in power (Committee to Protect Journalists, 2011, 1). While the elites in power and their allies bask in affluence, a preponderant majority of its citizens live below the poverty line. In the oil-producing areas, the citizens despite their obvious lacks are also faced with environmental problems caused by oil production and the corrupt political elites have turned a blind eye to plight of the endangered population. This chapter examines the paradigm of resource curse vis-à-vis the Angolan question. It will also explore the nexus between emerging conflicts and environmental degradation in parts of Angola. It will also analyse the characteristic leanings of the Angolan petro-economy.

Socio-Economic Characteristics of Angola

Angola has a population of about 30 million (World Bank, 2018). The Angolan population is relatively small when compared its surface area of about 1,300,000 km^2. Angola has a larger popular of young people. Over 14 million Angolans are below 15 years (Statista, 2021). People below

15 years are the largest age bracket in the country followed by people between 25 and 54 years which constitute 9 million citizens (Statista, 2021). Angolans aged 65 and above are in minority. Life expectancy in Angola as at 2019 is 61 years (World Bank, 2019).

At the beginning of the twenty-first century, Angola was a country ravaged by war, having been engulfed in violent conflict for over two decades. The country faced myriads of socio-economic problems ranging from widespread poverty, lack of proper health care, malnutrition, high infant mortality, prevalence of diseases, distorted production system, lack of social cohesion, among others. In the immediate aftermath of the Angolan civil war, the MPLA-led government began to implement an economic development plan aimed at reconstructing the Angolan economy. The development model adopted by the country falls midway between centrally economy and market economy which some authors termed liberal peacebuilding. The development plan according to Soares de Oliveira (2011) was a strategy by the oligarchy to consolidate themselves in power for effect exploitation of Angolan resources. The focus of the Angolan post-war reconstruction was the production system and infrastructure destroyed in the course of the long conflict. The war paralysed the production system and distorted the economy. Following the exit of the Portuguese with their oil production facilities, Angola was left with non-functional facilities for oil production. In 1976, Angola nationalized Portuguese capital and private oil and mining companies through the State Intervention Act. Angola, however, beckoned on private sector and foreign investor to partake in the oil and mining sector. This was facilitated through the Petroleum Activities Act of 1978 and Foreign Investment and Mines Act of 1979. It should be noted that revenue from oil production after the exit of the Portuguese which was exclusively under MPLA control extensively financed the Angolan conflict which ended in favour of the party (Garcia-Rodriguez et al., 2015). During the war year and post-war year, the few elites in power collaborated with private oil and mining companies and gained unduly from oil wealth and mineral wealth. This privileged minority and their associated grew in affluence which a larger chunk of the populace wallowed in penury.

Angola's oil sector has been much enhanced since the end of the civil war. The country has continued to be one of the largest oil-producing states in Africa. Also, significant mining activities are going on in the country with many interests striving for control and government exercising overwhelming control. Some authors consider Angola to be a perfect paradigmatic instance of resource curse considering the lingering human suffering that the citizens of the country go through despite the growing oil wealth of the state. The government of the state has overtime demonstrated its incapacity to equitably distribute the benefits oil production and mining activities in parts of the state. A few elites on the corridors of power, their associates and military allies have been in control of the country's oil revenue and have skewed oil production agreements to benefit them at the expense of the generality of the citizens (Sachs, 2007). The elites in power protected themselves and oil production facilities from the largely disaffected citizens through their military collaborators. By maintaining a monopoly of violence, that state suppresses dissenting voices, and the public at large. The rentier state is overfocused on oil related production and mining activities with little effort given to other sectors of the economy. This has limited the limited the development of the private sector where a greater part of the citizens could have been actively engaged.

Angola's oil sector is often referred to as an enclave. This appellation arose from the fact that the sector lacks linkages to the rest of the nation's economy. Ferguson (2006) described the Angolan economy as a model in the global economy in which capital instead of flowing evenly across the territory, hops to spaces secured by private security contractors. Angola economy is an instance of petro-capitalism where wealth is accumulated without work through the connivance of the political class with transnational oil corporations (Hodges, 2004). The enclave sector permits the selected few in government to amass resource rents by virtue of their positions rather than their labour. The distribution of oil revenue in Angola does not flow to the populace equitably rather it is selectively distributed to a few citizens through a patronage system. The more revenue the government pumps into patronage, the government is left with little for redistribution to the wider population (Soares de Oliveira, 2007).

Angola's exclusive petro-capitalism has precipitated internal and external interventions aimed at challenging absolute stake in the oil sector by the MPLA-led government. Also, government's repressive actions towards dissident voices or groups have resulted to pockets of petro-violence, a term that relates to all forms of violent struggles aimed at gaining access to and control of oil revenue. The government in its bid to ensure the safety of oil bases and enclaves has put up security measures. These include the use of the armed guards provided by private security contractors to secure oil facilities and raising razor wire fences around oil facilities. Also, the strong backing provided by the military has enabled the government to thrive and continue to serve the interest of minority political elites at the expense of the wider populace.

Poverty and Political Corruption in Angola

Lack of accountability in governance has enhanced the covering of many dubious deals struck with multinational oil companies and siphoning of public fund by the leadership of Angola. The factor of corruption that is ingrained in Angolan leadership is instrumental to the emasculation of citizens and misappropriation of oil revenue (Roque, 2009). The Angolan situation is an irony of resource endowment. Rising oil price has enhanced the revenue base of the country yet the sufferings of the people are not being ameliorated. The connivance of transnational companies with the political elites in power led to the emergence of the term, nomenklatura petrola, which is used to describe the minority elite class that has enriched themselves from shady oil production deals prevented equitable distribution of oil revenue (Cameron, 2017). The national oil company, Sonangol, has been a major tool through which the political elites and their cohorts siphon Angola's oil money (Soares de Oliveira, 2007). Pervasive corruption among the political officeholders has led to the emergence of the political class as the richest class in Angola. In 2003, a Luanda newspaper, Angolense, published a list of wealthiest people in Angola which reveals that the seven (7) richest people in Angola were those in government (Human Rights Watch, 2003). The list did not contain names entrepreneurs or technocrats from the private sector rather those who fed fat from the public fund. Through corrupt oil deals, those in power divert oil wealth due to the state to their personal accounts. In 2013, Forbes Magazine revealed that the eldest daughter of the then President, Dos Santos was the first African woman whose fortunes crossed the barriers of 1000 million US dollars (Dolan & Marques, 2013).

The Angolan political class are notorious for shady oil deals and theft of petro-revenue. A significant fraction of revenues generated from oil rents, royalties from offshore oil flow and signing of bonuses bypass state coffers and are logged in offshore bank accounts. Koning (2012) reported that over four billion US dollars in oil revenue did not enter state treasury between 1998 and 2002. Corruption among the political class is a factor that has reinforced unfair distribution of oil revenue. This has led to the impoverishment of many citizens whose means of livelihood have been adversely affected by oil production activities. Furthermore, sustenance of opaque accounting system has obstructed the path to accountability and transparency thereby shading corrupt deals of the elites in power and misappropriation by same. There is no effective mechanism in the political and economic system that ensures accountability. This ugly scenario has resulted to the sustenance of a kleptocratic system that has succeeded in widening the chasm between the rich political class and the impoverished masses. The citizens are intentionally kept aloof from oil benefits while the elites in power amass same for themselves and their cronies. Corruption has been the major driver of the political economy of exclusion which characterize the state of Angola and has enforced the impoverishment of many citizens.

According to the World Bank, some common forms of corrupt practices that have characterized that Angolan public sector include political bribery or kickbacks given to highly placed public employees (World Bank, 2018). Another form of corruption noted by the World Bank African Development Indicator (2015) is known as quite corruption. It is a form of corruption that occurs when public servants fail to provide goods or services paid for by government (World Bank, 2015). According to the World Bank report (2015), this form of corruption is widespread and has led to loss of trust and confidence in the public sector by the poor masses. The corruption that is ingrained in the Angolan public sector is very detrimental to the plight of the poor in the country.

In terms of human development indicators, Angola has not been able to use its oil wealth to transform the lives of majority of its citizens. The country currently faces the crisis of poverty. According to CGTN African report (2020, June 3), Angola's poverty rate stands at 41%. That is to say that 4 out of 10 Angolans live below the poverty line. Poverty rate is more pronounced in the rural areas where the rate is given 57.2%. According to the UN Poverty and Equity Brief (2020, April), between 2018 and 2019, the number of persons living below the poverty line has changed from 37 to 41%. The report also indicates that there is high rate of poverty in the rural areas; the Cunene Province has a poverty rate of 54%, Moxico Province has a poverty prevalence rate of 52% while the Kwanza Sul Province has a poverty prevalence rate of 50%. Several millions of Angolans have very limited access to basic social amenities and services (Cameron, 2017). In 2019, Angola has a human development index value of 0.581 which places it at 148 position out of 189 countries (UNDP, 2020). According to the UNDP poverty rate in 2019 was

48.4, an average schooling years of 11 while life expectancy from birth was given as 61 years.

Angola has made significant progress in its macroeconomic and structural reforms which has accorded it a measure of stability. The country's GDP recorded steady increase from 2008–2014. The economic recession of 2014 and its attendant oil price slide led to reduced GDP from 2014. Poverty rate increased to 48.4% in 2019 and stood at 51.1% in 2020. Slowdown in economic activities brought about by the COVID-19 pandemic reduced the country's GDP earning and plunged many below the poverty line (World Bank, 2021). Poverty rate in Angola is expected to remain high within the next three years as economic performance of the state worsens (World Bank, 2021). According to the Oxford Poverty and Human Development Initiative (OPHI), 54% of Angolans is multidimensional poor and poverty is more pronounced among children under the age of ten. It further pointed out that in the urban areas, 1 in 3 persons is poor while 9 out of 10 persons on the rural areas are poor (OPHI, 2020).

Angola's oil wealth is indubitable concentrated in the hands of a minority group, the political elites and their allies at the detriment of the generality of the populace. Unemployment rate in the country is high. The oil companies and mining companies have not provided significant job opportunities for the teeming job seekers in the country. Less than 20,000 persons are employed by the oil and mining companies. Furthermore, a significant number of rurally based Angolans that depended on fishing has suffered great losses in recent time as a result in oil spillage and other forms environmental degradation. This partly explains while most Angolans are living with poverty. Having emerged from a long period of warfare, Angola faces social problems such as dilapidated infrastructures, deficiency of essential services such as healthcare and education, weak national economy. The ruling party, MPLA and their representatives in power have not been able to alleviate the sufferings of the people through development programmes and social/welfare service schemes.

Oil Exploitation and the Angola Environment

Oil was discovered in Angola as early as 1910, however, commercial production of crude oil in Angola only started in 1956, when Campanhia de Petroleum de Angola (Petroangol) began oil extraction in the basin of the River Kwanza. Petroangol later discovered oil in the Congo Basin.

Petroangol was the major operator of most of the on-shore oil fields. Petroangol worked in partnership with Texaco, a US company and Angol, a subsidiary of a Portuguese oil company, Sacor. In 1954, while oil exploration was going on around the Congo Basin, a US Gulf Oil Company and Cabinda Gulf Oil Company also explored the Cabinda and began oil production in the area by 1968 (Koning, 2012). As a result of additional discovery of oil fields, Angolan oil production scaled up from 2.5 million tons in 1969 to 8.2 million in 1973 with a corresponding increase in export. By the time the Portuguese left Angola in 1975, oil had overtaken coffee as the leading export commodity with an output of 172,000 bpd (Sonangol, 2009). Following Angola's independence from Portugal, the MPLA-led government implemented some reforms in the oil sector. In 1976, the Angolan Government nationalized the Sociedade de Lubricants and Fossil, Angol, a subsidiary of Portuguese Company, Sacor and created a national fuel company known as Sonangol. Sonangol was a state-owned oil company which served as the sole licensee of oil resources in Angola. Through the Sonangol, government made and implemented its oil policies and related with multinational oil companies that operate in Angola.

Oil exploration and exploitation in Angola was predominantly on shore, however, with the entrance of multinational companies such as British Petroleum, Chevron, Total Tina-Elf, Texaco, Agip, Exxon Mobil and Statoil, most oil exploration took place offshore. These companies secured exploration agreements and established oil rigs. Angolan oil production rose from 100,000 bpd in 1976 to 2.1 million bpd in 2009. In 2011, Angola's oil production exceeded Nigeria's due to sabotage faced in the Nigerian Niger Delta region. In February 2021, oil production in Angola was 1.25 million barrels per day (Statista, 2021).

Angola's oil production activities have very significant environmental consequences. Incessant oil spills at sea, air pollution, deforestation and soil erosion are some of the problems which oil production activities have created in Angola. Sea pollution caused by oil spillage has led to significant catch drop in some fishing communities in the coastal areas. It has also led to death of fish and degradation of the environment. Furthermore, wastes from refineries have resulted to degradation of land in oil bearing communities. Some communities that depended on farming and fishing have been adversely affected by oil production-related activities and have remained uncompensated for their misfortune (Sayagues, 2021).

Petro-Violence in Angola

Violence which has characterized some oil-bearing communities of Angola is an outcome of enforced exclusion. These communities whose resources sustain the economy have continued to clamour for inclusion in the distribution oil revenue. Also, considering the huge loss these communities incur from environmental degradation arising from oil production activities, they have hoped that their access to oil revenue would mitigate their misfortunes. However, government's insensitivity to the plight of these communities has pushed them into violent agitations. In its bid to muffle up dissident voices in some oil-bearing communities, the Angolan Government have repeatedly used repressive measures against agitators. In Cabinda where such resource control agitations are popular, government troops have been used to terrorize the people. Also, in Soyo in the south of the Congo River, government troops have occupied the area to starve off or clamp down on any protesting group, thereby creating an atmosphere of fear.

The Angolan Government through its violent agenda has continued to terrorize the oil-producing communities and suppressed agitating voices without enhancing their inclusion in the share of oil revenue. The narratives of oil-bearing communities that have been victims of state terrorism are quite pathetic. Harsh treatments given to communities that demanded for their due share of oil benefits have made such societies see their separation from Angola as the only way for their redemption from enforced poverty. Angolans in the Cabinda city area do not see themselves as Angolans but as Cabindans and have continued to sustain their demand for independence from Angola. This arose from years of neglect and violent repressions.

The Resource Curse Model and the Angolan Question

The resource curse model is a deterministic approach that is used to analyse conflicts and economic development challenges that are usually associated with in petro-capitalist or rentier economies. According to the resource curse literature, abundant endowment of resource wealth relative to the size of the economy tends to, or can, lead to slow economic growth, greater economic (and political) volatility, more corruption, more authoritarianism and greater violence. The model from a holistic view does not constitute a perfect explanatory tool to the political economy of oil-rich and dependent economies of sub-Saharan Africa. Some states such as Canada, Norway and Botswana were not affected by some of the features that are associated with natural resource endowments as given by the resource curse model (Soros, 2007). From a clear point of view, the bane of development in oil-rich sub-Saharan Africa states is inequitable distribution and misuse of petro-revenue, lack of rule of law and weak institutions. Lack of rule of law, political corruption and weak institution in sub-Saharan Africa have given way for poor accountability in governance thereby giving kleptocrats opportunities to siphon and misappropriate public funds with impunity. Weak institutions allow political officeholders to become more autocratic if not absolute in power and lose accountability to the citizens. Absolute leaders who have lost legitimacy use violent repressive as the only means of maintaining political power and starving off critiques. Such absolute leaders use state fund to maintain their clique of patrons and loyalists who give them support. When states fund is used to maintain patronage less amount of fund is left for distribution to the populace.

Most African oil-dependent states started enjoying petrodollars when they were newly independent without well-established institutions of governance to checkmate the excesses of the political elites. Hence, they became prone to abuse of power and misuse of public funds. Lack of strong political institutions allowed political leaders to become absolute and reckless. The political elites misused public funds and were not held accountable. The notion of resource control is deterministic and is bereaved of fundamental explanatory parameters. It is a doctrine of hasty conclusions and misguided generalization. The focus of studies on underdevelopment of the oil-dependent sub-Saharan African states such as Angola should be on the nature and characteristics of their political economies to identify factors that have inhibited development and address them adequately.

Conclusion

Good and accountable governance founded on the principle rule of law is the way out of the mire of exclusiveness that characterizes the Angolan petro-economy. Enhanced inclusion in the distribution of oil revenue will stem the tide of violent conflicts in the oil-bearing provinces of Angola. Furthermore, a more humanistic approach to environmental degradation brought about by oil exploitation will go a long way in placating the affected communities and give them assurance of hope for a better life in the state. Continued use of repressive forces to maintain political power and oil production activities will continue to aggravate the already bad situation. The MPLA should know that they are in power to serve the Angolans. The party should look inwards and find out where they have failed Angolans. Furthermore, the government should create platform through which it can interface with the oil and mineral bearing communities to identify their key areas of concern and through medium seek ways of resolving identified problems. The state should also as a matter of necessity put up strategies for ensuring environmental protection, clean energy usage and sound industrial waste management.

References

Ani, K. J. (2017). Ezza-Ezillo conflict and national implications in Nigeria: The need for multi-dimensional peace-building. *Affrika: Journal of Politics, Economics and Society*, 7(2): 143–159.

Cameron, L. (2017). Reversing the resource curse in Angola. Will discover undergraduate conference, 5. https://scholar.uwindsor.ca/uwilldiscover/2017/posters2017/5.

CGTN Africa. (2020, June 3). Angola poverty rate at 41%. https://africa.cgtn.com.

Committee to Protect Journalists. (2011). Attacks on the Press 2010: Angola. https://Cpj.org/2011/02/attacks-on-the-press-2010.angola/.

Dolan, K. A., & Marques, R. (2013, September 13). Dadd's girl: How an African princess banked $3 billion in a country living on $2 a D. *Forbes*. www.forbes.com.

Ferguson, J. (2006). *Global shadows: Africa in the neoliberal world order*. Duke University Press.

Garcia-Rodriguez, J. L., Garcia-Rodriguez, F. J., Castilla-Gutierez, C., & Major, S. A. (2015). Oil, power and poverty in Angola. *African Studies Review*, 58(1): 159–176. https://doi.org/10.1017/asr.2015.8.

Hodges, T. (2004). *Angola: Anatomy of an oil state* (2nd ed.). Indiana University Press.

Human Rights Watch. (2003). Violations of the right to freedom of expression: Arbitrary imprisonment, violence and threat against Journalists.

James, W. M. (2011). *A political history of Civil War in Angola*. Transaction Publishers.

Koning, T. (2012). Milestones in Angola's oil history. *GeoExPro*, pp. 20–26.

Roque, P. (2009). Angola's façade democracy. *Journal of Democracy*, 20(4): 137–150.

Sachs, J. (2007). How to handle the macroeconomics of oil wealth. In M. Humphreys, J. D. Sachs, & J. E. Stiglitz (eds.), *Escaping the resource curse* (pp. 173–193). Columbia University Press.

Sayagues, M. (2021, July 4). Environment-Angola: Losing trees to war. Inter Press Service News. http://www.ipsnews.net/1999/09/environment-angola-losing-trees-to-war/.

Soares de Oliveira, R. (2007). Business success, Angola-style: Postcolonial politics and the rise and rise of Sonangol. *Journal of Modern African Studies (45)*: 595–619.

Soares de Oliveira, R. (2011). Liberal peacebuilding in Angola. *The Journal of Modern African Studies*, 49(2): 287–314.

Sonangol, P. P. (2009). Corporate strategy. http://www.sonangolpp.com/pnp Estrategia_en.shtml.

Soros, G. (2007). Foreword. In M. Humphreys, J. D. Sachs, & J. E. Stiglitz (eds.), *Escaping the resource curse*. Columbia University Press.

Statista. (2021). Population of Angola in 2021 by age group. Statista. www.statista.com.

UN. (2020, April). Poverty and equity brief.

UNDP. (2020). Angola: Human development report. https://Hdr.undp.org/file/MPI/AGO.

Univeristy of Oxford. (2020). Oxford poverty and human development initiative. ophi.org.uk.

World Bank. (2015). Gross domestic product 2015. http://databank.worldbank.org/data/download/GDP.pdf.

World Bank. (2018). Angola overview: Development news, research data. World Bank. www.worldbank.org.

World Bank. (2019). Life expectancy at birth, total (years)—Angola. World Bank. www.data.worldbank.org

World Bank. (2021). Angola overview: Development news, research and data. https://www.worldbank.org/country/angola/overview

CHAPTER 8

Conflict in Democratic Republic of Congo: Framework for Resolution

Ogunnowo Ruth Oore-Ofe and Victor Ojakorotu

Brief Historical Background

Conflict in itself is an inevitable phenomenon in the globalized world where relationships exist between and among states. This chapter proposes a framework for the resolution of the lingering crisis in the Democratic Republic of Congo (DRC) where there have been the challenges of insecurity and instability since its independence. A brief historical background of the DRC conflict is provided, clarifying the root cause of the conflict. The conflict is thereafter analyzed as the actors are well indicated; the strategies devised by them. The study presents the international, national and regional actors in managing the conflict as well as the outcomes of these plans and activities. The frustration–aggression theory is used to analyze the conflict situation in the DRC. A proposal of the structure to douse tensions in the Eastern region of the

O. R. Oore-Ofe (✉) · V. Ojakorotu
Department of Political Studies and International Relations, North-West University, Mafikeng, South Africa
e-mail: kajewoleruth@yahoo.com

K. J. Ani (ed.), *Resource Conflict and Environmental Relations in Africa*,
https://doi.org/10.1007/978-981-19-7343-7_8

DRC is thereafter offered. This paper would, therefore, demonstrate how peaceful coexistence could be attained and sustained in DRC as well as other African states.

The DRC gained its independence from Belgium in 1960 (Human Rights First 2014), with Patrice Lumumba as the Prime Minister and Joseph Kasavubu, the President (Enough Project 2014). After the election, multiple forms of political alliances developed leading to tensed political climate. A variety of threat of wars and secessionist movements surged (Enough Project 2014), thereby leading to the murder of Lumumba in 1961 (Enough Project 2014). Consequently, Kasavubu took overpower notwithstanding the rising ethnic and political tensions in the country. The division after the death of Lumumba was widespread. Kasavubu was overthrown after a coup in 1965 (Enough Project 2014). The overthrow of Kasavubu worsened the ethno-political tension as his loyalists joined forces to undermine the new military regime. The state continued under the military regime of Joseph Mobutu for more than three decades (Enough Project 2014). The regime was characterized by; corruption, fraudulent election, despotism, and dictatorship (Arieff 2014). In fact, observers viewed Zaire—as it was called under the Mobutu government, as a 'kleptocracy' (a country whose government's major aim was to loot public funds) (Enough Project 2014). The situation was worsened by the total disregard of Mobutu to nation building. However, the combination of the use of excessive force to intimidate the citizenry and widespread imprisonment of opposition voices sustained his leadership.

Worthy of note is the fact that the DRC was and still is rich in water resources, agricultural potentials (Arieff 2014) and mineral resources which include; gold, diamond, cobalt, among others (BBC 2012). These resources if adequately harnessed would give the country a global economic edge. Unfortunately, the resources of the state were mismanaged, allowing for a dwindling economic growth and, the intrusion of neighboring states. The state gradually slid out of the control of Mobutu in 1997 (BBC 2012; Namangale 2015). It is a natural truth that there can be no sustainable resource management in a country that have been overtaken by dictatorship, insecurity of lives and properties as well as mass mis-governance. While those factors contributed in weakening nation building in DRC, they also fueled the conflict.

There would be a need to briefly recount the events that led to the Genocide in Rwanda, so as to understand its relationship to the outbreak of Conflict in DRC. The Conflict in Rwanda may be regarded as an ethnic conflict that existed between the Tutsis and Hutus. The Hutus are regarded as the minority. The colonial government had given the impression that the Tutsis were superior to the Hutus and this had fueled tensions among both ethnic groups, even after independence. Many of the Tutsis had as a result fled to such neighboring countries as; Burundi, Tanzania, Uganda, and DRC to seek refuge (BBC 2011).

Although the Hutus took overpower after Rwanda's independence in 1962, the state witnessed a dwindling economic situation. The Tutsi refugees in Uganda were interested in recovering their rights, returning to their country and taking over government. The several mechanisms employed to put an end to the tension were abortive. In April 1994, the President Juvenal Habyarimana's aircraft was shot down. The President of Burundi and other members of the Chief of staff were in the same aircraft. This was the last straw that broke the camel's back; the conflict was on the increase, thereby leading to the genocide in Rwanda (BBC 2011). This conflict as well spilled over to DRC and contributed to the lasting crisis in DRC.

The spilling over of the conflict is due to the place of concentric cycles in conflict development. The genocide in Rwanda allowed for the influx of people into DRC. In July 1994, about 2million Hutus fled into DRC (BBC 2011), many of who were involved in the Rwandan Genocide. These men associated with the Mobutu government and decided to launch attack on the Tutsis who had lived in DRC for a very long time (BBC 2012). War broke out in DR Congo in the early '90s, though declared over in 2003, there still seems to be a level of instability in the Eastern part of DR Congo that has its border close to Rwanda (UNECA 2015). The former United Nations Secretary General stated in 2013 that DRC happens to be among the three African countries with setback in stability and conflict resolution (Annan 2013, cited by UNECA 2015).

Observers having studied the DRC conflict submit that it has no specific cause, but its root is founded on the 'needs, interests and grievances' (Prendergast 2014) of the people who are not necessarily Congolese but also foreign migrants especially those from Rwanda. There are basic political, military, and economic dimensions to the causes of the DRC conflict. Politically, the different ethnic groups crave for political power in order to access the state's income and resources. Economically, government, rebel groups and external actors desire to control the vast natural resources evident in the state. They are caught up in deep-rooted resource wars, where militia take arms and engage in resource exploitation and trade. Militarily also, the government has been unable to control its security services hence resulting in a high level of human right violation and revolt (Prendergast 2014).

Thus, the nature of conflict in DRC is complicated. Observers refer to the Democratic Republic of Congo (DRC) conflict as "Africa's World War" (BBC 2016). In fact, about 5.4 million people have died in this conflict since 1998, and about 45,000 Congolese lose their lives monthly to diseases and starvation among other consequences of violence (Enough Project 2014). The state is yet gradually recovering from conflict. The devastation done by the massive deaths and loss of properties that follows remains unquantifiable.

Analysis of the Conflict

Actors

There are many forms of actors in the DRC conflict. Both state and non-state actors have hitherto featured in the DRC conflict. The actors could be further classified as internal and external actors. The internal actors include; the Congolese government and its military force that is saddled with the responsibility of protecting its territory, the ethnic militant factions, and the rebels. The external actors include the ruling Tutsis government in Rwanda, other local groups around neighboring states who gain from the furry of conflict in DRC, as well as the international community that comprises of international forces and militia arrangements of regional and international institutions mainly on peacekeeping (BBC 2012; ACLED 2013). Consequently, the DRC conflict is influenced by a large number of actors; the strategies and outcomes of some of the actors would be examined in this discourse.

In the DRC, the Mayi-Mayi faction is a militia group saddled with the responsibility of protecting the local communities of the DRC against external forces (ACLED 2013). The Armed Conflict Location and Event Dataset records in the country's report of 2013 that there were about thirty distinct Mayi-Mayi groups operating in the state at the time. This group initially—in the 1990s—acted as a substitution for the national military force. They opposed the Rwandan radicals and the Rally for Congolese Democracy (RCD) dissidents during the Second Congo War [1998–1999] (ACLED 2013; CHD 2009). The group was as well a major opposition force against the rebellious Alliance of Democratic

Forces for the Liberation of Congo-Zaire [AFDL] (ACLED 2013). Unfortunately, as years went by, the Mayi-Mayi groups degenerated from positive minded patriots to a militia network.

There is also the National Congress for the Defense of the People (CNDP), which is another rebel group based in the DRC and alleged to have been at a time led by Laurence Nkunda (Dagne 2011, 6). It aimed at protecting the Tutsi population in Eastern Congo and opposing the FDLR. Some of the members of this group later on were incorporated into the Congolese armed forces or joined other military groups, yet engaged in molesting Congolese Civilians (Dagne 2011).

There was more so the seeming peacekeeping activities of the militant rebel group, the March 23 Movement (M 23)—alleged to be predominantly Tutsis and located in North and South Kivu. The group takes its name from the 2012 March 23 peace agreement written between the government and the National Congress for the Defence of the People [CNDP] (ACLED 2013). The M23 could be regarded as a predecessor of the CNDP. It is recorded that between 2006 and 2008, CNDP fueled about 8 conflicts every month, while M23 rather than ensure peace after the peace talks, fueled more conflicts recorded at 17 per month (ACLED 2013). This was much more havoc than the former groups had caused. Not only did the M23 rebels wreak havocs targeted at the civilian population, but it also had several clashes with the Mayi-Mayi factions and the UN Peacekeeping troops (ACLED 2013).

The Lord's Resistance Army (LRA) had also been an active rebel group evident in the Orientale province of DRC since 1999. This group perpetrated many violent acts and recruited more people into its sect. It should be noted that the group also had its presence and violent activities in the Central Africa Republic which was also close to DRC. It targeted majorly the civilians in DRC (ACLED 2013).

The Democratic Forces for the Liberation of Rwanda (FDLR) was established in 2000. It acted as one of the rebel groups in the DRC conflict. This group, predominantly Hutus, comprises of some of the Rwandan armed forces that were once active in the Rwandan conflict. They had not only launched attacks on the Rwandans but had the opportunity to wreak havoc on the Congolese civilians (Dagne 2011, 6). Analysts and regional officials have estimated the population of the FDLR to number between 6,000 and 8,000 individuals, as more people were recruited on a regular basis to join the group. Observers argue that the FDLR receives support from: some of the Congolese government forces,

Rwandans in the United States, Europe, and other parts of Africa (Dagne 2011, 6).

The United Nations (UN) peacekeeping mission in DRC became active in 1999 (ACLED 2013). It initially operated as United Nations Missions in the Democratic Republic of Congo (MONUC). However, even after the cease-fire had been signed in 2003, the atrocities still seemed to linger in the state. The UN was alleged to have contributed less efforts than expected. The UN then adjusted its obligations to include protecting the individuals and assisting in the reconstruction of the state. Hence, it was re-positioned as the United Nations Organization Stabilization Mission in the Democratic Republic of Congo (MONUSCO) in July 2010 (ACLED 2013; Namangale 2015, 78). The latter was to demonstrate the novel stage reached in the state (ACLED 2013, 7). Namangale (2015) records that the UN Peacekeeping force was the largest DRC ever had as it covered virtually every area of the state particularly Eastern Congo which was the major concentration (Namangale 2015, 76).

As the conflict dawdled and became increasingly dreadful, the UN Peacekeeping forces required additional troops. The International Conference on the Great Lakes Regions (ICGLR) and the Southern African Development Community (SADC) saw the need to review approaches for lasting peace and security in the state, especially for the civilians. Troops were, therefore, contributed by "Malawi, Tanzania, and South Africa" (Namangale 2015) to the UN. There was a continent-wide determination to find a lasting solution to this conflict. The MONUSCO troop gradually increased to about '19,815 military personnel all over the DRC – 760 military observers and staff officers, 391 police personnel and 1050 formed police units' (Namangale 2015, 78).

The European Union in its aspiration to act and contribute to global peace and security also acted in the DRC conflict. The EU presumes that for a country to achieve development, a level of peace and stability should be attained. In essence, peace, stability, good governance, and development are to a large extent linked together (Martinelli 2006, cited by Arnould and Vlassenroot 2016, 4). If the DRC which has an abundance of resources that could contribute to global development was experiencing a disturbing degree of instability, there may be a need to intervene in its case, hence the motivation to act in the DRC crisis.

The United States was not left out as one of the actors that played mediation roles in the DRC conflict to ensure peace and stability is realized. After the Secretary of States—Hillary Clinton in 2009 visited the

Eastern region of DRC; she observed that the state faced series of challenges that include the lack of development and investment, corruption in governance, sexual and gender-based violence that was targeted predominantly at the women and children. The United States was, therefore, interested in assisting the state to be free from this menace (Dagne 2011, 13).

Strategies

In November 1999, the United Nations Security Council passed Resolution 1279 to approve the operations of MONUC in the DRC conflict resolution under the Chapter VII of the UN Charter (Dagne 2011, 10). This authorization permitted the use of force if need be. Furthermore, in order to strengthen the MONUC force, Resolution 1291 was passed by the Security Council certifying MONUC to perform certain tasks, such as executing a cease-fire agreement, authenticating the disengagement and redeployment of forces, supporting humanitarian work as well as observing human rights activities (Dagne 2011, 10). More so, the MONUC by virtue of the Resolution was saddled with the responsibility of protecting personnel, activities and civilians under the threat of physical violence.

Another Resolution 1565 was approved in 2004. This increased the MONUC recruits. Similar to the previous Resolution, it aimed at protecting civilians and seizing of arms (Dagne 2011, 10). To this effect, National Unity of Government institutions as well as government staff were given temporary protection against violence. As the Kabila government in 2011 pressed for the removal of the MONUC forces from the state, the UN made efforts to begin dialogues with the ordinary Congolese. UN Delegates led by the Ambassador of France—Gerard Araud were sent to discuss with the senior Congolese officials. The objective of the mission according to the Ambassador was to have a dialogue with the authorities, population and civil societies in the DRC as regards the future of the presence of the United Nations in the state (Dagne 2011, 10).

As incessant acts of violence and atrocities prevailed especially in the Ituri and Kivu regions of the DRC, even with the increase in the number of the MONUC troops, the DRC government persisted in its request for the gradual withdrawal of some of the UN peacekeeping force. However, it should be noted that while peacekeeping force members as often accused of harassing ladies, their threat to societal security cannot be compared to that of the militia and armed groups in the country at war. The United Nations Security Council passed a Resolution 1925 on 28 May 2010. This Resolution changed the name of the initial peacekeeping force from MONUC to MONUSCO and in June 2010, commanded the removal of about 2,000 troops of the force (Dagne 2011, 9 & 11). In all, Faubert Carrol (2006, 12) summarizes the strategies of the UN in the DRC as Security and it comprises of such components as; 'Disarmament, Demobilization and Reintegration [DDR].'

The EU adopted the strategies of "humanitarian assistance; development aid; democracy and human rights support as well as a Common Foreign and Security Policy that includes (Common Security and Defence Policy [CSDP])" (Arnould & Vlassenroot 2016, 9). The humanitarian assistance expended on DRC extends even to the remote areas where the road networks are not easily accessible. Support has been given to the Internally Displaced Persons (IDPs), as well as the refugees from within the states and neighboring states (Arnould & Vlassenroot 2016).

The EU contributed to the refurbishment of the state, especially the health, transportation, security, and finance sectors as well as other institutions of the state (Arnould & Vlassenroot 2016). During the transition period, security personnel, and election observers were mobilized for the electoral process in 2006. Similar contributions were made by the EU during the 2011 elections in DRC. To strengthen democracy and promote its elements in the DRC, the EU has funded such projects as; 'independent local media, civic education, citizen participation in local governance, and the fight against impunity' (EIDHR 2011, cited by Arnould & Vlassenroot 2016, 9).

In addition, the EU in fulfilling its obligation of contributing to global peace and stability undertook five CSDP missions in DRC; two of which were military missions and others civilian. Although European-led, both military missions were authorized by the UN (Arnould & Vlassenroot 2016). The Artemis mission was to join in salvaging an urgent crisis situation at the time—the Ituri Conflict (Homan 2006). The EURFO DRC was also deployed as the second military mission to assist the MONUC in securing the election process in 2006 (Arnould & Vlassenroot 2016). The Civilian missions, on the other hand, had a longer-term restructuring drive. The missions include EUPOL Kinshasa, EUPOL DR Congo, and EUSEC DR Congo. It had the collective aim of supporting the Congolese police force in the security and police reform processes (Arnould & Vlassenroot 2016, 10).

In order to promote law and order and uphold democracy, the EU funded the process of reformation of the state's judicial system. Asides other expenses incurred on the judicial restructuring of the DRC, about 20 million Euros was invested in the court rehabilitation projects in the western regions including Bandundu, Bas-Congo, and Kinshasa. Funding was also provided to encourage the mobile court arrangement that was intended to reach the citizens in the remote areas, and the areas affected by the conflict in Eastern Congo (Arnould & Vlassenroot 2016, 12). Scholars and observers submit that the strategies adopted by the EU have its basis in the elements of Human Security approach (Arnould & Vlassenroot 2016, 10). This is evident in the; merged employment of the military and civilian personnel to ensure security, efforts to protect the lives of the people alongside their belongings, and the strategies to prevent war in the DRC (Arnould & Vlassenroot 2016, 10).

The United States in addition through the United States Agency for International Development (USAID) Program intervened in the crisis situation. It supported the transition to democracy initiative, the health, and educational sectors. Funds were designated for the prevention and treatment of AIDS. The Economic Support Funds (ESF) were designed for the government of DRC to ensure reconciliation, conflict mitigation, and resolution. There was also the International Military Education and Training (IMET) fund directed at "training the Congolese officers on military justice, human rights and joint operations" (Dagne 2011, 13). Furthermore, in 2010, the Wall Street Reform and Consumer Protection Act were signed into the United States' law. This was with the aim of modifying the Congo Conflict Minerals. American Companies were obliged to reveal measures taken to ensure that minerals imported from Congo are not "Conflict minerals" (Dagne 2011, 13&14).

Outcome

At the earlier stage of the war in 1999, at a Summit in Lusaka, Zambia, a peace agreement was signed by leaders of Uganda, Rwanda, Congo, Zimbabwe, Namibia, and Angola (Dagne 2005, 5). The agreement further established a Joint Military Commission (JMC) saddled with the responsibility of investigating cease-fire violation and the disarmament of militia groups. The Lusaka Accord—as often referred to—constitutes the following actions; the removal of foreign forces from Congo, the deployment of UN military observers, a political dialogue among Congolese forces and armed rebel groups for a peaceful settlement of dispute and to work out a new political episode for the state (Dagne 2005, 5). This agreement was to take effect in the space of 24 hours after it had been concluded by all parties. Unfortunately, every party to the conflict constantly violated the pact (Dagne 2005, 5). Rather than witness peace in DRC, the conflict continued dreadfully.

Following many years of the conflict, Laurent Kabila was assassinated in 2001 and his son Joseph Kabila succeeded him. Thereafter, in 2002, DRC and Rwanda signed an agreement widely referred to as the Pretoria Agreement. The elements of the agreement include 'cessation of hostilities, an inter-Congolese dialogue, withdrawal of foreign forces, and the disarmament of the negative forces' (Dagne 2005, 2)—referring to the rebel groups responsible for the 1994 Rwandan Genocide and has contributed to the conflict in DRC. Impressively, all the requirements were met except for the elimination of the negative forces that one could submit are the reasons behind the consistent conflicts in DRC persistent most especially in the Eastern part (Dagne 2005, 2).

In June 2003, President Kabila named a Transitional government in DRC to make efforts to lead the country out of Civil War that has claimed the lives of millions since its outburst, and to take the state to democratic elections (Agence France-Presse 2003). The transition government comprised of 36 ministers and 25 deputy ministers. Some of those who held the positions are the rebel movements [Congolese Rally for Democracy (RCD) and Congolese Liberation Movement (MLC)], the government officials, and members of the political opposition (Agence France-Presse 2003).

Again in 2004, Rwanda and DRC signed an agreement—Joint Verification Mechanism (JVM) to address cross-border concerns, especially to deal with threats of the Interahamwe and the negative forces of the 1994 Rwanda Genocide (Dagne 2005, 2). The device included the Joint Verification Team of experts from each of the parties, representatives of MONUC and the African Union (AU). In addition to the operative formulas being designed by the Joint Verification Team, the United States enabled a 'tripartite talk' between Rwanda, DRC, and Uganda. Having held several meetings in Washington, the parties agreed the negative forces actually posed the most dangerous threats to the peace of DRC. A Tripartite Joint Commission was thereafter inaugurated with the focus to; 'disarm, demobilize and repatriate foreign armed groups' within a year (Dagne 2005, 2 & 3). In sum, other commitments and agreements made between the DRC and its neighbors include "the Principles on good neighborly relations and cooperation between the DRC and Burundi, Rwanda and Uganda of 25th September, 2003; the pact on security, stability and development of the Great Lakes Region of 15th December 2006; the commitments made by the Tripartite-plus members in Lubumbashi on 8th June, 2007 and Kampala on 17th September, 2007" (Nairobi Agreement 2007).

There was also the Nairobi agreement on 9 November 2007 between DRC and Rwanda in order to end the threat posed to peace and stability in both states and the Great Lake Regions. The first multi-party election in about four decades was held in 2006—national and provincial elections in July, and the presidential run-off in October. Joseph Kabila was said to have won the presidential elections with 58% of the votes over Jean-Pierre Bemba who had 42% of the votes (DFID 2009). More so, Kabila's supporting political party—Alliance de la Majorite Presidentielle (AMP)—won the National Assembly elections over 'Bemba's Union Pour la Nation (UN) alliance.' Election observers considered the election to be somewhat fair and well-coordinated by the Independent Electoral Commission (CEI). The international community not only provided security mechanisms but also provided support for 'the justice system for election disputes'—the International Criminal Court [ICC] (DFID 2009).

A second 'national democratic elections' took place in 2011, this time coordinated by a new independent national electoral commission (CENI). In terms of logistics, observers submit that the voters' registration process was faulty. Violence had begun even before the election started, the election calendar did not provide adequate time for proper preparations, and the stage of registration of voters was not transparent enough as many international observers did not witness it (Eastern Congo Initiative 2012). However, once again, the Supreme Court ruled that Joseph Kabila was the winner of the election.

Violence and threats of war did not cease in DRC, it heightened most especially at the Eastern regions. The Democratic Forces for the Liberation of Rwanda (FDLR) was alleged to be the major perpetrators of these violent activities. Human Rights Watch records that most victims were women, children, and the elderly whom the rebels hacked to death with machetes or hoes or burned to death in their homes. The deliberate killings of civilians between 2012 and 2015 has been estimated to

94. These attacks were accompanied by widespread rape and other sexual violence. Abuses were made by Rwandan and Congolese soldiers during the military campaign (Human Rights Watch 2015).

The ICC on July 13, 2012, issued an arrest warrant for Sylvestre Mudacumura, the military commander of the FDLR, 'on nine counts of war crimes in eastern Congo's North and South Kivu provinces. The alleged crimes include attacks on civilians, murder, mutilation, cruel treatment, rape, torture, destruction of property, pillage, and outrages against personal dignity' (Human Rights Watch 2015).

It is important to understand that the FDLR is predominantly a Rwandan Hutu rebel group grounded in eastern Congo, some of whose leaders participated in the 1994 genocide in neighboring Rwanda. 'UN experts estimate the group to have around 1,400 active fighters in 2015, compared to the 6,000 in 2008' (Human Rights Watch 2015). Hence, the lingering rebellious and violent activities in the Eastern part of Congo. The atrocities tend to be once more on the increase as the FDLR perpetrated more crimes, such as 'Summary executions, abductions, sexual violence, and forced recruitment of children into the group' (Human Rights Watch 2015). In spite of the various Conflict Resolution strategies implemented in the DRC, the crisis lingered.

Theoretical Framework

To analyze the conflict in the DRC, the study considers the need theory; frustration–aggression theory. This theory was enhanced by John Dollard and his colleagues from Yale University. It was, however, modified by scholars such as Karl Menninger and J.P Seward. The theory assumes that frustration births instigations to various types of responses, one of which could be aggression. This means that there are other causes of aggression asides frustration. Frustration according to these proponents is defined as "an interference with the occurrence of an instigated-goal response at its proper time in behavior sequence." When interference or barrier is interrupted continuously, an extra amount of energy is mobilized which tends to overflow into generalized negative behavior (Dollard et al. 1980; 5).

The theory posits that the individual experiences an urge to attack whatever obstruction in the way of his goal. The direct barrier target may, however, be physically, psychologically, or socially resistant to attack from the frustrated individual or such attack may attract punishment. This leads to a displacement of aggression in which the individual directs aggression toward someone or something not responsible for the frustration. A scapegoat is used as target intended to wish injury to the interfering agent.

While attempting to transfer the frustration–aggression syndrome from the individual to the societal level, psychologists explain that the process of acquiring social habits consistently gives rise to frustrations; in as much as every strained change of impulsive behavior interferes with goal response. It could, therefore, be said that frustration–aggression patterns are, therefore, cultural bound; both the factors that make for frustration in human beings and the directions in which aggressive impulses are turned and the targets of the aggression will to a large extent be dependent on the values of the particular cultural system.

Consequently, every cultural system or society produces in its members' frustrations that might in the long run lead to fear, hatred, and violent aggression. Such a society must, therefore, develop its own solution to the problem it creates in those frustrations by means of managing the aggressive impulse of its members (Bandura 1978).

Proposal of a Framework for Resolving the Conflict

The framework proposed here revolves around the concepts of peacebuilding and peacemaking. Peacebuilding seeks to enthusiastically resolve the root of the conflict, if necessary, to forcefully create the conditions for a sustained peace (Richmond 2004, 84, cited by Kenkel 2013, 134). Peacemaking is an action to get antagonistic parties to agreement (UN 1992 cited by Kenkel 2013, 128).[1]

Peace education may be important in addressing the root of the conflict and allow for peacebuilding in DRC. It should be noted that the notion that the Tutsis are superior to the Hutus had existed in Rwanda and by extension in the DRC even before the independence of these states. Evolving generations grow with the idea that the Hutus are to be relegated in the affairs of the state, hence, the incessant conflict.

Youths and children should, therefore, be dissuaded from such indoctrination and taught that the ethics of; equality, 'mutual understanding, peace and tolerance' (World Education Forum 2000, cited by Ramsbotham et al. 2011, 239) are important values the young and old should imbibe. School curricula could include principles of; 'humanism, tolerance, diversity, democracy and critical thinking' (Ramsbotham et al. 2011, 240)[2] to promote peace in the state. The children soldiers should also be persuaded to drop their arms and embrace education at appropriate levels.

There is a need to train the security personnel—the police and the armed forces on the best ways to handle conflict situations rather than the shootings, killings, rapes, and the training of children soldiers which the forces are alleged to have indulged in. More so, foreigners should be repatriated and the borders made less porous to avoid illegal immigrants and rebels. These are some of the elements of the Fourth generation peace support operations as described by Boutros-Ghali in his *Agenda for Peace*.[3] He outlines some of the comprehensive techniques to uphold peace that could be adopted in conflict situations as the DRC's. These techniques in sum include "disarming the previous warring parties and the restoration of order, the custody and possible destruction of weapons, repatriating refugees, advisory and training support for security personnel, monitoring elections, advancing efforts to protect human rights, reforming or strengthening governmental institutions, and promoting formal and informal processes of political participation" (UN 1992, 55, cited by Kenkel 2013, 132). However, to ensure an effective Conflict Resolution process, interveners should carefully ensure that the approaches are sincere and that it is in the interests of those on whose behalf the intervention is being discharged (Ramsbotham et al. 2011, 170).

Conclusion

Africa in general has witnessed series of conflict but that of DRC seems to be the most violent and somewhat challenging especially to actors who have hitherto applied various techniques of Conflict Resolution. There is no doubt that conflict is inevitable in the international system, however, it is essential that a state attains a level of stability and co-operation for growth and development to be evident. DRC that is plenteous in natural resources and sound minds should not be left to the destructive pangs of violence which is eating deep into its resources and existence. Hopefully, the aforementioned roadmap if considered and applied could restore the peace of the state.

This idea of peace education may not be concentrated on the young ones only, but taught the older population through the media and the social media. More so, it should be practiced on a regular basis. That is, institutions (schools, government parastatals and private organizations) should ensure there are no discriminations in the treatments of any citizens of the state. For democracy to flourish, it is essential that political participation is encouraged. Governance should not be in the control of a few nationals especially not in the hands of the Kabila family members or relations only. The principles of democracy should be upheld as the state has transitioned into such system of government. Every citizen, groups and civil societies should be allowed to participate in the political affairs of the state. This promotes transparency especially in the economic sector that happens to be one of the major sources of the conflict. By so doing, no individual or party appears to be excluded from governance.

More so, to ensure a violent-free election process, as well as a fair or credible election in subsequent times, the states' electoral commission should consider itself responsible to the public. Adequate time for preparation should be provided; every eligible citizen should be captured and registered for elections, and the activities to be carried out during elections properly communicated to the public through every available medium. In addition, the electoral body should be trained to understand the best techniques for conducting elections in a state recovering from chaos.

Notes

1. See Boutros-Ghali's *Agenda for Peace*, UN 1992.
2. See Ramsbotham et al. (2011, 240).
3. See United Nations (1992).

References

Agence France-Presse. (2003). *Transitional government named in DR Congo*. Available at http://reliefweb.int/report/democratic-republic-congo/transitional-government-named-dr-congo [Accessed 12 May. 2016].

Arieff, A. (2014). Democratic Republic of Congo: Background and U.S policy. *Congressional Research Service*. Available at https://www.fas.org/sgp/crs/row/R43166.pdf [Accessed 14 Mar. 2016].

Armed Conflict Location and Event Dataset. (2013). *Country Report: DR Congo*. Available at http://www.acleddata.com/wp-content/uploads/2013/12/ACLED-Country-Report_DR-Congo_December-2013.pdf [Accessed 16 Apr. 2016].

Arnould, V., and Vlassenroot, K. (2016). *EU policies in the Democratic Republic of Congo: try and fail?* London: Security in Transition.

Bandura, A. (1978). Social learning theory of aggression. *Journal of Communication*. Wiley Online Library.

British Broadcasting Corporation. (2011). *Rwanda: How the Genocide happened*. Available at http://www.bbc.com/news/world-africa-13431486 [Accessed 3 Mar. 2016].

British Broadcasting Corporation. (2012). *Q&A: DR Congo conflict*. Available at http://www.bbc.com/news/world-africa-11108589 [Accessed 4 Mar. 2016].

British Broadcasting Corporation. (2016). *DR Congo country profile*. Available at http://www.bbc.com/news/world-africa-13283212 [Accessed 4 Mar. 2016].

Center for Humanitarian Dialogue. (2009). *The challenge of building sustainable peace in DRC*. Available at http://www.hdcentre.org/uploads/tx_news/69DRCpaper.pdf [Accessed 16 Apr. 2016].

Dagne, T. (2005). Democratic Republic of Congo: Transitional process and U.N mission. *Congressional Research Service*. Available at https://www.fas.org/sgp/crs/row/RS22089.pdf [Accessed 12 May. 2016].

Dagne, T. (2011). The Democratic Republic of Congo: Background and current developments. *Congressional Research Service*. Available at https://www.fas.org/sgp/crs/row/R40108.pdf [Accessed 3 Mar. 2016].

Department for International Development. (2009). *Elections in the Democratic Republic of Congo 2006*. Available at https://www.gov.uk/government/uploads/system/uploads/attachment_data/file/67652/elections-cd-2006.pdf [Accessed 12 May. 2016].

Dollard, J., et. al. (1980). *Frustration and aggression*. Westport: Greenwood Press.

Eastern Congo Initiative. (2012). *Democratic Republic of Congo 2011 presidential elections*. Washington: Eastern Congo Initiative's Final Report.

Enough Project. (2014). *The Democratic Republic of the Congo: Roots of the crisis*. Available at http://www.enoughproject.org/conflict_areas/eastern_congo/roots-crisis [Accessed 4 Mar. 2016].

Faubert, C. (2006). *Evaluation of the UNDP assistance to conflict-affected countries: Case study of Democratic Republic of Congo*. New York: United Nations Development Programme Evaluation Office.

Homan, K. (2006). Operation Artemis in the Democratic Republic of Congo. In European Commission, *Faster and more united? The debate about Europe's crisis response capacity*. Clingendael: Netherlands Institute for International Relations. pp. 151–155.

Human Rights Watch. (2015). *DR Congo: Arrest rebel leader wanted by ICC*. Available at https://www.hsrw.org/news/2015/07/13/dr-congo-arrest-rebel-leader-wanted-icc [Accessed 9 May. 2016].

Human Rights First. (2014). *The Democratic Republic of the Congo: Ravaged by conflict, human rights atrocities and impunities.* Available at https://www.humanrightsfirst.org/wp-content/uploads/pdf/DCR_Bckgrnd(3).pdf [Accessed 3 Mar. 2016].

Kenkel, K.M. (2013). Five generations of peace operations: From the "thin blue line" to "painting a country blue". *RevistaBrasileira De PoliticaInternacional.* Vol. 56. Vol. 1. pp. 122–143.

Nairobi Agreement. (2007). Joint Communique of the Government of the Democratic Republic of Congo and the Government of the Republic of Rwanda on a common approach to end the threat posed to peace and stability in both countries and the Great Lakes Region. *Nairobi: African Union.*

Namangale, C. (2015). Dynamics of conflict management in the Democratic Republic of Congo. *PRISM* Vol. 5, No. 2. Available at http://cco.ndu.edu/Portals/96/Documents/prism/prism_5-2/PRISM5-2_Dynamics_of_Conflict_Mgmt.pdf [Accessed 16 Apr. 2016].

Prendergast, J. (2014). *What is the main cause of the conflict in Democratic Republic of Congo?* Available at http://www.huffingtonpost.com/quora/what-is-the-main-cause-of_b_5133945.html [Accessed 4 Mar. 2016].

Ramsbotham, et al. (2011). Contemporary conflict resolution (3rd edn). *Cambridge: Polity Press.*

UNCEA. (2015). Conflicts in the Democratic Republic of Congo, Causes, impacts and implications for the Great Lakes region. *United Nations Economic Commission for Africa, Addis Ababa.* https://repository.uneca.org/handle/10855/22687.

CHAPTER 9

Mining, Crush Rock Nigeria Ltd and Environmental Problems in Ishiagu

Victoria Nnenwogo Okafor, Nnenna I. Enwo-Irem, and Emmanuel Obiahu Agha

INTRODUCTION

Mining is as old as man, and its operation have continued to evolve with the advance in science and technology. A known mine on archeological record is the "Lion Cave" in Swaziland, which radiocarbon dating shows to be about 43,000 years old.[1] Mining the earth is the process by which the earth is drilled by machinery to extract economic materials such as gold, coal, diamonds, sand, limestone, lead and rock to name but few.[2]

V. N. Okafor · N. I. Enwo-Irem · E. O. Agha (✉)
Alex Ekwueme Federal University Ndufu-Alike, Ndufu-Alike, Nigeria
e-mail: emmanueloagha2002@gmail.com; aghatophel@yahoo.com

V. N. Okafor
e-mail: 08100vic@gmail.com

N. I. Enwo-Irem
e-mail: nnennaeirem@gmail.com

K. J. Ani (ed.), *Resource Conflict and Environmental Relations in Africa*,
https://doi.org/10.1007/978-981-19-7343-7_9

Mining operation is across the globe and has contributed heavily to environmental issues. These mining activities can have serious negative effects on the environment. These effects occur from the exploration stage to the closure stage of a mine's operation. Nigeria is a country endowed with different minerals such as gold, oil, coal, tin ore, gold among others and exploration and exploitation of these minerals affects the environment ranging from pollution of the environment, contamination of body of water to health hazard which affects the host communities where mining operations are undertaken.

Ishiagu is a community in the present Ivo Local Government Area of Ebonyi State of Nigeria, it is located within latitude 6′ N and longitude 6′ E and with an altitude of 137 metres.[3, 4] Ishiagu is a community with the highest deposit of mineral resources in the state, with the huge deposit of limestone, zinc and lead in the community, Ishiagu was able to attract many mining companies such as Nigeria Railway Corporation at Amalokpa Ishiagu (1945–1970), C.C. Daniels and son's Niger (1962–1987), Okwuosa and Son's Niger (1962–1987), Crushed Rock Nigeria Limited 1976—present, just to mention but a few. Presently, eight (8) mining companies are operating in the community with Crushed Rock Industry as the oldest among them. Crushed Rock Industries Nigeria Limited came to Ishiagu in 1976 and commenced mining operations in 1 January 1978 after entering into a land lease agreement with the landlords of the area to enable the company operate freely.[5] The land was bounded in the West by the junction of two roads to Eke market, in the South by the road to Amaokwe hill and in East by Okue and Ngwogwo villages all in Ishiagu.[6]

Against this background, this study seeks to examine the environmental hazards posed by Crushed Rock Nigeria Limited to the host community (Okue Ishiagu) from 1976 to 2008. The area of study had over the years, served the socio- economic needs of Igboland, Colonial government, post-colonial and Nigeria government, non-governmental organizations and private individuals. This was partly made possible by the availability of the solid mineral in the area, which at various times during our period of study were exploited by mining companies to their advantage and to some degree the interest of Igboland and indeed Nigerian society at large. Yet this important mining exercise had never attracted the attention of scholars for study. This means that there exists lacuna in our knowledge of the economic development triggered by the mining operations and its environmental impact. The present study endeavours to seek to remedy the lacuna. Also, a historical investigation is necessary to find out what the operators did and how they organized themselves, so much attention has been devoted to mineral oil, but in the recent past the government is increasingly getting interested in solid minerals because of obvious economic advantage derivable from this source. It is in this regard that this present study becomes necessary. This research adopts historical research method using qualitative approach. Primary and secondary sources are adopted. The primary source materials utilized are oral interviews, intellectual reports and company registers among others. Secondary sources utilized include; books, journals, articles and internet materials.

Literature Review

Issues relating to quarrying in Nigeria have been examined in recent years by scholars. However, studies or publications which examine the consequences of quarrying in Ishiagu are few, necessitating the need to carry out this current study. In the past, Christopher Simmon,[7] in his book "Global Environmental History" stressed that the environment is principally affected in two ways through its resources, including cropping or extraction of the resources and in using the atmosphere as a sink for waste products. Simmon's book only examined two ways the environment is affected rather than being holistic or exhaustive.

Detwyler T.R.,[8] in his book "Man's Impact on Environment", submitted that quarrying, opencast mining, or scarification, generally destroys natural vegetation and reshapes land surface. The book, however, failed to examine all the underlying effects of mining on the environment. Also, Langer W.H.,[9] in his book "Environmental Impacts of Mining Natural Aggregate", confirmed that mining has drastic visual impacts on the environment, as it can lead to the blockage of active groundwater conduit or disappearance of groundwater bodies inhabited by small site endemic fish and snail species, among others. In all, Langer's book affirmed that mining has drastic impact on the environment, but it focused more on its effects on the water bodies.

Adekoya J.A.,[10] in his book "Environmental Effect of Solid Mineral Mining", drew attention to the fact that certain social environmental problems are linked to mining activities, especially as mineral deposits are exhaustible and non-renewable. One of such problems is the creation of "ghost town" or forced migration of people from mining areas to other habitable places as a result of stoppage of mining activities due largely to depletion of mineral resources. The work discussed forced migration as one of the effects of mining but it did not take into consideration the fact that the people of Okue has never migrated to other areas because of the impact of mining on them. The people's migration in the study area is based on personal decision, and even people from other areas migrated to okue because of the mining companies and activities.

The Wikipedia Encyclopedia[11] noted that the effects of mining on the environment become adverse or drastic in the absence of protective measures. Resultantly, mass scale contamination and destruction of the environment are unavoidable when protective measures are not exercised by mining companies or relevant government agencies. This position is essential to the present study as it states the effects of mining, but it focused more on the effects of mining on water. Similarly, a report presented by Reinford. O[12] on mining and its effect on land degradation to the Ministry of Mining and Energy in Jamaica explained that mining is a major human economic activity which often affects the earth's surface and beneath and thus leaves clear visual imprint on the landscape. However, he further explained that mining does not necessarily cause land degradation, especially when proper mining practices, post land use planning and effective land rehabilitation are put in place. Finally, he averred that wanton negligence of mining practices by mining industries often leads to the impacts of mining on the environment, including reduced soil fertility, loss of biodiversity, degradation of surface and groundwater quality, air pollution and creation of "poisoned lands", among other impacts. This work is essential to the present study as it states that the environmental effects of mining are not only limited to land degradation or water.

Bowel R.,[13] in his book "*Impact of Mining and Quarrying on the Water Environment*", explained that mining activities inevitably affect local water environment and cause potential damages to it if appropriate mitigation measures are not observed. As a result, he stressed that appropriate environmental legislative and regulatory policies can mitigate or stem the tide of adverse environmental impacts by mining activities and companies in any country. This work specifically examined the impact of mining on local water, but its mitigation measures would be discussed here.

According to Okonkwo Ivo[14] mining operations have severe impact on the environment of the host community as it has resulted in building cracks and collapse of certain buildings. This interview identified other environmental effects of mining aside its effect on water and land. The U.S. Environmental Protection Agency (EPA)[15] has stated that emissions from mining can contaminate both air and water. They listed as many as hundred different air pollutants issuing from the nation's mining industry including dust particles and sulfurdioxide, which can create acid precipitation. This work stated that mining does not only affect water but also air, which in turn hampers the health of host communities. Although a relationship between environmental damage and mining has been documented in the past years, there are only a few reports that include major discussions of the environmental consequences of mining. This necessitates the present study.

Geographical Location of Ishiagu

Ishiagu is a community in Ivo Local Government Area of Ebonyi state of Nigeria, located within latitude 6′ N and Longitude 6_E and with an altitude of 137 metres.[16] Ishiaguland lying on a slightly vast undulating plain in South-eastern savannah region of the Igbo speaking part of Nigeria is situated between the Western fringes of Cross River at the Afikpo point and the Eastern foot of the Agwu Okigwe range of hills. The land is bounded on the East by Akaeze and Ugwueke, on the West by Umuchieze, on the North by Ndeabor and on the South by Uturu and Acha. Consequently, the Ishiagu people regard the sun as rising from the Akaeze/Ugwueke area and setting behind the Okigwe Agwu range of hills.[17]

The Okigwe-Akaeze-Afikpo road passes through the eastern portion of the town, cutting off to the East some village communities, and the farmlands of Amagu, Ogwor and Okue communities, while the other major areas of the town lie on the Western side of the road. The Okigwe-Enugu express way is about a few kilometres to the West of the Agwu and Lokpa borders, the Eastern Railway line starting from Port-Harcourt, passed from the otamkpa through Afikpo Road Railway station and the Ishiagu Railway station (Kwari), to the Northern town of Ndiabor from where it continues to Enugu and then to the Northern parts of the country.

Some rivers, streams and brooks flow from the South-west regions towards the North-east. The Ivo River, the largest river of the area rises from the region of Uturu and Umuchieze and meanders its way through the farmlands of Amaonye, Ihie, Amagu and Ogwor from where it continues to journey to Okue and after Amaokwe it turns east wards after Ike river. In the words of Ibina 1 of Okue,[18] "there is also the Ike river which passes from the region of Ndiabor through the farms of Amaeke/Amaokwe and Ngwongwo to join the Ivo river neat the Amaokwe farm. The river dries up during dry season. It is bounded, forested and surrounded with Achi trees providing useful hunting exercise during the dry season". He also said that "a number of small lakes (Ogwu) in ishiagu dialect could be found in some parts of the community and fishing in the lakes is not allowed, these lakes were often the people's source of water supply". According to Agu[19] of Ishiagu,[20] "there is presence of granite stones, lead, zinc, marble and a number of other types of rocks and minerals in the area". He added that "lead and zinc deposits are found in abundance in the farmlands of Ihietutu and parts of Amata while marbles are found in Amaokwe, Ngwongwo and Okue communities in Ishiagu".

Brief History of Ishiagu

Ishiagu is made up of eleven villages originally founded by one (Agu, a hunter from Ishiagu Ukwu in the present day Anambra state), who first settled permanently with his family in a place at Ishiagu, now known as Ngwongwo village. Thus, Ngwongwo became the oldest village in Ishiagu.[21] At Ngwongwo, Agu begot four sons who later founded other villages. However, the first son Echelle succeeded Agu the father as the head of Ngwongwo village. The rest of the sons namely: Amaonye (the second son), Ogwor (the second son) and Amata (the fourth son), each founded a village of his own which he named after himself. Thus, Ishiagu have in order of seniority Ngwongwo, Amaonye, Ogwor and Amata villages. These sons of Agu later had their sons who in turn founded other villages that were named after them. Thus, Amata begot Amaeze, the founder of Amaeze village, Ogwor begot Amagu the founder of Amagu village, Ogwor also begot Okue (his second son) who founded the Okue village.[22]

Furthermore, these grandsons of Agu had their sons who later founded other villages. Thus, Amagu had a son called Amaeke, the founder of Amaeke village, he (Amagu) also had another son called Ihie the founder of Ihie village, Amaeke begot a son called Amaokwe the founder of Amaokwe village. The exact periods of the above settlements are not known, but it is likely that before the nineteenth century this had come to pass. However, about the second half of the nineteenth century few hamlets emerged resulting from secondary waves of migrations and settlements which were part of the responses to the various stresses and strains of population increase and incessant inter-clan wars. The emergent hamlets included Obilegu (Obinagu), Amaisisi and Ndiokoroukwu.[23] In the words of Paul Chukwu,[24] "it was mainly to protect and safeguard Ishiagu from the menace and constant harassment of the Edda and Aro invaders, that some warriors like Oche, Eze and Okoroukwu moved and founded military outposts in Obilegu (Obinagu), Amaisisi and Ndiokoroukwu respectively, from these places as vanguard groups". They mounted checks on the advances of their enemies.

Further still, other hamlets later sprang up, each being a product of the circumstances. For instance, the establishment of a Railway station in Afikpo Road (Ishiagu) in 1917 naturally attracted a good number of people to the area. Some of these people were railway workers and traders, they gradually settled in the area and with the growing population, it (Afikpo Road) become one of the known village in Ishiagu.[25] Similarly, about this time, the Mile Two Road Junction due to its strategic position attracted a large population of people mainly from Uturu, Isuochi and Arochukwu in the present day Abia state and Imo state. Some of these people were initially road workers (under public works department), while some others were craftsmen or artisans. Like their Afikpo Road counterparts, they settled and grew in population that today they are numbered as one of the villages in Ishiagu.[26]

Economic Activities in Ishiagu

The mainstay of Ishiagu economy like other parts of Igboland is agriculture. Ishiagu's location in the rain forest region made some positive impact to the growth of agriculture, as there was large expanse of land and this encouraged productive agriculture. This was chiefly in form of subsistence farming; each family had parcels of land scattered all over the village farmlands. In the month of February, the eldest member of one particular family in Ngwongwo would make a heap in the farm. Thus, declaring the beginning of farming season.[27] Among the several crops produced in Ishiagu yam assumes a unique position. Yam is part and parcel of Ishiagu society, this reflects in the degree of the people's commitment to the cultivation and preservation of Yam culture. After each planting season and harvesting season, the man with the highest number of yam barns takes the title Okoji which means Great Cultivator of Yam. Species of yam cultivated in Ishiagu includes white Guinea Yam, Yellow Yam and water Yam. In addition, Okro made so many families wealthy as the Calabar people came down to Ishiagu to buy them (Okro) in very large quantities. In the words of Ajah Ekeh,[28] "a typical Ishiagu man had farmlands where he cultivated the aforementioned crops and reared animals as well. "For this reason, agriculture for centuries remained not only the mainstay of Ishiagu economy but also the chief employer of labour not only in Ishiagu, but indeed the entire Igboland".[29]

Another important economic activity of the area of study is the non-agricultural production, generally referred to as local industries. This sector of the people's economy has remained viable and has made positive impact on the people of the area as well as that of their neighbours. Among the local industries that thrived in the communities were palm wine tapping, smithery and pottery. Kindred known as Amauzu (Smiths) in Amagu village were professional smiths, they produced cutlass and hoes which a farmer needed to clear the bushes and make mounds. They also produced guns and arrows for hunting.[30]

Furthermore, Ishiagu was reputable for the pottery industry, hence the name Ishiagu okpu ite (Ishiagu the pot maker). The prosecution of this industry was made possible by the availability of clay deposits in parts of Ishiagu. The clay was mined by women and used to produce various types of earthwares. These earthwares served the domestic and religious needs of the people.[31] The types of pottery ranged from large water pots, large wine jars, water coolers, saucers, trays, palm oil containers and kolanut trays among others. The growth of this industry had made some impact on the economy and culture of the area, it made Ishiagu very popular as people from various parts of Igboland came there to buy all sorts of earthwares, it also made women relatively rich.[32]

Another aspect of the people's traditional economy was trade, the people were involved in two kinds of trade namely local and long distance trade. In the local trade, the people assemble at the Eke market on Eke days to exchange or carry out buying and selling, Ishiagu communities such as Okue, Ogwor, Amaokwe, Amaeke to mention but a few as well as Ishiagu neighbouring communities like Mpu and Uduma came together to practice the local trade while in the long distance trade Ishiagu people travelled to far places like Calabar to sell their goods. It should be noted that agricultural products formed a major item of trade. However, there were in addition locally made crafts such as various types of baskets, earthwares, knives, arrows, hoes and host of other non-agricultural products traded.[33]

It is pertinent to note that colonial rule in Nigeria marked the beginning of granite, lead and zinc mining in the study area. About two major factors were responsible for the growth and development of granite mining in Ishiagu. One was colonial rule which started with development projects like construction of rail lines, motor roads and housing projects and these projects demanded the use of pebbles or stones of various sizes. Second was the availability of granite deposits in the study area, at the inception of colonial rule various engineers and contractors initiated and executed projects such as roads, culverts, bridges to name but few, for these projects, concrete structures were inevitable.[34] Granite mining in Ishiagu started in about the fourth decade of the twentieth century via external agencies, Crushed Rock Industry, one of the mining companies that operated in Ishiagu commenced their mining operations in 1976 specifically.[35]

Brief History of Crushed Rock Industry in Ishiagu

After the Nigerian-Biafra war in 1970, more efforts were made to establish industries in the areas of quarrying and mining. The Monier Construction Company (MCC) which was a West German construction company came to Ishiagu to acquire a site at Okue hill.[36] In the words of Okoro Uche,[37] the East Central government in 1974 awarded a contract to a construction firm namely Monier Construction Company (MCC) to rebuild the Ivo river bridge which was damaged during the Nigeria Civil war. It was in the course of executing this contract that the company (MCC), prospected for granite stone in Ishiagu and found a very mighty hill called Ugwu Ejirija in Okue Ishiagu.

According to Ajah Paul,[38] MCC entered into an agreement with Okue community to enable them commence mining in the area. He further said that (MCC) was a specialist in road construction and not mining, therefore, plunging into an unfamiliar area of mining was not in the best of its interest. So it opted to make a way for a company that specialized in mining so that it would be a special customer to the Crushed Rock Industry who would in turn give it (MCC) discounts for all its purchase of chippings from the company as compensation for its role.

So by 1976, Crushed Rock Industries made its appearance at Ugwu Ejirija mining site in Okue Ishiagu. Before the company commenced operation, it first of all met with the landlords of the area and entered into a land lease agreement with them to enable it (company) to freely operate. This land was leased to the company for a period of ten years commencing from 1 January 1976, at a rent of one hundred naira per annum, the tenant company would, apart from the annual rents pay 50,000 every year to the landlords for the celebration of New year festival.[39] The agreement was signed by Orieji Ajah, Uche Agwu, Chukwu Ubani, Akachukwu Ogbu among others, for and on behalf of the landlords, the manager of the Crushed Rock Industry signed for the company.[40] Among the mining companies in Ishiagu, Crushed Rock Industry was said to be the best operators with the most sophisticated equipment. The work force of the company was high, the output of its mining machines were too high and the demand and supply ratio of the company was also high.[41] At the beginning of the company's operation in the 1970s, it made use of driller machine of small size. It also made use of small size crusher machine. The company never made use of hand drilling machine as did by some other mining companies in Ishiagu.[42] This is because of the large expanse of the company's mining pit. By the close of 1980s, the company witnessed a high growth rate. Various factors were responsible for this. One was the high quality chippings products produced by the company. Also the company made use of mass media in advertising her products. This further attracted more customers to her. Aside, mass media the company sent her field agents who made contacts with various construction companies across the world with the aim of advertising the company's product increased appreciably.[43]

Increased demand for the company's product inevitably required that the company must adjust appropriately to accommodate this situation. In 1919, the company acquired very high equipment on granite mining. This equipment was a giant drilling machine and a giant crusher machine.[44] The production strength of the crushing machine was about 750 tons per day.[45] The giant driller was said to have the capacity of drilling up to a depth of 30 metres through a bedrock before explosion took place.[46] These high equipments made some negative impact in the host community, in the words of Okafor Chukwu[47] the heavy equipments caused noise pollution and building cracks in the host community.

According to the company's geologist, Iheanyi S. Njoku,[48] Crushed Rock products had been tested in the laboratory and found to be a very superior grade with a density of 2.6. The location of this industry at a place without any natural barrier to companies and individuals demanding for the products, also added its advantage to the growth of the company. With increased output and increased demand for the company's products, the total sales per day was between 1000 and 1500 tons of chippings.[49] This in turn allowed the haulages and driver's opportunities to make more profits.

Environmental Hazards Associated with Mining by Crushed Rock Industry in Okue Ishiagu 1976–2008

Environmental hazard is a state or event which has the potential to threaten the surrounding natural environment or adversely affect people's health, including pollution and natural disasters such as storms and earthquakes.[50] Mining which involves removal of rock from the ground could be undertaken in diverse methods such as hard rock mining, using rock drills, explosion of dynamite and other sophisticated methods.[51] At the construction of Crushed Rock Industry in Okue Ishiagu, various development projects were undertaken. The aim was to minimize the negative impacts and maximize the positive impact on the biological and physical resources. However, some negative implications were inevitable for a project of this magnitude inspire of the precautions undertaken.

One of the environmental hazards associated with the activities of the Crushed Rock Industry is the cracking effects of explosives on buildings as Crushed Rock Industry unlike other mining sites was situated within the homestead and the bedrock in the site was greater than what existed in other mining sites. A geologist under the service of Crushed Rock Industry had remarked that granite chippings produced by Crush Rock Industry granite was 5.1 in density.[52] This was because of the size of the bedrocks and as a result of this, the volume of the explosives applied to blow-up bedrocks had shattering effects on people's houses, these damaging effects also became part of the landlord/tenant agreement. According to this term of agreement, the company undertook to pay compensation to owners of buildings damaged by explosives used by the company.[53] However, this term of agreement was rarely honoured by the company, only when there are certified evidence been duly approved by relevant community leaders were applications for compensations honoured by the company, even where the company accepted to pay compensation, it had control over its criteria for payment. In other words, whatever it decided to pay was what is paid.[54] For buildings outside the landlord community, the company had rejected claims from such victims, even when it was clear that the damages on the buildings were as a result of the explosives applied by the company. The reason given by the company was that there was no agreement obliging it to undertake such compensations. This had been a source of discord between the company and victims of the explosives outside the landlord community.[55]

Furthermore, according to Ibina 1 of Okue[56] the mining activities of the Crushed Rock Industry had severe negative impact on Ivo River which was the only source of water supply for Okue and its neighbouring communities as the company disposed its waste inside the river, this in turn shoots life out of all the river animals and the water was not conducive for drinking, bathing nor cooking. He further stated that at some point Okue community had to journey to Uturu or Lokpa to get water to drink, bath and cook.

Also, the existence of Crushed Rock Industry had caused series of accident that has led many youths to their early grave and the survivals with permanent defects. In the words of Chukwu Igwe,[57] Ekeh Otuomasirichi's life was cut short because of Crushed Rock Industry, as the quality stone produced by the industry attracted so many contractors to the area, trailers were always parked at both sides of the road from the location of the industry to Amaeze Ishiagu, the drivers were reckless in driving as they all dragged the road in order to meet their daily turn-ups. He further stated "on that faithful day 25th August 2004, a beautiful and tall teenager of about 19 years by name Ekeh Otuomasirichi, the last born of her family and an SS1 student of Blessed Iwene Tansi Memorial Secondary School, in Okue Ishiagu, was sent on an errand with a kymco motorcycle, at about 12:30 pm, an eyewitness attested that she was crushed into pieces by a trailer owned by Chukwuma B.M.C". He also said that if Crushed Rock Industry was not situated in Okue Ishiagu, the poor girl would not have undergone such a painful death. It is pertinent to note that so many other accidents took place in the area and the company never compensated the family of the deceased.

Furthermore, the mining operations of the Crushed Rock Industry had a negative impact on the land, especially through erosion/leaching of top-soil nutrients. Mining, explained by A.S. Hornby, means digging hole in order to excavate minerals, such as coal, gold, stones and mineral oil. For each mining operations, large pits are made. The Crushed Rock Industry's pit measured about 100–150 m^2.[58] This pit was a total loss to agriculture as the top-soil which was loamy and humus and contained the need soil nutrient that supported agriculture was totally erased for actual mining to take place. E. U. Okoro pointed out in his work that poor management of the soil such deforestation, overgrazing and over cultivation damage the soil structure, thereby exposing the soil to other erosion agents.[59] This means that the cutting down of trees in the study area by Crushed Rock Industry has hampered the soil fertility of the area. Aside the erosion caused by the mining activities of the Crushed Rock Industry in Okue community, it has accelerated the level of leaching in the area. Leaching is the washing away of plant nutrients from the top-soil down the soil profile by heavy rainfall. The mining pit of the Crushed Rock Industry cut deep inside the earth and whenever there was rainfall. It was very easy for the flood to leach the soil nutrients at the top-soil of the surrounding earth surface into the pits. This loss of soil nutrients affected farm yields and thus the farmers demanded for compensation but the company paid deaf ears to them.

Another environmental impact of the Crushed Rock Industry on the host community is noise. Noise are various sounds usually unwanted. The noise from Crushed Rock Industry has induced hearing impairment. In the words of Okoro Ajah,[60] more than 100 persons from the host community have disabling hearing difficulties courtesy of Ugwu Ejirija, he further stated that when crucial meetings are conducted in the host community, the noise results in problem of concentration and fatigue, information shared in the meeting will be misinterpreted oftentimes, and people stress their vocal cord as they automatically raise their voice to overcome the masking effect of noise upon speech. The noise from Crushed Rock Industry also affect the mental health of the host community as it causes anxiety, emotional stress, nervous complaints, nausea, headache, change in mood, increase in social conflicts as well as general psychiatric disorders.

In addition, the Crushed Rock Industry has cost the host community a great deal of health hazards by contamination of the environment. In the words of Okoro Samuel,[61] the dust particles from Crushed Rock Industry penetrate into the respiratory system and induce respiratory diseases such as silicosis on the people. During excavations, volumes of dust are emitted in the air, similarly various caterpillar machines operating at the mining site, emits smokes, these smokes and dusts with their debris settle on nearby houses and individuals.

Okue Crushed Rock Industry Riot and Government Intervention

If a government fails at its duty to spearhead national development initiatives provide basic infrastructures and improving the functionality and diversity of rural sub-economies then the immediate result is that communities will transfer these expectations into mining entities.[62] There is no doubt that Crushed Rock Industry had related well with Okue community, given the fact that it had complied to a large extent, with the provisions of the agreement with the Landlord community and Ishiagu Community Development Union (ICDU). However, the relationship between Crushed Rock Industry, the host community and Ishiagu Community Development Union cannot be said to be problem free or problem proof. The major problems affecting this relationship emanated from lapses in the terms of the agreement. A perusal through the 1992 agreement between the host community and Crushed Rock Industry would reveal that the Ishiagu Community Development Union (ICDU) team was a mere agent of the company rather than true representatives of the community. By error of omission or commission, basic genuine interests of the community were not given due attention.[63] Among the teething problems not taken care of by the said agreement were:

(i) conditions for recruitment and termination of employment of Ishiagu indigenes in the service of the company,
(ii) compensation of people whose houses were cracked through the effects of explosives outside the host community and
(iii) paying of bursary and giving scholarship.

According to Ibina 1 of Okue,[64] on 5 January 2008, the people of Okue community, men, women as well as youths moved down to the location of Crushed Rock Industry, destroyed some of their mining machines in display of their anger and stopped the company from working. None of the workers were allowed in or out of the company premises. The community youths spent two weeks at the company to ensure that the company did not carry out mining operations (5–18 January 2008). According to Chukwu Ajah[65] the then governor of Ebonyi state Chief Martin Elechi deployed about 30 soldiers to Ishiagu on 19 January 2008. The soldiers tried their best to calm the people down but their efforts proved abortive. On 21 January 2008, the governor sent his deputy to Ishiagu and he was able to calm the situation. The company (Crushed Rock Industry) was given ultimatum to meet the people's demand in a month time.

In the words of Agu 3, Okoro Moses[66] "the community's demand was never met as the company bribed some leaders and influential personalities in Ishiagu, and these leaders come to the company's rescue each time the community tries attacking the company". He further stated that till date the demands of the host community has not been addressed, the company only empowered some youths with motorcycles. This is a ploy by the company to shut the youth up.

Ishiagu Women and Crushed Rock Industry

In as much as men played significant roles in Crushed Rock Industry as some worked as drivers, miners and many others as haulage contractors, the role of women in the company cannot be underscored. In the words of Ajah Nwaajah Udu,[67] "Ishiagu women cooked food, carried them in coolers inside wheelbarrows to the location of Crushed Rock Industry, where they sold them to the workers ranging from low to senior staffs". He further stated that one of the renowned women who made millions from this business was Ossi Nnenna popularly known as Nne Igwe by her customers. In the words of Lawrence Eze,[68] women worked in the company as clerks and nurses in the company clinic. He stated that the people employed as clerks were mostly young girls who knew how to read and write and as well knew the different sizes of stones and their prices. He revealed that there were also female haulage contractors who were seen as Nde Agbara nwanyi in Ishiagu. According to Fredrick Chukwu,[69] the work women were allowed to undertake in the company was limited to clerks, nurses, hawkers and other minor jobs. They were not allowed to work underground (in the pits) or handle the mining equipments because women were seen as fragile beings In Ishiagu. He further stated that some women who felt they were strong went into the company to carry big stones and then take it to their bashers were they break it in different sizes. The sizes of stones included $3^{1/2}$, 1 inch, 2 inch, 3 inch, lumps, stone base or 0.50, 3/8 and 1/2 inch.

Conclusion

Okue community in Ishiagu has witnessed some developments in granite mining business from 1970 till date, among the mining companies that operated there were: Onyeso Nwachukwu company, Rapheal Obasidey company, Crushed Stone Nigeria, Dumez Nigeria limited, MCC Nigeria Limited, Setraco limited and Crushed Rock Industry among others. Crushed Rock Industry no doubt made fantastic gains from their mining operations at the expense of the host community. This was because the community was peaceful and loving, only on few occasions did the people carry out demonstrations against the exploitative tendencies of the company. The government at all levels should intervene and force the mining company to initiate projects in favour of the host community as their (Crushed Rock Industry) mining operations has badly affected the lives of the people, the company should be made to provide the host community with electricity, good road, good water and scholarship scheme for a given number of community indigenes. Provision of these amenities will aid development of the community and work in favour of the individual communities in Ishiagu at large. This work has been able to trace and discuss the environmental hazards associated with mining by Crushed Rock Industry in Okue Ishiagu from 1976 to 2008. It looked at the history of the industry in Ishiagu and its mode of operation. It has also examined the crisis between Crushed Rock Industry and the host community as well as how government has tried to mediate between them.

Notes

1. Rock O. Mkpuma, O.C. Okereke, Ema M. Abraham, Environmental problems of surface and underground mining: a review. *The International Journal of Engineering and Science* (IJES), vol(4), 2015, 1–2.
2. Adeyinka O. Omotehishe, Bankole D. Ako, The environmental implications of the exploration and exploitation of solid minerals in Nigeria with a special focus on Tin in His and coal in Enugu. *Journal of Sustainable Mining*, vol(18), 2019, 18–24.
3. Joseph C. Chukwu, Mining operations in Ishiagu, Lekwesi, Lokpaukwu and Uturu communities in Nigeria 1900–2005. Unpublished PhD thesis, University of Nigeria Nsukka, 2006.

4. Joseph C. Chukwu, Mining operations in Ishiagu, Lekwesi, Lokpaukwu and Uturu communities of Nigeria, 1900–2005, Unpublished PhD Thesis, University of Nigeria.
5. Chimbo A. Uluma, Environmental consequences of quarrying in Ivo L.G. A of Ebonyi State Nigeria. Unpublished PGD project, University of Nigeria Nsukka, 2006.
6. Anyata Eugene, *Ishiagu in cultural perspective.* Owerri Alphabet Nigeria Publishers, 2001.6.
7. Christopher Simmon, *Global environment history.* London Edward Amolds Publishers, 1976.6.
8. T.R. Detwyler, *Man's impact on the environment.* McGraw-Hill, New York, 1977.5.
9. W.H. Langer, Potential environmental impacts of quarrying stone in Karst. *Open File Report*, vol(10), 2001, 1–7.
10. J.A. Adekoya, Environmental effects of solid mineral mining. *International Journal of Physical Science*, vol(2), 2003, 625–640.
11. Wikipedia Encyclopedia, Surface mining, Wikipedia Foundation Inc, 2006.
12. O. Reinford, Mining and its effect on land degradation, a paper presented at the ministry of water conference on desertification and land degradation. *Jamaica*, 2000, 1–8.
13. R. Bowel, *Impact of mining and quarrying on the water environment.* SRK UK LTD, 2004.7.
14. Okonkwo Ivo, Retired Civil servant, aged 72 years, interviewed at his residence in Amagu Ishiagu on 14th June 2020.
15. Bioethics education project pollution, mining and quarrying, http://www-beep.al-uk/content, 2008.
16. Anyata Eugene, *Ishiagu in cultural perspective.* Owerri Alphabet Nigeria Publishers, 2001.6.
17. Ibina 1 of Okue, Retired teacher, aged 90 years interviewed in his residence at Okue Ishiagu on 16th April 2020.
18. Agu 3, Okoro Moses, traditional leader, aged 65 years, interviewed in his palace at Amata Ishiagu on 17th April 2020.
19. Rock O. Mkpuma, O.C. Okeke, Ema M. Abraham, Environmental problems of surface and underground mining: a review. *The International Journal of Engineering And Science* (IJES), vol(4), 2015, 1–2.
20. George Okorie, Retired Civil servant and community leader, aged 70 years, interviewed in his residence at Okue Ishiagu on 19th April 2020.
21. George Okorie interview cited.
22. George Okorie interview cited.
23. George Okorie interview cited.
24. George Okorie interview cited.

25. Anyata Eugene, *Ishiagu in cultural perspective.* Owerri Alphabet Nigeria Publishers, 2001.63.
26. Beatrice Njoku, A trader, aged 50 years, interviewed in her residence at Ngwongwo Ishiagu on 20th April 2020.
27. Ajah Ekeh, A gateman at Ishiagu Central School, aged 70 years interviewed in his residence at Ihie Ishiagu on 22nd April 2020.
28. Ude Ajah, Retired civil servant, aged 50 years, interviewed in his residence at Amaonye Ishiagu on 23rd April 2020.
29. Maxwell Okoro, Retired civil servant, aged 70 years, interviewed in his residence at Amaonye Ishiagu on 24th April 2020.
30. Nwannediya Ajah, Retired potter, aged 75 years, interviewed in her residence at Amagu Ishiagu on 30th April 2020.
31. Nwannediya interview citied.
32. Nwannediya interview cited.
33. Maxwell Okoro interview cited.
34. Maxwell Okoro interview cited.
35. Fidelis Nwachukwu, Civil Engineer, aged 70 years, interviewed in his residence at Okue Ishiagu on 1st May 2020.
36. Anyata Eugene, *Ishiagu in cultural perspective Owerri alphabet.* Nigeria Publishers, 2001.252.
37. Uche Okoro, A teacher in Ishiagu High School, aged 52 years, interviewed in his residence at Amagu Ishiagu on 3rd May 2020.
38. Paul Ajah, Lecturer in Federal Collage of Agriculture Ishiagu, aged 45 years, interviewed in his residence at Amagu Ishiagu on 5th May 2020.
39. Tony Makwe, Former staff of Crushed Rock Industry and now a haulage contractor, aged 67 years interviewed in his residence at Okue Ishiagu on 7th May 2020.
40. Tony Makwe, interview cited.
41. Cosmas Orji, Driller operator, aged 75 years, interviewed in his residence at Okue Ishiagu on 9th May 2020.
42. Cosmas Orji interview cited.
43. Joseph C. Chukwu, Mining operations in Ishiagu, Lekwesi Lokpaukwu and Uturu communities in Nigeria 1900–2005. Unpublished PhD thesis, University of Nigeria Nsukka, 2006.
44. Joseph C. Chukwu thesis cited.
45. Joseph C. Chukwu thesis cited.
46. Joseph C. Chukwu thesis cited.
47. Okafor Chukwu, Retired teacher, aged 72 years, interviewed in his residence at Okue Ishiagu on 10th May 2020.
48. Iheanyi S. Njoku, Geologist with crushed Rock Industry, aged 50 years, interviewed in his office at Crushed Rock site Ishiagu on 12th May 2020.
49. Joseph C. Chukwu thesis cited.

50. Andrew MacPherson, Meta A. Synder, H. Lilian, Nursing, health and the environment strengthening the relationship to improve the public health. Institute of Medicine, ISBN 0585-02694-7, 1950.
51. Rock O. Mkpuma, O.C. Okereke, Ema M. Abraham, Environmental problems of surface and underground mining, a review. *The International Journal of Engineering and Science IJES*, vol(4), 2015, 3.
52. Chimbo A. Uluma, Environmental consequences of quarrying in Ishiagu in Ivo Local Government Area of Ebonyi State Nigeria. Unpublished PGD project, University of Nigeria Nsukka, 2006.
53. Joseph C. Chukwu's thesis cited.
54. Joseph C. Chukwu thesis cited.
55. Joseph C. Chukwu thesis cited.
56. Ibina 1 of Okue, Retired teacher, aged 90 years, interviewed in his residence at Okue Ishiagu on 15th May 2020.
57. Chukwu Igwe, Retired soldiers, aged 80 years, interviewed in his residence at Okue Ishiagu on 3rd June 2020.
58. Joseph C. Chukwu's thesis cited.
59. E.U Okoro, *Intensive agricultural science for Junior Secondary school.* Onitsha Elites Publishers, 2001.55–56.
60. Okoro Ajah, Retired teacher, aged 62 years, interviewed in his residence at Ogwor Ishiagu on 5th June 2020.
61. Ajah Samuel, Geologist, aged 40 years, interviewed in his residence at Ngwongwo Ishiagu on 17th June 2020.
62. Mining review in Africa, The relationship between the mining industry and communities' September 10, 2019.
63. Joseph C. Chukwu, Mining operations in Ishiagu, Lekwesi, Lokpaukwu and Uturu communities in Nigeria 1900–2005, unpublished PhD thesis, University of Nigeria Nsukka, 2006.
64. Ibina 1 of Okue, Retired teacher, aged 90 years, interviewed in his residence at Okue Ishiagu on 1st June 2020.
65. Chukwu Ajah, Retired teacher, aged 70 years, interviewed in his residence at Amagu Ishiagu on 5th June 2020.
66. Agu 3, Okoro Moses, Traditional leader, aged 65 years, interviewed in his palace at Amata Ishiagu on 7th June 2020.
67. Ajah Nwaajah Udu, A loader in Crushed Rock Industry, aged 30 years interviewed in his work place at Okue Ishiagu on 9th June 2020.
68. Lawrence Eze, Haulage contractor, aged 45 years, interviewed in his residence at Amaokwe Ishiagu on 15th June 2020.
69. Frederick Chukwu, Haulage contractor aged 40 years, interviewed in his residence at Ngwongwo Ishiagu on 18th June 2020.

Bibliography

Adekoya, J.A., Environmental effects of solid mineral mining. *International Journal of Physical Science*, vol(2), 2003, 625–640.

Bioethics education project pollution, mining and quarrying. http://www-beep.al-uk/content, 2008.

Bowel, R., Impact of mining and quarrying on the water environment SRK UK Ltd, 2004:7.

Chimbo, A.U., Environmental consequences of quarrying in Ishiagu in ivo L.G.A of Ebonyi State Nigeria, unpublished PGD project, University of Nigeria Nsukka.

Chukwu, A., Smart Chika Obiora Wholerock geochemistry of basic and intermediate rocks in Ishiagu, 2014.

Chukwu, J.C., Mining operations in Ishiagu, Lekwesi, Lokpaukwu and Uturu communities in Nigeria 1900–2005, unpublished PhD thesis, University of Nigeria Nsukka, 2006.

Detwyler, T.R., *Man's impact on the environment*. McGraw-Hill, New York, 1977:5.

Eugene, A., *Ishiagu in cultural perspective*. Owerri Alphabet Nigeria Publishers, 2001:6.

Langer, W.H., Potential environmental impacts of quarrying stone in Kasrt. *Open File Report*, vol(10), 2001, 7–11.

Mkpuma, R.O., Okereke, O.C, Abraham, E.M., Environmental problems of surface and underground mining a review. *The International Journal of Engineering and Science (IJES)* vol(4), 2015, 1–2.

Omotehidhe, A.O., Ako, B.D., The environmental implications of the exploration and exploitation of solid minerals in Nigeria with a special focus on Tin in Jos and Coal in Enugu. *Journal of Sustainable Mining*, vol(18), 2019, 18–24.

Reinford, O., Mining and its effect on land degradation, a papper presented at the ministry of water conference on desertification and land degradation. *Jamaica*, 2000, 1–8.

Simmon, C., *Global environment history*. London Edward Almonds Publishers, 1976:240.

Wikipedia Encyclopedia, Surface mining, www.Wikipedia foundation inc, 2006.

CHAPTER 10

The Anthropocene: An Alternative Lens in the Study of International Relations

Lawson Onyema Chukwu, Anthony Dibua, and Kelechi Johnmary Ani

Introduction

The discipline of international relations (IR) is chastised for having a purely human perception and as well-paying slim attention to other array of nonhuman inhabitants and things (Cudworth and Hobden, 2013). The goal of present scholars in the discipline is to discover alternative

L. O. Chukwu (✉)
Department of History and International Studies, University of Nigeria, Nsukka, Nigeria
e-mail: lawson.chukwu.pg001216@unn.edu.ng

A. Dibua
Department of International Relations, University of Westminster, London, UK

K. J. Ani
Department of History and Strategic Studies, Alex Ekwueme Federal University Ndufu-Alike Ikwo, Abakaliki, Nigeria
e-mail: Kelechi.ani@funai.edu.ng

K. J. Ani (ed.), *Resource Conflict and Environmental Relations in Africa*,
https://doi.org/10.1007/978-981-19-7343-7_10

means to include natural world into IR theory and analysis in a meaningful way. This is a difficult task, but it is not impossible (Corry and Hayley, 2017). The Anthropocene, an epoch in which human actions have influenced the Earth's geological processes, is currently hanging over humanity (Crutzen and Stoermer, 2000). For a long time, the term "Anthropocene" was unofficial term. However, it is now used in numerous academic disciplines and has been included into those that are not into the natural sciences. Numerous social scientific areas also take part in the debates about Anthropocene. They provide criticism as well as innovative explanations to international environmental issues. The discipline of international relations (IR) is not immune to this tendency. After all, it is 'the ideal home for thinking about how humankind (split as it is) cope with the difficulties of sharing a single, constrained environment' (Simangan, 2021). Environmental issues have remained marginalized in international relations studies, and Western ideas have dominated talks on Anthropocene, while voices from the Global South remain marginalized.

Moreover, the discipline is based on a geopolitical-examination of how geography and climate affect global politics. The value of geography in international relations research has long been recognized. History has been described as "geography in motion" on numerous occasions. "A country's foreign policy is defined by its topography," Napoleon reportedly observed (Palmer and Perkins, 2010). Civilizations and country development have been greatly influenced by geographical considerations. With modern modes of transportation and communication, the world has shrunk, increasing interdependence and bringing people closer together in a variety of ways. A fundamental understanding of political, economic, and human geography, as well as physical geography, is required to comprehend today's world (Palmer and Perkins, 2010). This demonstrates that international relations are not immune to environmental concerns, but also that it has a long history of neglecting them. While "contemporary literature often depicts nature as a novel role in politics," Daniel Deudney claimed that "the impression that environment is a resilient power influencing human political systems is exceedingly old" (1999, 25–26).

This work adopts a qualitative research method. It draws its sources largely from available sources such as text books, journals, and unpublished works on Anthropocene and international relations. This paper discusses how Anthropocene has transformed international relations as a discipline. It sets off by introducing the concepts of Anthropocene and international relations. It proceeds to analyze the nexus between Anthropocene and international relation and how the former has transformed the latter as a discipline. Finally, the paper concludes that Anthropocene has made scholars of international relations to go beyond power struggle among nation and include environmental issues into the discipline.

The Concept of Anthropocene and International Relations

Scientists have differing views on when the Anthropocene began, although various research point to distinct periods in Earth's history. The advent of humans and their invention of fire, as well as agricultural revolution, European colonization of other parts of the world, the Industrial Revolution in Europe, and the Great Acceleration, which began in 1950s and changed Earth's normal system. This change was as a result of climate change, ocean acidification, and terrestrial biosphere degradation are among them. The extraordinary and unsustainable human effect on the ecosystem is the unifying denominator of all transformations (Acharya, 2014).

The word 'Anthropocene' has sparked vibrant curiosity in many institutions and an astonishing range of individual scientists and scholars after it was introduced by Stoermer and Crutzen in 2000. The Anthropocene which was proposed to have started the period about 1800 A.D. has sparked debate, but there is widespread agreement that the definition of Anthropocene is the inception of processes in which human action instigated the movement of vital features of Earth System outside the previous cover of variability. Human race has increased its mark on Earth throughout the Holocene, and especially since the switch to farming, but it was after the onset of the Industrial Revolution that this impact of human on earth's system has matured to a main problem influencing numerous worldwide biogeophysical progression to the sense where it has become a powerful, essential, and controlling power in the Earth System. Because of the steam engine's adaptability to industrial production and transportation, various scientists, including Crutzen, argued that the year 1784 is the date the Anthropocene stated. This is because it was a year Scottish inventor James Watt invented steam engine (Encyclopedia Britannica, 2013). The globalization of international system—interconnectivity among nations in all the facets of human life in recent years, is the major feature of the Anthropocene (Oldfield et al., 2014). Anthropocene is an Earth that the atmosphere has been impaired by billions of tons of carbon dioxide that human spilled by burning coal and other fossil fuels (Bonneuil and Fressoz, 2016).

The Anthropocene is characterized with impact of human on global atmosphere and this imprint has become too much and effective to the extent that it dominates some of the forces of Nature in the functioning of the Earth system (Will S. et al., 2011). The impact has been felt on climate. The global dilapidation of Earth's living tissue is evidence proving that we are into the Anthropocene. Destruction of the world's ecosystem, climate change as well as the breakdown of biodiversity is also evident.

However, international relations today are characterized by a great interconnection and interdependence among states and non-state actors. Obviously, the international system is changing in innumerable ways. The study of international relations like other academic discipline is modifying. In a swiftly changing and progressively multifaceted world, it embraces more than the relations between and among states and non-state actors. It encompasses a great variation of intermediate relationship, at various levels among states and non-state actors in international system although; states still remain the prime actors (Palmer and Perkins, 2010).

Contemporary international relation is a discussion of the international community in transition. The discipline of international relations encompasses many subjects, for example, international organizations, globalization, ecological or environmental issues, international and regional peace and security, and nuclear proliferation, etc. (Khan, 2019). The discipline of international relations changed drastically with globalization of world politics and economy prompted by Industrial Revolution.

As an interactions or relations between states and non-state actors in the international arena, the study of international relations has changed from realist perceptive (struggle for power) of international system to encompass liberal view (multiple interdependence). International relations also entail covert and overt activities of actors across state borders and establishment of diplomatic ties (exchange of diplomatic personnel and diplomatic missions).

Ways Anthropocene Has Transformed International Relations as a Discipline

Words from the traditional IR agenda, such as peace and security, conflict, geopolitics, as well as governance, dominate the analysis on the Anthropocene within the IR discipline. Keywords linked with ecological studies, for example, climate change, biodiversity, and ecology, have been added into the discipline's terminology (Simangan, 2021). The ability of international relation to widen its horizon of inquiries from politics among states to include environment and natural science is demonstrated by the articulations of these nontraditional IR terminologies. The change in world climatic condition is not only a challenge for the environment, but also for national and human security (Barnett, 2003). As a result, it is only natural for the discipline of international relations to engross in a discussion outside its traditional themes to preparation for the Anthropocene's political needs (Burke et al., 2018). However, despite placing IR research in the context of the Anthropocene's concerns, the traditional subjects of IR study, as well as the persistence of statist and economic approaches, continue to dominate. The discipline's sturdy footing in its anthropocentric and modernist core indicates development priorities. In the context of the Anthropocene, Rossi, for example, discusses the increase of border disputes and migration (Rossi, 2017). In this case, the Anthropocene provides a new context for traditional IR challenges, making them more urgent. The logic behind focusing on human-centered issues is to maintain the field's logical precision. IR researchers have persisted to value the logic frameworks of IR. For instance, D'Souza considers how developing countries might adapt to the Anthropocene's borderless nature at a period that climate-related problems have posed additional pressing issues than politics (D'Souza, 2015).

International peace and security, globalization, development, etc., are still primary topics of study in international relations academics; however, they are increasingly being analyzed in a new light. The Anthropocene, in this sense, serves as a catalyst for international relations to widen its investigative structures, not just through multidisciplinary discussion but also include physical and temporal boundaries. This expansion is evident in the articles in this analysis; note how the terms 'earth system governance' and 'future' are linked to traditional IR terminology like politics, security, and global governance. These ties suggest that the discipline is interested in wider ontologies of time and space. McDonald's examination of climate change security discourse, for example, broadens the idea of susceptibility 'across interplanetary, period and android species' (McDonald, 2018). In the Anthropocene, the topic of security has been extended beyond human or national aspects to include the effects of human-prioritized security matters on other species (Waters et al., 2015). Politics and security, for example, are traditional IR subjects are now differentiated from socio-economic and ecological vulnerabilities, not only between states but also across intergenerational human societies and nonhuman counterparts, aggravate situations like conflict and environmental deterioration (Simangan, 2021).

In studying international security concerns, the Anthropocene presents a fresh lens as well as new subjects. For instance, the idea of the Anthropocene made Leep to examine the consequences of Iraq War on nonhumans (Leep, 2018). More so, Rossi uses exaggeration an article on the border clash between Chile and Bolivia over water to emphasize the importance of addressing water security concerns. As both countries lay long-standing claim over the Silala/Siloli Basin, there is a chance that this dispute will escalate into a major conflict. Concerns about fresh water, he claims, will be amplified in the Anthropocene, even in remote reservoirs of water-rich countries (Rossi, 2017).

The world we live in today is more complicated and unpredictable than it has ever been. The international community is threatened by a lot of worldwide issues that includes those are connected to environment, and without cooperation among international actors to resolve them; it will worsen and go above what we are experiencing presently. Environmental issues, particularly those involving the exploitation of natural resources, have become increasingly important. As a result, the survival of humanity is primarily dependent on the ability to construct a successful network of multilateral governance, both in terms of essence and scope of activity. Thus, based on environmental complication and our ability and unwillingness to deal with it, we can claim that the globe is progressing to a new global order or disorder (Pereira, 2015).

The rise of another global players, the increasing interdependence and interconnections among states and non-state actors on a global scale, the erosion of the customary distinction that exist between national and international as well as the emergence of a worldwide governance arrangement have shifted the focus of International Relations to globalization, as relations between states is no longer sufficient to study and comprehend the socio-political and economic, dynamics of the international community. Currently, there is an increase interdependence between states, these state can no more be viewed as sovereign and impermeable entities, that was characterized by Westphalian period, but interconnected and interdependent actors in the global system, forced to cooperate to resolve international challenges. The unlimited weakness of national economies to actions occurring in other parts of the world, the prevalent application of modern technologies which made individuals to interact with uncontrollable means by governments, and also with the fact that the international greatest persistent challenge, such as ecological issues, are fundamentally global, indicates that international system based on Westphalian is broken and it is becoming gradually doubtful. Furthermore, emergent of global governance system which made it possible for states to articulate and combine their interests, made choices, and as well execute policies, demonstrates that the global system of the twenty-first century has shifted from Westphalian characteristics to an era of interconnectivity (Zürn, 2012).

In this multilayered international system, governments' pursuit of national interest made them to join in a vast arrangement of collaboration as well as a variety of kinds of international cooperation. As a result, sovereignty is defined as the application of common public power and authority between and among national, regional, and international actors, which do entail the demise of state in any way. However, the position of states in the world is improving. Even while territoriality is still politically significant, sovereignty, and authority are progressively applied in international arena (Biersteker, 2012).

Despite the establishment of a world governance platform and increased interconnectivity between states, and with the close tie between national goals and global interest as well as actively participating in international stage, it appears that global organizations and governments that states uses their authority do not have suitable mechanism to address world issues—that is, issues that disturb world community entirely and whose effects necessitate an international controlling tactic (Bhargava, 2006). The inability of global community to resolve environmental issues such as change in climatic condition and other related issues highlights the need for restructuring of the United Nations, or even the formation of new ones that are extremely international-positioned and capable of managing and handling situations involving long-term issues. To evade pressures in the future, the growth of new powers and world challenges suggest to this course (Weiss, 2012). As a result, we are in a period of transition—a period that world order is characterized by Westphalian and post-Westphalian traits. The globe is at risk of pressures, clashes, and wars erupting, there is an extraordinary necessity for collaboration. Ecological challenges are important in this regard because they have characteristics that facilitate the emergence of conflict while also necessitating global collaboration and coordination. Ecosystem has appeared as an essential issue in the study of international relations in the twenty-first century, with enormous ability to adjust the course of globalization and the arrangement of the global system. Moreover, the international community treats the environment will defiantly have a great effect on the world (Pereira, 2015). External forces in today's world include population increase, globalization, socio-economic development, natural resource exploitation and scarcity, change in climatic condition, and urbanization. Global sustainability looks to be a civilizational need in the Anthropocene, an epoch distinguished by humankind's dominant involvement in geology and environment.

Environmental challenges overlap into a variety of area, including economy and security, major areas of critical significance to states; as a result, states have grown to play a prominent position in the world political plan, particularly after 2007. The United Nations Security Council met in 2007 to tackle climate change, first of its kind. Climate change has been a recurring theme in recent G20 Summits (Viola et al., 2013); a main public panel session was devoted to the dialogue of the future natural resource mining. In 2014 World Economic Forum, discussion was made concerning climate change, world food security, natural disasters, etc. Also, in 2014, China and the United States announced their Climate Agreement these are just a few examples that prove that ecological issues have taken center stage on the international arena.

Wars over water, drug, diamond, oil, etc., have shown the level of resource warfare during the era of deforestation, scarcity, climate change, and pollution increase which are increasingly common terms in discipline of international relations. The ecosystem and natural resources are inextricably tied to both national and global security, which have been a major theme in international politics. Very problematic to explain, it entails the lack of dangers to attained principles in a neutral sense, and lack of horror that such standards will be confronted in a subjective sense (Collins, 2010), particularly those that, if left unchecked, pressurize the existence of a specific entity (Williams, 2008). Security, in more broad way, can be seen as the conviction people have that they will continue to enjoy the entities that are most crucial to their existence and well-being (Barnett, 2003). Environmental challenges are presently linked to security concept in a changing world, because traditional security measures are no longer sufficient in a world with international events that are able to affect a broad range of human objects, concepts of security that are focused on military security are irrelevant (Greaves, 2012). Environmental or ecological security broadens the definition of security by looking into the threats that an environmental issue poses to the peoples' core values (Barnett, 2003). Change in climatic conditions, desertification, biodiversity loss, erosion and deforestation, air, land, as well as water pollution, ocean acidification, ozone layer reduction, and disruption of the nitrogen and phosphorus cycles are just a few of the risks.

The Industrial Revolution, which was fueled by technological advancements, agriculture, urbanization, and transportation development, encouraged high ingesting degree of goods and services that necessitate vast amounts of water, for example, consumption levels that appear to be becoming increasingly impossible to maintain. The situation has worsened because of change in climatic conditions (Pereira, 2015). World water consumption expanded in the same rate with population increase in the last six decades and future population growth, as well as Gross Domestic Product growth, when combined with pressures in energy and food revolution in numerous Global South countries, indicates a higher figure of places facing water scarcity. As a result, poor water resource management jeopardizes economic development and security. Water and climate change have inextricably linked, climate change has and will persist to have a significant influence on water supply, while water is the primary mediator of the impact of climate change on the economy, humanity, and the ecosystem, a connection essentially related to other sectors of human existence such as food production and energy.

Human activities have had a great impact on world ecological system. Environmental security, or environmental protection, includes economic, food, energy securities, and access to basic natural resources, all of which lead to the idea of human security and also shows that environment is a multifaceted trend. Security encompasses all sectors of human existence. It includes environmental, food, economic, health, community, political, and personal securities. This implies that security should be focused on individuals rather than just for national defense. Issues such as health, human right, poverty, malnutrition, justice, etc., can endanger security. At this juncture, ecological anxiety is linked with inequality, which leads to consideration of the increased disparities brought about by globalization and general economic policy (Pereira, 2015).

Issues concerning environment is conceivably the greatest world and multifaceted challenges in the global system, and the discipline of international relations as a scientific domain of inquire that draws from variety of disciplines and aims to syndicate information from other academic disciplines makes it the ideal academic discipline for analyzing and comprehending the modern international system. "Interdisciplinary knowledge is required to comprehend the current world and its future progress". It necessitates an awareness of the world in transition (Calouste Gulbenkian Foundation, 2014).

This implies that, as it concerns complex and world issue such as changing of earth's geological process, the discipline of international relations appears to be a major academic filed to develop and as well offer a framework for national, regional, and global stakeholders to understand world dynamics and their implications to entire humanity. It also recognizes risks and uncovers paths for cooperation. The discipline of international relations emerges as a particularly relevant academic filed in the twenty-first century's hybrid world system, where the globe faces geopolitical challenges; this necessitated the need for cooperation on a universal scale. International system is going for a new world order or disorder, which is inseparably from environment, thus, making it serious to investigate this emerging international setting so that humanity will not fall into world disorder.

Because the discipline of international relations immersed itself with the study of relations between states, trans-border operations of any kinds, and numerous scopes of modern globalization, it can help promote collective responses to problems that affect human existence and in which the solution cannot be found except the global community come together and combine forces to tackle it. This is because in today's international system, what happens inside a nation has great effect on the international arena, and what happens internationally has an influence on the national territory. This is the major feature of globalization and it is exacerbating, and this is what national and international actors need to realize concerning globalization. In order to create a cooperative and coherent international system, adjust to these present realities, evading wars, we must take advantage of is mutual challenges.

With respect to the Anthropocene, the global community needs to act with international concerns and, as a result, keep global interest in mind, which is not at odds with national interests. Both national and international actors approach national interest with different lens, nontraditional methods: We must develop a concept of national interest that is inseparable from world interest, bearing it in mind that it is impossible to achieve most of important national objectives without thinking globally, without achieving the goals of humanity, as the environment appears to prove. This made domestic and international interests a two sides of the same coin, not separate entities.

Conclusion

In this period of unparalleled world environmental challenges, the Anthropocene has become a rallying cry. I maintained that globalization operates in vague ways, and environmental or ecological problems are integral parts of volatile impact of globalization, arguing that international system has moved away from struggle for power between nations to an era of interdependence and interconnectivity because of threat the Anthropocene epoch is imposing to the entire humanity. I hoped to demonstrate how ecological problems have hint numbers of diverse sectors and the security risk it pose in global environment, as well as the need to move toward international collaboration, by reviewing the most recent works on Anthropocene, environment, and natural resources.

The work asserted that geopolitics and globalization are not commonly selected concepts, but opposite ideas that are vital for understanding the current international situation. Similarly, the importance of the Anthropocene in international affairs was emphasized. In a nutshell, I sought to show that a new international order is evolving, and the manner that environment is influencing and might alter the global social relations. Suggesting the discipline of international relations has the potential and tools to study the emerging international order and as well recommend institutional reforms and cooperative paths to global actors. Given their growing significance in the world system and its international character, and it capability to inspire cooperation, it is critical that academics of international relations pay additional attention environmental concerns. The world currently is becoming more multipolar; however, it does not infer that the United States is in decline. The idea is that new powers are developing, this makes imperative to move away from hegemonic international system, but a balance of power based on strong interdependence. Globalization is advancing the geopolitical principle of balance through interdependence.

However, because a multipolar system requires discourse, this world system will only function when authentic and real international governance institutions are formed. If wars and violence prevail, this international order will amount to loser's game, particularly, if it involves environmental concerns listed in this article. As a result, humanity will witness a new international disorder. Current trends indicate a global system typified by conflict and anxieties, as well as socio-political and economic disintegration. However, given the growth of new powers and international difficulties in the system, collaboration serves as the major appropriate tools to tackle imminent international problems, especially given the intensifying global program. For example, among the international concerns which required concentrated and mutual act is the rise in acute weather events; therefore, climate crisis could be among the drivers for a truly new world order. However, as I have demonstrated in this work, it does not remove the prospect of wars (the Russia invasion of Ukraine has shown that realist ideology is hard to eliminate in international politics). Presently, humankind is in menace of becoming overwhelmed by discord and war. However, international relations scholars have the ability to aid in discovering answers for a world in transition.

References

Acharya, A. (2014). Global International Relations (IR) and Regional Worlds. *International Studies Quarterly*, 58, (4), 647–659.

Anthropocene Epoch. (2013). Encyclopædia Britannica. *Encyclopædia Britannica Ultimate Reference Suite*. Chicago: Encyclopædia Britannica.

Barnett, J. (2003). Security and Climate Change. *Global Environmental Change*, 13, (1), 7–17.

Bhargava, K. (2006). *Global Issues for Global Citizens*. Washington, DC: World Bank Publications.

Biersteker, J. (2012). State, Sovereignty and Territory. In *Handbook of International Relations*, edited by Walter Carlsnaes, Thomas Risse and Beth A. Simmons, 245–272. London: Sage.

Bonneuil, C. and Fressoz, J. (2016). *The Shock of the Anthropocene the Earth, History and Us*. Verso: London.

Burke, A. et al. (2018). Planet Politics' Millennium. *Journal of International Studies*, 46, (2), 190–208.
Calouste Gulbenkian Foundation. (2014). *Water and the Future of Humanity, Revisiting Water Security*. London: Springer.
Collins, A. (2010). *Contemporary Security Studies*. New York: Oxford.
Corry, O. and Hayley, S. (2017). *Traditions and Trends in Global Environmental Politics International Relations and the Earth*. London, UK: Routledge.
Crutzen, P. and Stoermer, E. (2000). The Anthropocene. International Geosphere-Biosphere Programme, Newsletter.
Cudworth, E. and Hobden, S. (2013). Complexity, Ecologism and Post-human Politics. *Review of International Studies,* 39, (3), 643–664.
D'Souza, R. (2015). Nations without Borders: Climate Security and the South in the Epoch of the Anthropocene. *Strategic Analysis*, 39, (6), 720–728.
Deudney, D. (1999). Bringing Nature Back in: Geopolitical Theory from the Greeks to the Global Era. In *Contested Grounds: Security and Conflict in the New Environmental Politics*, edited by D. H. Deudney and R. A. Matthew. New York: Albany State University Press.
Greaves, W. (2012). Insecurities of Non-dominance: Re-theorizing Human Security and Environmental Change in Developed States. In *Natural Resources and Social Conflict: Towards Critical Environmental Security*, edited by Matthew A. Schnurr and Larry A. Swatuk, 63–82. London: Palgrave Macmillan.
Khan, A. (2019). International Relations Introductions. Researchgate, retrieved from https://www.researchgate.net/publication/337635265 on 31st March 2022, 1–7.
Leep, M. (2018). Stray Dogs, Post-humanism and Cosmopolitan Belongingness: Interspecies Hospitality in Times of War Millennium. *Journal of International Studies*, 47, (1), 45–66.
McDonald, M. (2018). Climate Change and Security: Towards Ecological Security. *International Theory*, 10, (2), 153–180.
Oldfield, F. et al. (2014). The Anthropocene Review: Its Significance. Implications and the *Rationale for a New Transdisciplinary Journal*, 1, (1), 3–7.
Palmer, D. and Perkins, H. (2010). *International Relations*, Third Edition. Delhi: AITBS Publisher.
Pereira, J. (2015). Environmental Issues and International Relations, A New Global (Dis) Order—The Role Of International Relations In Promoting A Concerted International System. *Revista Brasileira de Política Internacional*, 58, (1), 191–209.
Rossi, C. (2017). The Trans-boundary Dispute Over the Waters of the Silala/Siloli: Legal Vandalism and Goffmanian Metaphor. *Stanford Journal of International Law*, 53, (1), 55–87.

Simangan, D. (2021). Where Is the Anthropocene? International Relations in a New Geographical Epoch. *International Affairs*, 96, (1), 211–224.

Viola, E. et al. (2013). Sistema Internacional de Hegemonia Conservadora. *Governança Global Democracia na Era da Crise Climática*. São Paulo: Annablume.

Waters, C. et al. (2015). Can Nuclear Weapons Fallout Mark the Beginning of the Anthropocene Epoch. *Bulletin of the Atomic Scientists*, 71, (3), 46–57.

Weiss, G. (2012). *What's Wrong with the United Nations and How to Fix it*. Cambridge: Polity Press.

Will, S. et al. (2011). The Anthropocene: Conceptual and Historical Perspectives. *Philosophical Transaction of the Royal Society A*, 369, (1938), 842.

Williams, D. (2008). *Security Studies: An Introduction*. New York: Routledge.

World Economic Forum. (2014). *World Economic Forum Annual Meeting. The Reshaping of the World: Consequences for Society, Politics and Business*. Geneva: World Economic Forum. In Pereira Joana Castro. 2015. "Environmental Issues And International Relations, A New Global (Dis)Order—The Role of International Relations In Promoting A Concerted International System". *Revista Brasileira de Política Internacional*, 58, (1), 191–209.

Zürn, M. (2012). Globalization and Global Governance. In *Handbook of International Relations*, edited by Walter Carlsnaes, Thomas Risse and Beth A. Simmons, 401–425. London: Sage.

CHAPTER 11

The Impact of Climate Change in Egypt

Maryam Jungudo

Introduction

Climate change has been identified as an environmental and human crisis of the twenty-first century, which led to public, political, and academic attention being devoted to the issue of global warming and climate change. At the root of climate change is global warming caused by anthropogenic emissions of carbon dioxide, methane and other greenhouse gases (for example, burning of fossil fuels, like coal, petroleum and natural gasses and widespread deforestation). The warming occurs worldwide and temperatures are rising on the African land mass and in the surrounding oceans. A broad scientific and political consensus has been established that climate change poses a considerable threat to Africa, its ecosystems and many of its species. Concern over the negative impact of climate change has strengthened fears that environmental degradation and demographic pressures will displace millions of people in Africa and create serious social upheaval. Most scientists studying the potential impact of

M. Jungudo (✉)
Department of History, Nigerian Army University Biu, Biu, Borno State, Nigeria
e-mail: maryam.jungudo@naub.edu.ng

K. J. Ani (ed.), *Resource Conflict and Environmental Relations in Africa*,
https://doi.org/10.1007/978-981-19-7343-7_11

climate change have predicted that Africa is likely to experience higher temperatures, the drying up of soils, increased pest and disease pressure, shift in suitable areas for growing crops and livestock, increased desertification in the Sahara region, floods, deforestation, and erosion are all signs that climate change is already happening and represents one of the greatest environmental, social, and economic threats facing Africa.

Perhaps, Egypt is a typical example of a developing country that is highly vulnerable to climate change which exposes it to numerous threats to its economic, social, and environmental sustainability. Climate change is also expected to add to the growing threats to national security fueled by a growing population and an increased demand on the already constrained resource base. Egypt is highly vulnerable to climate change due to the dependence of its large and growing population on the Nile River for fresh water and its long coastline, which is already experiencing sea level rise. With 98% of its population living on 4% of its total land area in the Nile Valley and Delta, the largest oasis of the Sahara Desert, the future of Egypt is directly linked to the flow of the Nile River and its endangered delta.

This paper is poised out to examine the impact of climate change in Egypt, it further sheds light on the Egyptian Government adaptation strategy on climate change. This paper is a desk study, as the research was performed through an extensive review of academic and policy literature, these included reports of national, regional, and international organizations and relevant climate change published literature. The paper argues that climate change is happening and the evidence is all around us, unless we act, we will see catastrophic consequences including rising sea-levels, droughts and famine, and the loss of up to a third of the world's plant and animal species.

Climate Change and Egypt

There is no internationally agreed definition of the term 'climate change,' which has resulted in differences of opinion on the issue. However, climate change refers to the long-term changes in average weather conditions covering all changes in the climate system, including the drivers of change, the changes themselves and their effects; or can refer only to human-induced change in the climate system.

Geographically, Egypt forms the north-eastern corner of the African continent with coasts on both the Mediterranean and the Red Sea. Part of

Egypt's territory, namely the Sinai Peninsula, is located in Asia. The total area of Egypt is 1,001,450 km^2 with a coastline of 3,500 km. The surface level ranges from 133 m below sea level in the Western Desert to 2,629 m above sea level in the Sinai Peninsula. According to Egypt's Second National Communication (SNC) to United Nations Framework Convention on Climate Change (UNFCCC), the general climate of Egypt is dry, hot and desert, with a mild winter season with rain over the coastal areas, and a hot and dry summer season. Data collected by the Egyptian Meteorological Authority and local universities for the period between 1961 and 2000 indicate a general trend toward a warming of the air temperature, with an increase in the number of hazy days, misty days, turbidity of the atmosphere, frequency of sand storms, and hot days (EEAA, 2010). The country has particularly good wind regimes with ideal sites along the Red Sea and Mediterranean coasts with an excellent potential to produce wind power. Egypt is a lower-middle-income country with a population of about 90 million, of which nearly 56% are living in rural areas. The population is estimated to reach 100 million by 2020, assuming the population growth rate remains unchanged. About 97% of the population in Egypt lives on the Nile Valley and the Delta, which represent about 4% of Egypt's total area. In 2009, the Gross Domestic Product (GDP) per capita was US$ 56,731, and the average yearly economic growth rate for the period from 1990 to 2007 was 4.47%. Agriculture, which contributes nearly 14% of the annual GDP, remains an important part of the economy. An estimated 55% of the labor force in Egypt is engaged in agricultural activities and the sector consumes about 80% of the fresh water resources. There are a number of limiting factors for future agricultural growth in Egypt, which enhance the sector's vulnerability to climate change. These include:

1. Historically high reliance on low efficiency irrigation systems (30% or less), which poses increased pressure on water resources,
2. Land degradation and desertification due to poor water management, poor agricultural practices, and intensive utilization of fertilizers and other agro-chemicals, and
3. Urban sprawl over agricultural land due to population growth and poor land use planning. The industry and services sectors account for about 32 and 54% of the GDP, respectively.

Though attracting FDI is one of the major goals of the Egyptian development plans, it has been relatively low at 3.6% of the GDP. The current Egyptian exports are dominated by energy intensive and low-technology products. However, the vision of Egypt's "Industrial Development Strategy" is that by the year 2025, Egypt will be a leading industrializing nation in the Middle East and North Africa (MENA) region in terms of industrial performance as well as a main export hub for medium-technology manufactured products. The cement and fertilizers industries have intensively grown, and their impact on the GHG emissions in Egypt is remarkable. Though social indicators have improved over the last decade, the fight against poverty and illiteracy (about one third of the adult population) remains an important challenge to policymakers (UNDP, 2011). Over the past decade, 22% of the Egyptian population was living on less than 1.25 USD a day (national poverty line). Egypt was ranked 113th according to the 2011 United Nations Development Program (UNDP) Human Development Report (HDR). Increasing rural-urban migration inevitably results in the mushrooming of slums and informal settlement with frequently inadequate services. Concentration of industry and transport in the capital means that Cairo is home to 40% of all industrial production sites, 32% of all vehicles and 25% of Egypt's population. As stated earlier, a combination of urbanization and general population growth enhances expansion of residential areas into valuable agricultural land and puts strain on agricultural production. This is especially critical in view of the fact that Egypt is far from being food self-sufficient and relies heavily on food imports.

Egypt is highly vulnerable to climate change impact as noted in Egypt's Initial National Communication (INC) to the UNFCCC (EEAA, 1999), in the UNDP Global HDR 2006 (UNDP, 2006) and in the Intergovernmental Panel on Climate Change (IPCC) Fourth Assessment Report (IPCC, 2007). Egypt has an emission ranking of 28 out of 215 countries and regions contributing about 0.60% of global GHG emission (Global Carbon Atlas, 2016). For climate vulnerability, Egypt has a ranking of 91 out of 181 countries in the ND-Gain Index. Egypt is the 87th most vulnerable country and the 73rd least ready country. Climate projections make it clear that current and future changes in climatic conditions constitute a major environmental risk that may jeopardize Egypt's development gains and poverty reduction strategies.

The Impact of Climate Change in Egypt

Coastal Zones

Climate change would cause serious damage to human settlements, to large parts of productive agricultural land and to industrial areas in the North Coast. Estimates show that 0.5 m Sea Level Rise (SLR) would lead to the permanent submersion of 1,800 km^2 of cropland in low areas of the Nile Delta and accelerate the trend of desertification in the form of increased soil salinity in the remaining land (EEAA, 1999). TheIPCC estimates that the Mediterranean Sea will have risen by one meter by 2050 as a result of global warming, ending in the loss of one third of the most productive land in the Nile Delta (IPCC, 2007). Observations at various points along the Nile delta shoreline indicate that sea-levels have already been rising. This SLR is due to a combination of local factors that include coastal subsidence and reduced sediment loads due to the construction of the High Aswan Dam upstream. It is also associated with global warming and thermal expansion of the oceans and glacier melting (El Shennawy, 2008). Several studies on the vulnerability of Alexandria, the second largest coastal city in Egypt, indicated that a 0.3 m SLR would inundate large parts of the city, resulting in billions of dollars' damage to infrastructure, displacement of over half a million inhabitants, and a loss of about 70,000 jobs. Such concerns about future SLR are well-reflected in Egypt's NCR to the UNFCCC. Along with the loss of populated and agricultural area, some industrial cities and important historic cities like Alexandria, Damietta, Rosetta, and Port Said would be victims of SLR. Furthermore, the expected SLR's effects include threats to food security, damage to the large investments in the tourism sector along the North West Coast, and the relocation of more than 10 million people to the already over populated Nile Valley. This will have a direct and critical effect on Egypt's entire economy.

Agriculture

Agriculture contributes nearly 14% to the GDP, making it a key sector of the Egyptian economy. Egypt has a unique heavily irrigated agriculture system. Temperature rises due to climate change will likely reduce the yield of the major crops and increase their water requirements. The combined effect of temperature increase, SLR, water shortage and other environmental conditions would worsen agriculture productivity, and therefore Egypt's food security. Agriculture is also the main water-using sector in Egypt, using 80% of all fresh water that is mainly provided by the Nile River (USAID [2018] Egypt: Agriculture and Food security). The agricultural sector is dominated by small farms using traditional practices. About 80% of cultivated land is 'old-land' in the Nile Valley and the Nile Delta that has been irrigated and intensively cultivated for thousands of years. 'New-lands' that have been reclaimed from the desert relatively recently or are in the process of being reclaimed represent the remaining 20% of cultivated land. The Nile Delta region, that accounts for 30–40% of Egypt's agricultural production, is subsiding and becoming less fertile since it is no longer replenished each year by flood sediments from the Nile. There are two main cropping seasons a year winter and summer cultivation seasons. Fruit trees are the most important perennial crops. Field crops cultivated include maize, rice, cotton, and sugarcane as main summer crops, while alfalfa, wheat, barley, green bean, clover, and sugar beet are the main winter field crops. Agricultural production is at risk from the direct effects of climate change, including:

- Expected rise in temperatures and change of seasonal patterns as well as a change in environmental agricultural zones;
- Marginal agricultural areas negatively affected and increasing desertification;
- Higher temperatures increasing water evaporation and water consumption;
- Decreasing water supplies reducing the availability of water for irrigation;
- Sea Level Rise (SLR) inundating coastal areas and increased salinization.

Projections suggest agricultural will experience the largest loss in the Egyptian economy due to climate change with a significant decrease in agricultural production (except for cotton). Because of the rise in temperature and the increase in the number of hot days and nights, water needs for all crops are projected to increase with reduction in water supplies further decreasing agricultural production (Smith, 2014). The potential impact of climate change could decrease national food production by 11 to 51% (range reflecting projections of low to high temperature models). By 2050, it is expected that the productivity of two major crops in Egypt—wheat and maize—will be reduced by 15 and 19%, respectively. It is also anticipated that 12–15% of the most fertile land in the Nile Delta will be negatively affected by sea level rise and salt water intrusion. Climate change impacts in Egypt are not gender neutral. Agriculture employs about 45% of all women in the labor force (USAID, 2018). Rural women in agriculture are usually seasonal workers with unstable earnings and vulnerability to food insecurity. Illiteracy rates for women are higher than those for men (one third of adult women are estimated to be illiterate compared to 15% of males) which means that up to 10 million women cannot read or write and have limited opportunities outside of the agriculture sector for employment. While a large percentage of the female labor is engaged in agricultural labor, a very small percentage of women (5%) are agricultural land owners due to inheritance customs in Egypt. The vulnerability of Egypt's agriculture to climate change presents considerable risks to the fragile socioeconomic situation of many rural Egyptian women who are already facing the challenges of high illiteracy, little asset ownership, and a weak capacity for economic mobility and adaptation (Kandeel, 2017).

Water Resources

Egypt has just one major source of water supply, the Nile River, which supplies over 95% of the country's annual water needs. The mean annual rainfall is estimated at 18 mm/year, ranging from 0 mm/year in the desert to 200 mm/year in the northern delta region. Non-renewable underground fossil water supplies are accessible outside the River Nile valley, especially in the scattered oases. Consequently, agricultural development is closely linked to the River Nile and its management, which would be impacted by climate change. Models have predicted that the annual Nile flow will vary between an increase of 30% and a decrease that can reach 70%. These two extremes can have serious implications in terms of increased flood risks or droughts that would lead to a decrease in food production and an increase in the number of lost jobs and water conflicts.

Climate change in the Nile Basin Since Egypt receives very little rainfall and is dependent on the Nile River for all but a small percentage of its freshwater, the flow of the Nile is of greater importance to Egypt than rainfall variability. The Nile is one of the world's major rivers with a basin area shared among 11 countries: Burundi, Democratic Republic of the Congo, Egypt, Eritrea, Ethiopia, Kenya, Rwanda, South Sudan, Sudan,

United Republic of Tanzania, and Uganda. The Nile Basin extends over five climatic zones—Mediterranean, arid, semi-arid, subtropical, and tropical with landscapes ranging from mountains, grasslands, forests and woodlands, wetlands, lakes and desert to a delta. The two main tributaries of the Nile River are the White Nile, with sources on the Equatorial Plateau and the Blue Nile originating in the Ethiopian Highlands. The Blue Nile contributes more than 60% of the total flow of the Nile (measured at the Aswan Dam) and the White Nile about 18%. The other major river systems (e.g., Sobat and the Atbara) contribute less than 15% each (Regional Initiative for the Assessment of Climate Change Impacts). Since the Basin is sensitive to changes in rainfall and temperature, the potential impact of climate change on the Nile River regime is significant (NBI, 2012). According to the NBI (2012) the vulnerability of the Nile River Basin to climate change is due to:

- High fragility of its natural systems: two-fifths of the basin is arid and semi-arid drylands;
- Rapidly growing population putting unprecedented pressure on the natural resource base;
- Poverty of the rural people in the upstream countries that limits diversification from agriculture, fishing, and forestry into less climate-sensitive sectors;
- High exposure to natural disasters, including droughts and floods;
- High sensitivity of many of the Nile sub-basins to changes in precipitation;
- Agriculture sector in the downstream countries (e.g., Egypt) that is almost totally reliant on the Nile-fed irrigation;
- High dependency on hydropower for energy across the basin.

Since the Blue Nile is its major contributor, the Nile is particularly sensitive to the variability of runoff from the Ethiopian part of the basin. Potential climate change impacts on the smaller White Nile flows are mitigated by the Sudd in South Sudan and the other large wetlands in the White Nile Basin (NBI, 2012). Changes projected for temperature, precipitation, and related extreme events suggest an overall increase in temperatures with a continuing rise in temperature by 2100 for the Basin. For precipitation, some models suggest an increase in precipitation for the Basin until 2040, followed by decreases in rainfall by 2100. A significant rise in temperatures increases the possibility of enhanced water losses from evapotranspiration which will reduce the stream flows and stored water. According to current estimates, evapotranspiration losses account for more than 70% of the water balance in the wettest areas of the Nile Basin, such as the Blue Nile and the equatorial lakes sub-basins, with even higher percentages in the drier areas, such as Egypt and the Sudan.

Drought and Flood

Shifts in temperature and rainfall patterns due to climate change will also have an impact on the recurrence of extreme conditions (drought and flooding), as well as contribute to changes in the river's flow (NBI, 2012). The impact of climate change on the variability in the annual output of the Nile River is a major concern. The ability to predict the amount of the flow, especially the likely years of reduced flow, is of increasing importance, especially since the population of the Nile River Basin is expected to double by 2050. A recent well received study, using a range of global climate models and records of rainfall and flow rates over the last half-century, suggests an increase of 50% in the annual variation of the amount of flow this century (Siam and Elthahir, 2017). The study bases its analysis on the increase in the intensity and duration of the Pacific Ocean phenomenon of the El Niño/La Niña cycle, which is strongly connected to annual rainfall variations in the Ethiopian highlands and adjacent eastern Nile basins which provides an estimated 80% of the Nile river's total flow. While the changing rainfall pattern is likely to lead to an average increase of the Nile's flow of 10–15% until 2040, there will be substantially fewer 'normal' years and many more extreme years with greater flows and more years of drought. Current water storage capacity and current plans for additional storage capacity in the Basin do not consider the projected enhancement of inter annual variability in the future flow of the Nile river. Both increased and reduced flows will have negative effects on Egypt and other countries in the Basin. In years in which the natural flow is considerably increased, the storage capacity of water systems might not be sufficient to accommodate these high flows, resulting in destructive floods. Also, of concern is the high probability that the conveyance and distribution network of Egypt's canals and drains might not be able to cope with the high flows. In years in which the opposite happens (natural flows are substantially reduced), Egypt and other basin countries such as the Sudan will face drought. Changing climatic conditions have the potential to impact the operational regimes of dams built on the Nile River and its tributaries, with effects on hydropower generation and low volumes to downstream countries (RICCAR, 2017) As the most downstream nation of the Nile River Basin, Egypt is most at risk. Variability in Nile flows into Egypt is moderated by the High Aswan Dam, which has one year's worth of storage capacity that helps in handling periodic drought. However, Egypt remains vulnerable to the multi-year droughts that are likely to occur.

Conflict, Migration, and Climate Change

Population growth, unemployment, and climate change are anticipated to create a 'combustible mix' to its stability. Due to its geographic location, its large population, and its significant role in the politics of the Arab world, Egypt's stability affects the region as a whole. Contributing to Egypt's vulnerability is its lack of self-sufficiency in grain production—a situation that will not change in future due to its growing population and decreasing agricultural land—and its dependence on the international commodity markets. From 2007 to 2017 Egypt was the world's largest importer of wheat (for 2018 it is estimated that Indonesia will be the largest with Egypt a close 2nd) (https://www.ft.com/content/a6545786-0da8-11e8-8eb7-42f857ea9f09). Egypt's national system to supply the population with subsidized bread costs 3% of its annual GDP. While economically unsustainable, proposing changes to the subsidized bread system is politically volatile, as demonstrated by the bread riots in 2008 (http://www.world-grain.com/Departments/Country-Focus/Country-Focus-Home/Focus-on-Egypt.aspx). The reliance on the changing international commodity markets to meet domestic demand exposes Egypt to external forces, in particular fluctuations in wheat prices. In the past higher wheat prices influenced the cost and availability of bread in Egypt, motivated citizen protests, and indirectly led to regime change in Egypt (Sternberg, 2013). Climate-related flooding in the Nile Delta and the subsequent decrease in agricultural production will also push down employment in the agricultural sector. Scenarios conducted by the United Nations Environment Programme (UNEP) and other organizations suggest that a 0.5-meter rise in sea level could displace 2–4 million Egyptians by 2050 and encourage migration of people from the coastal zone to other areas.

Transboundary Management of the Nile

The impact of climate change and climate variability will further complicate the management of shared water resources of the Nile River (RICCAR, 2017). The riparian countries are members of the Nile Basin Initiative (NBI) established in 1999 and intended to transition to a Nile River Commission after the signing of a cooperative agreement by its members. Currently, there is no cooperative agreement in place for the Nile Basin, primarily because of the opposition of Egypt and the Sudan. There are colonial-era treaties governing the Nile that predominantly benefit the downstream states, Sudan and Egypt, without much benefit to the upstream states. The effect of these treaties is to inhibit upstream projects so as to secure a continuous and undiminished flow of water to the Sudan and Egypt. Egypt has adopted a position consistent with the colonial-era treaties and an Egyptian-Sudan treaty of 1959 that stipulate that Egypt has an historical right to the full volume of the Nile and that upstream states may not disturb that right by impeding or otherwise affecting that flow (Gelil, 2014). Since Ethiopia announced its plan to build the Grand Ethiopian Renaissance Dam (GERD) there has been tensions and threats by Egypt over interference in the natural flow of the Nile. In 2015 Egypt, the Sudan and Ethiopia signed a mutual do-no-harm agreement. While there have been discussions by Egypt, Ethiopia, and the Sudan (which supports the dam), a formal agreement for sharing the Nile resources has not been reached, in part due to the flare up of political tensions between Egypt and the Sudan over other issues (Sudan Vision, March 2018). The GERD, the largest dam in Africa, will have a reservoir that will ultimately store 74 billion cubic meters of Blue Nile water and will take an estimated 5–15 years to fill. During the period of fill, the Nile's fresh water flow to Egypt may be cut up to 25% with a loss of a third of the electricity generated by the Aswan High Dam and a potentially decrease in the availability of water for agricultural production.

Egypt's National Adaptation Strategy to Climate Change

The Intergovernmental Panel on Climate Change (IPCC) defines adaptation to climate change as any "adjustment in natural or human systems in response to actual or expected climatic stimuli or their effects, which moderates harm or exploits beneficial opportunities". According to the

UNFCCC 'Adaptation is a processes through which societies make themselves better able to cope with an uncertain future.' Adapting to climate change entails taking the right measures to reduce the negative effects of climate change (or exploit the positive ones) by making the appropriate adjustments and changes. Adaptation also involves learning to manage new risks and strengthening resilience in the face of change. As late as April 2007, a report by the IPCC warned that Africa was not acting quickly enough to stem the dire economic and environmental consequences of excessive greenhouse gas emissions (IPCC, 2007).

Logically, Egypt's national adaptation strategy primarily focuses on the most vulnerable sectors, namely: agriculture, water resources, and coastal areas. For agriculture, it is recommended to change crop patterns to stress-tolerant ones, to change farm systems and fertilization practices, to develop simple and low-cost technologies suitable for the local context, to establish a special adaptation fund for agriculture, to build scientific capacity, and to improve public awareness. It is also recommended to enhance the adaptive capacity of rural communities through social protection and economic diversification.

In terms of water resources, the country has been implementing the concepts and practices of Integrated Water Resources Management (IWRM). The national adaptation strategy recommends public awareness campaigns on impacts of climate change on water resources, the development of local and regional circulation models capable of assessing the impact of climate change on the Nile basin, building scientific capacity, and enhancing exchange of information among Nile basin countries. The strategy also promotes Integrated Coastal Zone Management (ICZM), recommends the creation of wetlands in low lying areas, building shore protection structures (including dams), and management of coastal lakes; raise public and policymaker awareness; and use of remote sensing in monitoring SLR (Gelil, 2014).

Several adaptation actions are planned and currently underway to minimize the potential adverse impacts of climate change. As a potential alternative to agriculture and living areas, the government of Egypt has developed a massive infrastructure project in Toshka in the south of the country, bordering Sudan. Toshka features one of the most powerful water pumps in the world that diverts water from the Nile to the desert for irrigation and living needs. Yet to date, there has been no relevant migration to Toshka, as was initially planned, due to the hot climate and inadequate social services. Several international organizations such as UNDP, the International Fund for Agricultural Development (IFAD), and the Food and Agriculture Organization of the United Nations (FAO) are collaborating with Egypt to assess vulnerability and adaptation of water, agriculture, and coastal zones to climate change. This collaboration also includes the implementation of a communication strategy to increase awareness of climate change risks and promote the integration of adaptation measures into national development plans. The Agriculture Research Center in the Ministry of Agriculture and Land Reclamation collaborates with IFAD and FAO to assess existing agricultural policies and advocate the adaptation of climate-sensitive strategies and practices, develop stress-tolerant crops, along with the dissemination of knowledge on these crops, and enhancing optimized cropping patterns that cope better with global warming.

Another study, financed by the Global Environment Facility (GEF), on the needs and gaps to adapt to SLR has been prepared jointly by the Stockholm Environment Institute, Alexandria University (AU), and the Coastal Research Institute of the National Water Research Centre. The overall aim of the study was to enhance Egypt's resilience and reduce vulnerability to climate change impacts. The study concluded that an ICZM plan is a key element for adaptation along the coastal zones of Egypt. A combination of spatial planning and enhanced coastal defenses to manage the risk of SLR and storm surge is needed. Proactive adaptation requires more effective partnerships among different stakeholders to facilitate the transition toward safe urban development in large port cities and to implement effective disaster management in the event of flooding.

Egypt ratified the UN Framework Convention on Climate Change (UNFCCC) in 1994, the Kyoto Protocol in 2005 and the United Nations Framework Convention to Combat Desertification (UNCCD) in 1995. Egypt has prepared three National Communications to the UNFCCC (1990, 2010, 2016). The Second National Communication (SNC) addressed the vulnerability and adaptation of various sectors in Egypt to potential impacts of climatic changes. The Third National Communication (TNC) updated the vulnerability and adaptation assessment with a focus on health, tourism, and biodiversity. Egypt signed the Paris agreement on climate change in April 2016 and ratified the agreement in September 2017. In Egypt, the Ministry of State for Environmental Affairs (MOE) is the responsible body for compiling the data needed for the National Climate Change Communications from the relevant ministries81. The National Council of Climate Change (NCCC) established in 2015 is leading the National Adaptation Plan (NAP) process. This Council replaces the National Committee on Climate Change, its predecessor, which was established in 2007. Egypt has a climate policy framework, underpinned by the 2011 National Adaptation Strategy (NAS) and high-level political institutions consisting of line ministries which have the mandate for implementation. The strategy aims to increase the flexibility of Egypt to tackle the risks and negative impacts of climate change in various sectors. It also aims at strengthening the capacity to absorb and reduce the risks and disasters to be caused by such changes. Egypt has also developed a 'Sustainable Development Strategy (SDS) — Egypt's Vision 2030' which provides the roadmap for achieving the sustainable development goals. Among its priorities are: expanding the scope of sustainable growth, increasing real per capita GDP to reach the level of middle-income countries; and promoting the dynamics of sustainable and decentralization development. Projects identified in the SDS, which are climate change related include: sustainable agriculture, protection of coastal establishments, and the efficient use of water resources. The updating of the SDS 2030, which is underway, provides an opportunity to mainstream climate change into national strategies, which will lead to better national budget allocation across key development sectors.

Conclusion

Egypt proves to be highly vulnerable to climate change impacts according to IPCC reports. Egypt started to realize very early on the threat that climate change poses to its future development. Immediately after signing the UNFCCC in 1992 and with the support of international donors, the Egyptian scientific community started to assess the vulnerability of different economic sectors to the potential adverse impacts of climate change. Furthermore, some government research institutions have established specialized centers on climate change such as the "climate change research center" at the Water Research Institute, and the climate research center at the Agriculture Research Institute. As time passes, Egypt recognized, as well, the different opportunities offered by involvement in the global climate regime especially those related to transfer of environmentally sound technologies, financial support, and capacity building. Since the entry into force of the KP in 2005, Egypt has topped the list of Arab countries participating in the CDM with 14 registered projects and more than 100 projects in the CDM pipeline. The climate policy seems to be driven by national interests and is in line with the energy policy aiming at improving energy efficiency, switching to low carbon fuels, and promoting untapped renewable energy resources. Further, there is strong evidence that Egypt's positions have changed along with the emergence of a national climate policy framework that was induced by, among other things, a broader understanding of Egypt's own vulnerability to climate change, as well as the awareness that both long-term development will require some development of national energy policy and that the CDM of the KP can have numerous benefits.

References

Adaptation to Climate Change-induced Water Stress in the Nile Basin: A Vulnerability Assessment Report. Available at https://www.unenvironment.org/resources/report/adaptation-climate-change-induced-water-stress-nile-basinvulnerability-assessment

Climate Analysis Indicators Tool (CAIT) Version 2.0. (2014). (Washington, DC: World Resources Institute, 2014). World Resources Institute

EEAA. (2010). Egypt Second National Communication. Cairo: EEAA.

Egyptian Environmental Affairs Agency (EEAA). (1999). Egypt Initial National Communication. EEAA. Cairo: EEAA

El Shennawy, I. (2008). Coastal Vulnerability to Climate Changes and Adaptation Assessment for Coastal Zones of Egypt. Coastal Research Institute

Gelil, I. A. (2014). History of Climate Change Negotiation and the Arab Countries: The Case of Egypt, Published by the Issam Fares Institute for Public Policy and International Affairs, American University of Beirut

Global Carbon Atlas. (2016). Available at http://www.globalcarbonatlas.org/en/CO2-emissions

Intergovernmental Panel on Climate Change (IPCC). (2007). Fourth Assessment Report. Cambridge Press.

Kandeel, A. (2017). Millions of Rural Working Women in Egypt at Risk from Climate Change. Middle East Institute. Available at http://www.mei.edu/content/article/millions-rural-working-womenegypt-risk-climate-change

Nile Basin Initiative (NBI). (2012). Nile River Basin Status Report. Climate Change and its implications for the Nile Basin. Chapter 8. Available at http://nileis.nilebasin.org/system/files/Nile%20SoB%20Report%20Chapter%208%20-%20Climate%20Change.pdf

Regional Initiative for the Assessment of Climate Change Impacts on Water Resources and Socio-Economic Vulnerability in the Arab Region (RICCAR). (2017). Arab Climate Change Assessment Report (2017). Available at https://www.unescwa.org/publications/riccar-arab-climate-change-assessment-report

Siam, M.S. and Elthahir, E. A. B. (2017). Climate Change Enhances Interannual Variability of the River Nile Flow. Nature Climate Change 7: 350–354 . Available at https://www.nature.com/articles/nclimate3273

Smith, J.B. (2014). Egypt's Economic Vulnerability to Climate Change. Climate Research, 62: 59–7. Available at https://www.researchgate.net/publication/269038349_Egypt's_economic_vulnerability_to_climate_change

Sternberg, D. (2013). Chinese drought, wheat, and the Egyptian uprising: how a localized hazard became globalized. The Arab Spring and Climate Change. Edited by C. E.Werrell and F. Femia. The Center for Climate and Security. https://www.americanprogress.org/issues/security/reports/2013/02/28/54579/the-arab-spring-and-climate-change/

Sudan Vision. (March 2018). Ethiopia's Grand Dam and the End of Egypt's Control of the Nile. Available at http://www.svdaily.net/index.php/new-posts/reports/13194-worldview-ethiopia-s-grand-dam-andthe-end-of-egypt-s-control-of-the-nile

UNDP. (2006). Human Development Report. UNDP

UNDP. (2011). Human Development Report. UNDP

USAID. (2018). Egypt: Agriculture and Food Security. Available at https://www.usaid.gov/egypt/agriculture-and-food-security

https://www.ft.com/content/a6545786-0da8-11e8-8eb7-42f857ea9f09

http://www.world-grain.com/Departments/Country-Focus/Country-Focus-Home/Focus-on-Egypt.aspx

CHAPTER 12

Concluding Remarks on Resource Conflict and Environmental Politics in Africa

Reuben Edafenene Ojighoro and Chijioke Francis Onyebukwa

Resource has become a major determinant of domestic economy. The quantity of resources that a state has in its sovereign geography determines its economic viability, which has direct implication for societal and nation building process across the globe. Similarly, the degree of resource inherent in a society is often transformed into finished products or sold directly to other consumers as well as producers in order to accumulate capital that is needed for the development of the different sectors of a states' economy. The quest for capital accumulation often increases the number of peoples, groups, countries as well as other actors that are interested in the game of resource exploration.

R. E. Ojighoro
Department of Religious Studies, College of Education, Warri, Nigeria

C. F. Onyebukwa (✉)
Faculty of Arts, Department of History and International Studies, Kingsley Ozumba Mbadiwe University, Ogboko, Nigeria
e-mail: chijioke.onyebukwa@komu.edu.ng

K. J. Ani (ed.), *Resource Conflict and Environmental Relations in Africa*,
https://doi.org/10.1007/978-981-19-7343-7_12

In many countries within Africa, the state has failed woefully in the quest to provide for the social needs of the masses, thereby placing the masses on the desperate quest for economic resources. Unfortunately, in many African States, mineral resources are owned, explored and marketed by the machinery of the state. The problem arises when the masses begin to challenge state access and ownership of resources that are domiciled within their ancestral land, communities and constituencies. Often, the challenge and resistance to state ownership is generated by communal or group sense of exploitation, negligence and widespread poverty in the face of high resource endowment.

Paradoxically, in Niger Delta of Nigeria and the Cabinda region of Angela, as discussed in different chapters of the book; the state has unleashed unlimited might upon all social groups and agitators thereby leading to the increased act of taking arms by such groups. When the informal resource agitators succeed in arming themselves, they begin to demand for social and environmental justice, thereby leading to mass armed conflict between them and the government. Sometimes the confrontation could be between them and other rival local resource actors in the informal sector of their country's economy bearing in mind that resources within their jurisdiction have become the central determinant of national commonwealth.

It is at that state of desperado to control access, extraction and sale of natural resources in a state by different armed groups that the process of natural resources extraction qualifies as the most visible cause of conflicts and crises around the African continent. This is quite understandable given that mineral resource is a gift of nature; and nature is that phenomenon that every human, group and nation claim to represent, or, believe to represent them.

The intensification of the resource conflict is worsened by the combined role of foreign countries and multinational corporations. Recently, China is progressively taking over from England, France and other colonial powers in the race for mineral resource exploration in the continent. Chinese demand for African resources has improved the global prices of these resources and consequently the revenue earnings of these countries. For instance, Ayodele and Sotola (2014) have observed the reverses in the dwindling global prices of aluminium, copper and other minerals on the continent since the incursion of Chinese into its extractive sector. More so, the Asians are investing in high risk countries where others would not, such as Angola, Democratic Republic of Congo,

Zimbabwe and Sudan. This reduces the economic volatility of these countries to Western dependency. Consequently, even the so called pariah states have received economic succour from the Chinese which has multiplier effects on poverty alleviation and employment in Africa (Kobylinski, 2012, Thrall, 2015). Again, some Chinese factories in the continent, often process raw materials, within their area of neo-colonialism and that provides employment for Africans, which also generates increased demands for over-employment beyond the capacities of the companies thereby creating new forms of conflict. In addition, the Asians have contributed to human capital development on the continent by training about 36,000 professionals of African origin between 2010 and 2012 (Ayodele & Sotola, 2014; Konings, 2007).

The recent Chinese interest in African oil and other mineral deposits is characterized by the exploration of non-renewable resources which are depleting as the extraction takes place. The import of this amongst others is that the current rate of resource exploitation cannot sustain future generations. Consequently, the continent is threatened by resource depletion (Alden & Alves, 2009; Cherp & Jewell, 2014). More so, the extraction of mineral resources come with enormous environmental pollution and degradation which affect the livelihood of communities. It also destroys the ecosystem with its flora and fauna, dislocate communities and lead to violent conflicts, which further destroy the environment in a cyclical manner as experienced in Niger Delta, Angola, Sudan, Democratic Republic of Congo amongst others. These are direct threat to environmental security on the continent (Ajala, 2016; Gonzalez 2010; International Crisis Group, 2002; Rodriguez et al., 2014).

Essentially in many parts of Africa, a number of contemporary conflicts within sovereign states revolve around one resource or another. Pragmatically, natural resource-related conflicts are driven along four fronts: (a) conflict over resource ownership; (b) conflict over resources access (Maphosa, 2012); (c) conflict over decision-making associated with resource management; and (d) conflict over the distribution of resource revenue as well as other benefits and burdens (Olaopa & Ojaorotu, 2016).

At least, 22 countries across the continent have experienced or are experiencing different forms of resource conflicts across the continent. These include countries such as Burundi, Cameroon, Central African Republic, Chad, Democratic Republic of Congo, Ethiopia, Libya, Mali, Mozambique, Nigeria, Somalia, South Sudan, Tanzania and Togo. Other countries like Angola, Liberia, Rwanda and Sudan are still licking the

Table 12.1 Recent natural resources related conflicts in Africa

Country	*Duration*	*Natural resources*
Algeria	1992–2002	Oil, gas
Angola	1975–2002	Oil, diamonds, timber, ivory
Angola (Cabinda)	1975–2002	Oil
Burundi	1993–2005	Land
Cameroon/Nigeria	1997–2008	Oil
Chad	1980–1994	Oil, uranium
Congo-Brazzaville	1993; 1997	Oil
DRC	1993; 2011–ongoing	Copper, cobalt, diamonds, gold, timber
Eritrean/Ethiopian	1998–2000	Land
Kenya	1991–ongoing	Water, grazing pasture, livestock
Liberia	1989–1996	Iron, diamonds, rubber, timber, drugs
Libya	2011–ongoing	Oil
Mozambique	1976–1996	Ivory, timber
Morocco	1975–ongoing	Phosphates, oil
Nigeria	1991–2009, 2016–ongoing	Oil, grazing pasture, livestock
Papua New Guinea	1988–1998	Copper, gold
Rwanda	1990–1994	Coffee, land
Senegal	1997–2014	Drugs
Sierra Leone	1991–1999	Diamonds, bauxite, timber
Somalia	1988–ongoing	Bananas, livestock
South Africa	1990s	Drugs, land, platinum
South Sudan	2013–ongoing	Oil
Sudan	1983–2005	Oil
Western Sahara	1976–ongoing	Phosphates
Zimbabwe	2000	Land

Source Adapted from Maphosa (2012).

wounds of related resource wars and conflicts, which they experienced (Alao, 2007). See Table 12.1 for more details on natural resource conflicts in Africa.

The table above has shown cases of resources conflict and its cost remain very huge. They are both direct and indirect costs. Some of the direct costs of violence include military expenditure, high cost of care for displaced persons, infrastructural destruction and medical costs, which divert funds from other productive uses. Indirectly, the cost of violence falter economic activities, bringing inflation, debt, underdevelopment, unemployment, inadequate public services, trauma, poverty and rise in inequality (Oxfam, 2014 April 03). African countries in conflict, compared to peaceful countries, for instance, have on average: 50 per cent more infant deaths; 15 per cent more undernourished people; life expectancy reduced by five years; 20 per cent more adult illiteracy; 2.5 times fewer doctors per patient; and 12.4 per cent less food per person (Oxfam, 2014 April 03).

Summary and Conclusion

The articles are divided into twelve chapters. Chapter 1 is the introduction to resource curse conflicts and environmental politics in Africa. It captures the rich mineral deposits in different parts of the African continent. The chapter reveals that Africa is richly endowed with all manners of minerals ranging from gold in Ghana and South Africa as well as crude oil that is found in their large numbers within Nigeria, Angola and Chad. However, the country is also richly blessed with Diamond, platinum, lead, limestone, etc. Unfortunately, the combination of inability to explore the resources as well as poor leadership, which tends to be include towards mineral resource smuggling more than development leads to increased impoverishment of the masses, which naturally generates conflicts. The peak of such conflict witnesses massive loss of lives and properties in almost every resource-endowed area in Africa.

The second chapter maintained that mineral resource conflicts in Africa is a phraseology in vogue. Thus, the intersection of a number of trends-rising global demand for mineral resource in Africa, fears of the dwindling supplies, increased conflict in many of the mineral-rich regions, and concerns about the potential future devastation wrought by climate change-ensures that the sources, locations and stability of world energy and mineral resource supplies to the Western world from Africa have become a common subject for debate. In the context of this chapter, that is, the place of mineral resource conflict in critical security analysis in Africa; the chapter shall survey briefly what I term 'energy security', the Gulf of Guinea suffered cataclysmic upheaval as a result of rich mineral deposit in the region. Against this backdrop, we will define 'energy security' inter alia: Energy security exists when there are energy sources large enough to meet the needs of the political community (the energy demands, which include all military, economic and societal activity. Mineral resource conflicts abound in the Niger Delta region of Nigeria; and large mineral resource deposits was responsible for the emergence of apartheid in South Africa. All these developments in Africa had security implications for the government, the general populace and ultimately, the abuse of human rights.

The next chapter engaged in a theoretical assessment of the roles of diamond in the Sierra Leone's Civil War. That was followed by the role of local autonomy in the Niger Delta peace building process. The study revealed how the Niger Delta has become a theatre of armed confrontation between the Nigerian State security and multi-national oil corporations' forces on one hand and the multiple militia groups on the other hands. Unfortunately, the quest for Western models of peace-building has not sustainably worked in the area due to the suspicion from the masses that the process is an extension of resource exploitation politics. The authors maintain that the only road to sustainable peacebuilding must be driven by the local needs of the masses through increased grass root autonomy. The Niger Delta challenge was further captured by accounting for how international organization has reacted to the Niger Delta crisis. It documented both the responses of governmental and non-governmental organizations in the Niger Delta struggle. However, it is noteworthy that the international actors have generally condemned the degree of environmental damage that the Niger Delta masses are living in, due to resource conflict in their area. They have also condemned the human right abuses and killings within the Niger Delta.

The environment is a major determinant of geopolitical influence. Environmental factors influence the nature of diplomacy between one country and another. Fulani Herdsmen and Farmers Conflict Relations in Idomaland 1999–2017 were also discussed. Poverty is often the direct consequent of environmental and resource conflicts. In the whole African continent, the threat of poverty has continued to increase as people struggled to live in jungles and squalors where conditions of life remain very terrible. The intractable nature of many of the conflicts even undermine the economy, as well as other environmental resources that the masses live in, thereby creating widespread penury, malnutrition, diseases and high mortality rates.

The second half of the book presents resource curse and environmental conflicts in Angola, and framework for resolution in Congo. These two countries have witnessed the history of multiple forms of environmental conflicts that undermined nation building in their post-independence history. Those conflicts threatened national security and remains viral in different forms till contemporary times. The last few chapters of the study presented the mining politics of Crush Rock Nigeria ltd and environmental problems that they created in Ishiagu as well as the impact of climate change in Egypt. The second to the last chapter is on the place of Anthropocene as an alternative lens in the study of international relations.

Finally, one can really argue that if private and public efforts are not geared to end conflicts in different parts of the globe, armed conflict, especially resource conflict that has all manners of national and international actors, the world and Africa in particular will not have sustainable peace needed for national transformation.

References

Ajala, O. (2016). Human security in the Niger Delta: Exploring the interplay of resource governance, community structure and conflict, *Journal of Sustainable Development, Law and Policy,* Vol. 7 (2): 81–103.

Alao, A. (2007). *Natural resources and conflict in Africa: the tragedy of endowment*. USA: University of Rochester Press.

Alden, C., & Alnes, C. (2009). *China and Africa's natural nesources: the challenges and implications. Occasional Paper* No-41. Johannesburg: South African Institute of International Affairs.

Ayodele, T., & Sotola, O. (2014). China in Africa: an evaluation of Chinese investment. Lagos: *IPPA Working Paper Series.*

Cherp, A., & Jewell, J. (2014). The concept of energy security: beyond the four As. *Energy Policy*, Vol. 75: 415–421.

Gonzalez, A. (2010). Petroleum and its impact on three wars in Angola, Nigeria and Sudan. *Journal of Peace, Conflict and Development*. Vol. 16: 58–86.

International Crisis Group. (2002). *God, oil and country: changing the logic of war in Sudan*. Brussels: International Crisis Group.

Konings, P. (2007). China and Africa: building a strategic partnership. *Journal of Developing Societies*, Vol. 23 (3): 341–367.

Kobylinski, K. (2012). Chinese Investment in Africa: checking the facts and figure. *Association for international Affairs, Briefing Paper,* July.

Maphosa, S. B. (2012). Natural Resources and conflict: Unlocking the economic dimension of peace-building in Africa. *African Institute of South Africa Policy Brief Series No 74*, March 2012.

Olaopa, O. l., & Ojakorotu, V. (2016). Conflict about Natural Resources and the Prospect of Development in the Democratic Republic of Congo (DRC). *Journal of Social Sciences,* Vol. 49 (3): 244–256.

Oxfam. (2014). Armed violence costs Africa $18 billion a year. Defence Web News online publication 3 April, 2014. Available at http://www.defenceweb.co.za/index.php?option=com_content&view=article&id=34253:armed-violence-costs-africa-18-billion-a-year-oxfam&catid=56:diplomacy-a-peace&Itemid=111

Rodriguez, J, Rodriguez, F, Gutierrez, C., & Major, S. (2014). Oil, poverty and environment in Angola. *Bolelinde la Associacion de Geografos Esparnoles* (64): 427–432.

Thrall, l. (2015). *China's expanding African relations: Implications for national security*. California: Rand Corporation.

Index

K. J. Ani (ed.), *Resource Conflict and Environmental Relations in Africa*,
https://doi.org/10.1007/978-981-19-7343-7

FSC
www.fsc.org
MIX
Papier | Fördert
gute Waldnutzung
FSC® C083411

Kolibri 360 GmbH
Ferdinand-Jühlke-Straße 7
99095 Erfurt, Deutschland
produktsicherheit@kolibri360.de